SKIPPING TOWARDS
ARMAGEDDON

SKIPPING TOWARDS ARMAGEDDON

THE POLITICS AND PROPAGANDA OF THE LEFT BEHIND NOVELS AND THE LAHAYE EMPIRE

Michael Standaert

Soft Skull Press
Brooklyn NY
2006

© 2006 by Michael Standaert
ISBN 1-932360-96-4
ISBN-13: 978-1932-36096-7

Cover design by Peter Garner
Interior design by Sarah Groff-Palermo

Editorial: Rachael Crossland & Melinda Haggerty

Published by Soft Skull Press
55 Washington Street, 804
Brooklyn, NY 11201
www.softskull.com

Distributed by Publishers Group West
800.788.3123 www.pgw.com

Printed in Canada

Library of Congress Cataloging-in-Publication Data

Standaert, Michael.
    Skipping towards armageddon : the politics and propagan-
da of the left behind novels and the LaHaye empire / by
Michael Standaert.
        p. cm.
    Includes bibliographical references and index.
    ISBN 1-932360-96-4 (alk. paper)
    1. LaHaye, Tim F. Left behind series. 2. Politics and litera-
ture--United States--History--20th century. 3. Christian fiction, American--History and criticism. 4. Antichrist--History
of doctrines--20th century. 5. Apocalyptic literature--History
and criticism. 6. Religious right--United States. 7. Rapture
(Christian eschatology) 8. End of the world in literature. 9.
Evangelicalism in literature. 10. Millennialism in literature. I.
Title.
    PS3562.A315L4437 2005
    813'.54--dc22
                                                        2005004293

FOR NANCY

CONTENTS

ACKNOWLEDGMENTS

First of all, I would like to thank Soft Skull publisher and editor Richard Nash for his patience, guidance, insight, and belief in this project, as well as all the people at Soft Skull who helped put this book together. I'd also like to thank Melinda Haggerty for her copy editing late in the process, and Rachael Crossland for her editing and content suggestions earlier on. An immense debt of gratitude goes out to Amy Cary at the University of Iowa Special Collections, for her time helping me wade through the extensive and remarkable Social Documents collection at the library there. And finally, I thank my wife Nancy for keeping me grounded in reality during the writing of this book.

SKIPPING TOWARDS ARMAGEDDON

INTRODUCTION: NO PEACE TILL JESUS COMES

There are perhaps few more influential, yet underacknowledged, belief systems working through the subconscious of American society today than the theology of dispensational premillennialism. These ideas are often referred to as the belief in the "Rapture" or the "End Times" theology, the theoretical premise that Christ's true believers will be taken to heaven before a great Tribulation lasting seven years. During this time of Tribulation would come the expected reign of the Antichrist, catastrophic plagues, earthquakes, fire and brimstone as the final punishment for those left behind not accepting Jesus Christ as their personal savior. The most well-known representations of this apocalyptic vision are contained in the best-selling series, the Left Behind novels.

This escape through Rapture, Tribulation of the non-believers, and return of Christ is the basic plotline for the Left Behind novels—a narrative that has become a powerful tool for the blending of religious and political activism for the authors and their supporters. Conceived by evangelist and religious right activist Tim LaHaye but penned by writer Jerry B. Jenkins, the novels have sold over 70 million copies in the past decade, including spin-off audio and children's book formats.[1] In anticipation of the final novel of the regular series *Glorious Appearing* early in 2004, bookstores pre-ordered the complete first print run of 1.9 million copies.[2] Estimates are that the series of books now generate revenues around 100 million a year.[3] Jenkins, who writes the

Left Behind books, is the conduit for LaHaye's brand of apocalyptic vision and gives the novels a touch of mainstream
respectability by smoothing out many of the wild-eyed edges—at
least on the surface.)

The original series of novels begins with *Left Behind: Novel
of the Earth's Last Days* and ends with *Glorious Appearing: The
End of Days*, the final of the first twelve books. A simple reading
says the books follow a group of converted new "believers" after
the Rapture has taken the "real Christians" to heaven, as they
battle the Antichrist and his forces during the seven-year
Tribulation. That Tribulation signals the time between Rapture
and the return of the resurrected Jesus Christ at the final battle of
Armageddon, the battle between Good and Evil, between the
Satanic forces of the "man-centered" world and the virtuous
forces of the "God-centered." The Tribulation, for premillennialists, is the time when God attempts one final test for mankind.
Will they return toward him, or away, toward Satan? [A full synopsis of each book is in the appendix.]

The theology of LaHaye and narrative of Jenkins alone do
not drive these widely popular novels. Instead, a mixture of popular fundamentalist religion, conservative politics, and long-
standing rightwing conspiracy narratives are the engine for these
books—books that portray the extermination of other worldviews considered old and "in the way": Catholicism, Judaism,
and Islam, mainly, but also any form of secular and modernist
thought considered outside the premillennialist worldview.
Essentially about power and not faith, these books can be read as
a guide to understanding this battle for the mind of America: the
battle between the moderate secular society, built on tolerance
over the past century for any number of views, and a new brand
of quasi–pop culture fundamentalist absolutism that wants to
roll back progress to Creationism's rule over science, to when
schooling was the domain of churches, and to a time when many
of the individual freedoms taken for granted today are replaced
by the law of Biblical morality.

For a growing portion of the population, perhaps now as
high as 30 percent of the country, Tim LaHaye is winning that
battle for minds.[4]

It's a battle LaHaye has been waging for the past thirty
years. One battle, in which the militant language of Revelation is

mined to create the Left Behind books, is an organized effort by active fundamentalists to influence the political direction of the United States. In this battle it has been important for premillennialists to take a rhetorical position based on vengeance and hate that is directly opposite that of their Christian faith, to ignore the Jesus of the Gospels. Instead that final book of Revelation focuses on constructing a vision that sees everything outside of it as the realm of Satan. For LaHaye, it is a world with no hope for peace and one in which the militant language of retribution and destruction has outstripped that of love and tolerance. Before Jesus can return to cleanse the world of sin and establish His thousand-year reign of peace on earth, the theology of dispensational premillennialism maintains that there will be no peace—no peace in Israel, no peace in Iraq, no peace anywhere until His glorious appearing. Peace, for adherents to this theology, is among the most satanic of words.

To get to the political reality of why premillennialists hate talk of peace, it is important to understand why the Antichrist character of the Left Behind novels, Nicolae Carpathia, the "peacemaker," is painted so deliberately as Satan. It is the "man-made" peace and utopia delivered through secular world order which Carpathia represents, in contrast to peace and utopia under Christian dominion, that the premillennialists fear. More, Carpathia is delivering his hope for humanity based on social progress outside the domain of Christian progress: "The day will come when we live as one world, one faith, one family of man. We shall live in a utopia of peace and harmony with no more war, no more bloodshed, no more death."[5]

The words of prominent TV evangelist and premillennialist Jim Robinson echo this fear of secular peace quite clearly. In his opening prayer to the 1984 Republican National Convention, Robinson said: "There'll be no peace until Jesus comes. Any preaching of peace prior to this return is heresy. It's against the word of God. It's anti-Christ."[6] These real words parallel the fictional words uttered by Pastor Bruce Barnes in the Left Behind series book *Tribulation Force*, where he relays Biblical prophecies to the group he has helped form to battle the Antichrist Carpathia: "You will never hear peace promised from this pulpit."[7] For these fictional and real-life believers, it is a battle on all fronts, a battle without quarter, and a battle that is becoming increasingly intertwined with the political realities of America.

From reading the books in the Left Behind series, and researching the political network of LaHaye, as well as looking at the history of how dispensational premillennialism and rightwing conspiracy narratives have come together during the latter half of the twentieth century, it is clear that LaHaye has had a central role in combining the narrative elements with the political elements to produce an influential and propagandistic framework that taps into the fundamentalist Christian and conservative Christian psyche of the nation. Focusing on LaHaye, his political activities, and his writings gives a view into one aspect of the larger movement often called the religious right and how it has become a powerful social and political force in America over the past three decades, including playing an important role in the past few presidential elections.

Much of the backlash coming from fundamentalist political activism can be attributed to the increasing number of ways that the world views realities. For example, a fountainhead of identities and along with them, identity politics has become a definning factor of our times. The democratic world of choices, freedoms, and responsibilities goes hand-in-hand with a postmodern world less certain of these absolutes which fundamentalism wraps around itself in an attempt to offer hope amid confusion for the believer. Being so, it is also worth noting that the theology of dispensational premillennialism has often been called the theology of despair, the result of fundamentalist segments of the Protestant evangelical community coming to the conclusion that their absolutist world is rapidly careering toward a chaotic and final end. The only thing left to do is find an escape hatch, a direct pipeline to heaven where they can sit out the final collapse and return along with the triumphant Jesus to a millennium of peace and harmony. Tim LaHaye and the Left Behind books are the most important and visible means for delivering these ideas to those fundamentalist communities and beyond into a nonfundamentalist and largely Christian American society.

This book describes the history of that narrative in America, how LaHaye—one of, if not *the* most important, leaders of the religious right—has used this narrative for political as well as personal gain. The Left Behind books are conscious propaganda

on the part of LaHaye and his network of fundamentalist institutions. The books' cores uncover many of the anti-Semitic, anti-
Catholic, and anti-Democratic beliefs long thought lessening
from this segment of society, and the capital gain—both financial
and psychological—is being spent to further LaHaye's fundamentalist agendas, which have little to do with spiritual faith and
a great deal to do with power over how millions of Americans
view the intersection of faith and politics.

A HOUSE DIVIDED

In the mid-1990s, around the time the Left Behind novels first made their way onto bookstore shelves, I was living in the small town of Carterville, in southern Illinois. I was renting a room for about $50 a week from a middle-aged man named David who occupied the second story, while I had the bottom half of the house. I was enrolled in two classes at the time—Existential Philosophy and Russian Realist Literature—two heavy and demanding subjects with reading lists that helped fill my small room with stacks of books. Upstairs, David had his own course of study, one that he would tell me about every day, every time I saw him. Part of my rent went toward an evening meal, which put me in direct contact with David at least once per day. I became something of a captive audience for him, and, for the first time in my life, came into contact with the all-encompassing worldview of dispensational premillennialism.

According to Thomas Ice, a steering committee member of Tim LaHaye's Pre-Trib Research Center and author of *The Truth Behind Left Behind*, premillennial dispensationalists believe that the Bible is "God's inspired, inerrant revelation to man" and through that revelation the Bible "provides the framework through which to interpret history (past and future)" to be "interpreted literally and historically (past and future)." The dispensations of premillennial dispensationalism are the different "ages, or epochs of history through which His creatures (men and angels) are tested" and that "Jesus Christ is the only way to a relationship with God." Furthermore, "only genuine believers in Christ are open to the teachings of the Bible" though what *genuine* is has been vaguely left undefined. Here are the following points verbatim, from Ice:

> God's plan for history includes a purpose for the descendents of Abraham, Isaac, and Jacob—that is, Israel. This plan for Israel includes promises that they will have the land of Israel (biblical land of Israel), will have a seed, and will be a worldwide blessing to the nations. Many of the promises to a national Israel are yet future; therefore, God is not finished with Israel.[1]
>
> God's plan from all eternity also includes a purpose for the church; however this is a temporary phase that will end with the Rapture. After the Rapture, God will complete his plan for Israel and the Gentiles.
>
> The main purpose in God's *master plan* for history is to glorify himself through Jesus Christ. Therefore, Jesus Christ is the goal and hero of history.[2]

This summary gives a good overview of how premillennialists view the world, especially in how they view history as both past and pre-ordained future, due to the eschatological framework they have constructed that lets them view the world in this way. All future is known in this construction. Only the time frames, or dispensations, are hidden.

It is this clock-watching that gives this ideology much of its power. For my landlord, clock-watching was his life.

David had a bad back and was in immense physical pain daily. He needed a walker to get around the apartment, and a mechanical Lay-Z-Boy lifted him to a standing position when he finished watching television. He hardly ever changed his clothes. Besides spending his money on generic cigarettes and green stamps on staples like milk, canned goods, and frozen food from Aldi, most of his savings went toward buying apocalyptic Christian books and videos. Other than a collection of old Hollywood videos, all I ever saw him watch besides Christian television on his basic cable service was *Jeopardy* and the evening news, the latter which he followed intently. A bombing in Israel? The Apocalypse is coming soon, he would say. Russians interfering in Iraq? The End is very near. Virtually any story that surfaced in the news had relevance for David as signifying that we were living in the End Times. The endless parade of images across the screen, the stories of murders, wars and rumors of wars, the "identity" politics of feminism, abortion, homosexuality, all the corruption and lack of hope in the world signaled one thing for David: the Day of Doom. This is one major seduction of being attuned to the eschatological time bomb of Revelation— the sense that believers are in the front-row seat for the End of Time. The other major seduction is that the only escape hatch would be the Rapture of those believers followed by the destruction of this fleshy corrupted world and the dawning of the new and glorious spiritual kingdom of Christ—the Millennial Reign of Jesus and the return of the triumphant Raptured to this newly created utopia.

And as if this wasn't enough, all the moral decay in the world is not due to the actions of individuals dealing with their own destinies or of larger social forces and societal inequities crashing into one another, but to a secretive and widespread conspiracy enacted by shadowy forces in international banking, by satanic global leftist elites, distant foreigners, apostate Catholics, fanatical Muslims, and demonical Jews. Through the last hundred years, conspiracy theories like those promoted through the *Protocols of the Elders of Zion*, *The Turner Diaries*, and McCarthyist Communist conspiracy narratives have united with premillennial interpretations of Revelation based on the writings of John Darby. These in turn have been woven into how the founding myths of American exceptionalism are understood to produce a paranoid vision of America's place in the world.

The Protocols of the Elders of Zion was a fraudulent document that appeared in Russia (with a previous birth from other falsified documents in Europe) at the end of the nineteenth century. It was alleged to be a guidebook for the plans of a secret Jewish society bent on world domination, an "international Jewish conspiracy," if one will, and was used by a variety of political groups in Russia at the time to fuel hatred and pogroms against Jews. It has been used by anti-Semites, Christian and Muslim, ever since. During the rise of the Nazis, the book was disseminated as a compulsory text in the Third Reich's schools. Today, Muslim extremist groups such as Al Qaeda, Hamas, and Islamic Jihad, as well as some Muslim governments, distribute these materials as fact. Textbooks in Saudi Arabian schools often contain references from the book as factual truth, much in the same way as the book was used by the Nazis. Looking back at the more white supremacist end of American premillennialist literature and pamphlets of the pre–civil rights era in the early and middle part of the twentieth century, the *Protocols* were also taken as a matter of fact. Recently in 2004, Wal-Mart was forced to remove the books from their online catalog, which had suggested that the books were accurate, after protest from American Jewish groups.[3]

The *Turner Diaries* is a book of white supremacist fantasy portraying a time when all non-white Americans have been annihilated in a massive race war started by antigovernment white supremacist militias. Written in 1978 by William Pierce, the now deceased leader of the white supremacist National Alliance, the book circulated through mail order for many years but is now available through mainstream sources. Some speculate that the Oklahoma City Federal Building bomber, Timothy McVeigh, was influenced by this book in his own decision to rise up against the government and car bomb the innocent people there; the book was found in his possession when he was arrested and opens with a similar bombing of the FBI headquarters. Many of the assumptions of the book, the points which lead to the race wars, are similar to conspiracy theories promoted by such books as the *Protocols of the Elders of Zion*.

There are striking similarities to what is depicted in both of these books and what is insinuated in the Left Behind books, mainly in regards to anti-Semitism, anti-Catholicism, and anti-Islamism, and the depictions of race. It is worth noting here the sleight-of-hand portrayed in the Left Behind books about *imminent future events*, or this knowledge of historic-future, is on par with those of *The Turner Diaries*—but instead of race war we are presented with a war between the forces of the "Global Community" led by the Antichrist character Nicolae Carpathia and the "believing Christians." In that Global Community are a wide variety of suspects worth eliminating—Jews, Catholics, and Muslims, as well as the usual suspects of liberals and humanists, atheists, and any other group portrayed as outside this worldview. These enemies are portrayed as evil, subhuman, and not worth the earth they stand upon. There is one significant difference here between the Left Behind books and the aforementioned racist conspiracy narratives: the supreme slayer, the ultimate instrument of genocide in this case, is Jesus Christ himself. The configuration of Christ as the "hero" in this massacre fits into a Christian fundamentalist context, as opposed to the strictly white-supremacist and largely secular one of the *Turner Diaries*.[4] As for the similarities to the *Protocols of the Elders of Zion*, this is also sleight-of-hand: much of the ideology LaHaye uses as his basis for the books is complexly intertwined with conspiracy theories such as those used in the *Protocols*. But, instead of using the old conspiratorial line "international Jewish bankers," the Left Behind books simply drop "Jewish" out of the phrase, and we are left with shadowy "international bankers." For anyone familiar with the old conspiracy phrase, "Jewish" certainly springs to mind. By combining all this with the maze of interpretation that is the Book of Revelation, LaHaye delivers a Christian context, or at least a premillennialist Christian one, and injects it with hints of Christian nationalism of a specifically American nature.

Second Coming, Coming Soon

Often while watching the nightly news with David, I would find myself perplexed by the intense connections he made with events happening on the screen and events which he said fit into this prophetic scheme—all of which revolved around Jews, Israel, and the Second Coming of Christ. Where did these connections or presumptions about current and future events come from? Where did he learn, for example, that all the violence happening in Israel was a harbinger for events that signaled the End? What interested me most about David's beliefs wasn't so much that he harbored them, but where they developed. Obviously to draw so many conclusions from daily news reports, there had to be some overarching narrative besides the Bible that fed these assumptions. Conspiracy theories have long floated about, but their traction has often been suspect, open to ridicule, and limited to the few unless disseminated actively by groups who can use them politically, such as how extremist Muslims and various anti-Semitic groups and governments in the recent past have used the *Protocols*. Here, in David, those conspiracy theories mixed with a militant Christian fundamentalist religiosity fixated mainly on interpreting the Book of Revelation as a guide to the future had become whole, ingrained, and personalized. These ideas were so alien to my own core beliefs, beliefs that I considered were fundamentally Judeo-Christian as well, beliefs concerned with personal and individual morality, not as a mass movement or mass reality constructed for spiritual and political power.[5] That they largely spoke to people's fears and alienations rather than their hopes and aspirations also made me wonder where their influence lay.

From researching the material surrounding LaHaye and the premillennialists, it became clear that much of the dissemination of these ideas had been due to a relatively small number of people and these ideas themselves came from a relatively marginal segment of Protestant fundamentalist theology. The power of this narrative, and one which feeds its dissemination, is how inherently it is tied to the fears, hopes, paranoias, beliefs and myths of society as a whole. And it is one that is prepared to consume them—millions of potential consumers of a radical, militant ideology that is specifically packaged and branded to play off these fears and paranoias. Once this relatively small segment of society penetrated those fears, hopes, myths, and the like, the memes established by their efforts have multiplied and been reinforced by the continued and relentless marketing and dissemination through a growing media structure and through tapping into individual churches and Christian groups—book clubs, political activist groups, church groups, prophecy seminars—all these work as spokes to the wheel of the Left Behind and premillennialist ideology. What is fascinating, and frightening, is how LaHaye and others like him have successfully tapped into those social manias to create a complex political and social force that traffics in fear and hatred.

While I was downstairs reading complicated and not easily digested books, where absolutes are questioned and truth murks—books by Soren Kierkegaard, Mikhail Lermontov, Albert Camus, Leo Tolstoy, Jean Paul Sartre, Fyodor Dostoyevsky, or Martin Heidegger—David was upstairs leafing through books that lay everything out in strict detail, often portrayed as absolute truth—books like the latest works by Hal Lindsey, Tim LaHaye, Arno Froese, Ed Hindson, Mark Hitchcock, John Walvoord, or Jack Van Impe. It was something of a parallel universe of modernism versus fundamentalism, a house divided in miniature. The division between these worldviews, the absolutism of the fundamentalist and the skepticism of the modern couldn't have been greater. On a number of occasions David would force a book into my hand and later quiz me about my beliefs. I often told him that I didn't believe in the literal word of the Bible, but had taken it as an allegorical teaching, especially the Revelation. I had always thought the Bible is a great and complex, often paradoxical and not very easily understood piece of literature. From over twelve years of parochial schooling, I'd gained a wide understanding of the Bible and faith, but then I'd also gained an understanding of the theory of evolution and science, something that doesn't jive well with those who take the Bible as the literal word of God. David once gave me a copy of *The Final Battle* by Hal Lindsey, a book that discusses the prophecy of the Battle of Armageddon, which I read with interest at the time, though also with great skepticism. For a number of years I'd been interested in this sub-genre of literature, as well as the segment of society which consumes it. As the years passed I also largely forgot about David and his all consuming interest in these subjects—that is, until the Left Behind series became such a publishing phenomenon.

Left Behind Books, Publishing Success

The only other publishing phenomenon that equals the success of the Left Behind novels in the past decade is the Harry Potter series, the latter of which had sold an estimated 250 million copies worldwide before the release of the sixth book in the summer of 2005. Another notable, *The Da Vinci Code,* has sold somewhere around 7 million copies in the U.S. and 15 million worldwide. But where both of these books have a worldwide reach, the Left Behind novels are specifically American. Before the release of the final book, *The Glorious Appearing,* the Left Behind series had sold over 60 million copies in less than ten years in the U.S., with another 20 million in spin-offs. Three weeks before the final book of the original twelve went on sale, in late March 2004, the initial hardcover print run of 1.9 million had already been sold out through bookstore pre-orders. The first novel in a three-novel prequel series to Left Behind called *The Rising: Antichrist is Born* was released in early 2005, while the second of the series, *The Regime*, is came out in November 2005.

By October 2001, the Left Behind series had sold more than 45 million copies, more than the estimated 24 million Harry Potter books sold in the U.S. during the same timespan. Yet while two-thirds of American adults were aware of Harry Potter, just one-quarter had heard of the Left Behind books. Around one out of ten people in the country had read at least one book of LaHaye's series.[6] A survey commissioned by Tyndale House, publishers of Left Behind, found those who read the Left Behind series were mostly between the ages of thirty-five and fifty-five, Protestant or born-again Christian who lived in the South and the West, while Catholics and non-Christians living in the Northeast were the least likely to have ever heard of LaHaye's books. Far from being strictly limited to Christian fundamentalist readers, the Left Behind series reached an estimated three million non–born again readers by 2001.

George Barna of the Christian polling company Barna Research Group notes: "The series represents one of the most widely experienced religious teaching or evangelistic tools among adults who are not born again Christians." It "reached a larger unduplicated audience of non-believers than most religious television or radio ministries draw through their programs."

Specifically, Barna looks at the Left Behind series as a religious and evangelistic tool, and not as a political and propagandist tool. It is difficult to discern what pulls and what pushes readers—the religiosity or the politics—to come to the books. For example, many people who are drawn to the conspiracy theory thriller style of the *Da Vinci Code* may purchase the Left Behind books, just as many may buy it for its evangelistic use in order to give to friends or relatives. Likely both groups of readers will have their suspicions confirmed each in his or her own way, one the conspiracy and the other the religiosity. In the middle the political messages of the books reaches both spectrums. rightwing assumptions about the conspiracy of secular society, which feature prominently in nonreligious rightwing media, mix with the self-help and identity-style religiosity of more mainstream proselytizing media. Where publishing success meets spiritual success is where the figures often become inconclusive, though this isn't for a lack of trying. Each Left Behind novel has at least one or more conversion stories, a detailed narrative about how one of the characters has come to accept Jesus Christ as her personal messiah. All the main characters in the books go through the story of their conversion at least once. Since these conversions are all post-Rapture, all have something to do with the loss of loved ones, almost a battlefield conversion, often with a sense of guilt that they had not converted before the Rapture.

Here is one such passage from *Assassins* in which a minor character named Annie came to believe:

> "I want to hear you guys' stories, David," Mac said. "I know you still have family in Israel. Where you from, Annie?"
>
> "Canada. I was flying here from Montreal when the earthquake hit. Lost my whole family."
>
> "You weren't a believer yet?"
>
> She shook her head. "I don't guess I'd ever been to church except for weddings and funerals. We didn't care enough to be atheists, but that's what we practiced. Would have called ourselves agnostics. Sounded more tolerant, less dogmatic. We were tight. Good people. Better than most religious people we knew."
>
> "But weren't you curious about God?"
>
> "I started wondering after the disappearances, but we became instant devotees to Carpathia. He was like a voice of reason, a man of compassion, love, peace. I applied to work for the cause as soon as the U.N. changed its name and announced plans to move here.[7] The day I was accepted was the happiest day of my life, of our whole family's life."
>
> "What happened?"
>
> "Losing them all happened. I was devastated. I'd been scared before, sure. Knew some people who had disappeared and some who had died in all that happened later. But I had never lost anyone close, ever. Then I lose my mom and dad and my two younger brothers in the earthquake, not to mention half the people in our time, while I'm merrily in the sky."[8]

After her loss, Annie goes looking for answers on the Internet and comes across the teachings of Tsion Ben-Judah, a Jewish scholar who has become what the authors call a "believing Jew," and devours all the information she can about this new line of belief, eventually turning to God through the prism of the teachings of Ben-Judah.

"Dr. Ben-Judah explained God and Jesus and the Rapture and Tribulation so clearly that I desperately wanted to believe. All I had to do was look back at his other teachings to realize that he was right about the Bible prophecies. He had predicted every judgment so far."

Mac nodded, smiling.

"Well," she said, "of course you know that. I switched back to the archived message and read how to pray, how to tell God you know you're a sinner and that you need him. I laid facedown on my bed and did that. I knew I had received the truth, but I had no idea what to do next. I spent the rest of the day and night, all night, reading as much of the teaching as I could. It became quickly obvious why the GC tried to counter Dr. Ben-Judah. He was careful not to mention Nicolae by name, but it was clear the new world order was the enemy of God. I didn't understand much about the Antichrist, but I knew I had to be unique among GC employees. Here I was, in the shelter of the enemy of God, and I was a believer."[9]

Most of the other conversion stories are simply reworked renditions of Annie's—the terrible tragedy and loss inflicted through both the Rapture and through the catastrophic Tribulations following—both God-induced we might add—bring believers to the flock.

In effect, what the Left Behind novels attempt to promise those who come to them is that if they convert before all this tribulation, they will be saved in the Rapture and miss out on the destruction brought on by a wrathful God. It is a message that tries to interpret current social and political happenings today through the prism of *future* prophetic actions taken as the truth of what will eventually occur. By tapping into these fears, linking them with prophecy, and filtering them through political messages, LaHaye's message becomes one of propaganda in the novels rather than simply Christian fantasy fiction or thriller novels. These messages are a powerful political tool bent on rendering more of a fear of God than a love of God, a fear of anything outside this line of belief and a love of the destruction of all that is outside of it, an embracing of "God's master plan" to destroy all unbelievers and usher in the "hero of history" in the form of a militant Jesus Christ.

This is where the political manifestation of resentment politics enters the scene. Nearly everything outside the worldview is considered evil, the books perpetuate this, and LaHaye taps into this for political gain by further radicalizing those believers who buy into his picture.

Blessed Success

Some of the commercial success of Left Behind is due to the authorial relationship between LaHaye and Jenkins, argues Amy Frykholm in her book *Rapture Culture*. While LaHaye is heavily steeped in the dispensational premillennialism of his theology, some of the theology is toned down by Jenkins's more moderate position and relative knowledge of contemporary culture, which is alien to LaHaye. It is a "negotiation with contemporary American culture," writes Frykholm, "amending traditional dispensationalism" while at the same time "continuing to assert a claim of a special place within unfolding world history." Frykholm, in her study of the readers of the Left Behind series, found that most readers approach the interpretation of the books as a group experience, much like the Bible itself—in their churches, book clubs, and through family members—instead of as a solitary activity. "Readers of Left Behind connect to one another and use the books to provide ground for those connections," writes Frykholm. "The popularity of Left Behind lies in its passage from hand to hand."[10]

Frykholm attributes the popularity of fiction as the vehicle to the essential individual interpretations readers make and the inherent multiplicity of fiction in general. More than the premillennialist vision itself, what made Left Behind so successful is that the characters set against the backdrop of this apocalyptic conspiracy narrative—even though they are often wooden and each character is largely indistinguishable from the next—allow a diverse group of Christian readers the ability to identify with the daily decisions or supernatural adventures these characters go through.

Yet one thing most researchers like Frykholm fail to recognize is how the Left Behind books are also functioning as bridges to LaHaye's political writings and his network of activists. By using God and faith as that bridge, LaHaye is able to manipulate the devout religious beliefs of the nation for political ends. Depending on which interview with LaHaye one reads, he either came up with the idea for the series while watching a wedding ring–wearing pilot flirt with a stewardess on an airplane or "the Lord" gave him the idea. The distinction is not arbitrary but varies depending on whether he is talking to the perceived secular or avidly Christian press. "What if the Rapture occurred right now?" he says he thought on that fateful ride, wondering what would happen to that sinner-flirting pilot when he realized his "believing" wife had been Raptured with all the other good folks.[11]

"People are searching for the truth and that's what leads them to our novels," says Jenkins in an interview at *Food For the Hungry*, adding that he and LaHaye have created a "series of books about the greatest cosmic event that *will happen* in the history of the world." In sporting lingo, LaHaye often talks of "winning souls" like it is some great game. But nothing LaHaye and Jenkins describe in the Left Behind books seems like much of a game at all—billions on the losing and the winning sides are wiped off the map in detailed, gory fashion.

LaHaye acts as the planner, promoter, and the "brand" name attached to the books. Before writing the books, Jenkins receives a detailed outline from LaHaye along with a liberal splashing of Biblical passages, then works from there. LaHaye says he began to pray to God to send him a fiction writer, but it was actually his agent, Rick Christian, who introduced the two.[12]

"I hoped it would sell 100,000 copies," Jenkins said when talking about the first Left Behind book's release in 1995. Taking cues off apocalyptic author Hal Lindsey's own successes in the 1970s, as well as the massive market for similar Christian apocalyptic books that had sprouted up since, contributed to this Revelation inflation, though they couldn't foresee how massive those sales would eventually become. Mark Taylor of Tyndale House, the Left Behind publishers, hoped for 500,000—but the figure reached 5 million for the first Left Behind book by late 2000 and 11 million for the entire series by the end of that year. As evidence of the effect the series has had, during 2000 the Left Behind website was getting around forty thousand visitors a day and Jerry Jenkins dropped in occasionally to respond to readers and connect with fans.[13] In 1999 alone, the first book sold nearly 2 million copies, 1 million of these in the final four months leading up to the millennium.[14] Banking on the success of Left Behind is the publisher that brought it to the marketplace. In the last decade Tyndale House has built a new sixty-thousand-square-foot warehouse, doubled its number of employees, and become one of the rising Christian publishing houses.

According to LaHaye and Jenkins, they only planned one novel. That soon grew into a trilogy, which eventually grew into a twelve-book series. However, if one reads the books at all closely, they appear to be carefully planned and set out from the beginning, slowly, methodically tracing the lives of the heroes through the various tribulations they encounter on the way to the final book—*Glorious Appearing*—and the return of the Messiah. The authors start peppering the series with the phrase "glorious appearing" by the third book, *Nicolae*, lighting the path to that final book of the original twelve. As the series stretches out, it seems a very careful and remarkable amount of planning went into constructing of the books, taking into account how the "detailed Biblical outline" is presented. "I've never done one thing to cultivate that," LaHaye remarked in a *Book Page* interview about the success of his books, instead crediting God himself as the mastermind behind the publicity.[15] Toward the middle of the series, and on the verge of the millennium in 1999, LaHaye and Jenkins released a defense of the premillennial version of eschatology with their book *Are We Living in the End Times?* This also seems to be a carefully calculated, if regurgitated, version of past works on the same subject, meant to deflect the growing criticism of their ideas on the Rapture.

Further capitalizing on the success of the Left Behind series, LaHaye reportedly received a $42 million advance from Bantam Books for a new series called Babylon Rising. This four-book series, which is written by lesser known co-writers attaching themselves to the LaHaye brand a la Jerry Jenkins, continues along the quasi-thriller-Biblical-prophecy genre line by tracking the adventures of Biblical archeologist and Indiana Jones clone Michael Murphy through his search for artifacts such as Noah's Ark. Like Left Behind, this series also delves into the black magic of conspiracy, describing a secret organization that is murdering people all around Murphy. The first and title book of the series debuted among the top ten on the *New York Times* bestseller list. LaHaye's more politically combative book, *Mind Siege*, co-authored with David Noebel, debuted on the *New York Times* hardcover nonfiction bestseller list in 2001 at number seventeen, at the same time as five of the Left Behind books were on the hardcover and paperback bestseller lists. "Brand LaHaye" has become so successful that LaHaye has signed onto a three-book fiction deal with Kensington to be co-authored by novelist Gregory Dinallo.[16] LaHaye has also teamed up with former Focus on the Family alum Bob DeMoss for a young adult series called Soul Survivor, of which the first book is a familiarly titled *Mind Siege Project*.[17]

Just a year before releasing the Left Behind book *Babylon Rising*, LaHaye had a reported income of around $15 million a year, adding in the earnings from his Tim LaHaye Ministries, which brings in around $500,000 a year from his speaking at prophecy conferences, and through his other book sales.[18] Another of the LaHaye holdings, founded during the 1980s, was the not-for-profit Tim LaHaye Ministries, based out of El Cajon, California. The Pre-Trib Research Center, organized in late 1992, and the Family Life Seminars lecture program on sex, marriage, and Christian lifestyle, started in the early 1980s, are two other important arms of the LaHaye's personal empire. The nonprofit Tim LaHaye Ministries, which brought in about one million dollars in 2002, hosts LaHaye's website www.timlahaye.com, promotes the LaHaye books, asks for donations to his Pre-Trib Research Center, steers people to LaHaye appearances at prophecy conferences, and pushes his Christian Family seminars.[19]

Expanding beyond print media, an audio drama series of Left Behind was syndicated on over 350 radio stations nationally by early 2002.[20] In 2004, Left Behind went wireless with an agreement between Tyndale House and mobile channel management company Airborne Entertainment, a company that reaches nearly 100 percent of all enabled mobile subscribers in North America. The Left Behind series has now been converted to SMS alerts, cellphone wallpaper, ringtones, MMS messaging and a number of other downloadable applications. LaHaye and many premillennialists have been actively using new technology to reach audiences and market their ideas. Having virtually secured Internet, radio, film, TV, and print, they have aimed a direct and ferocious marketing campaign at children in this battle for minds and wallets.[21] For all their disaffection with modernity, it is surprising how these fundamentalists have been among the most ardent in embracing technology. "Millennialists are cutting edge in com-

God loves you!
Seek Him —

Love,
Jesus

dership,

rage,

tributions

12 • 1–3 p.m.

munications technology," says Richard Landes of the Center for Millennial Studies. "This makes cyberspace's implications for the twenty-first century what paintings were to the sixteenth."[22]

The children's audio books and comics series, Left Behind: The Kids, now grosses around $100 million per year and the children's book series had sold over 11 million copies by the end of 2004.[23] Marketing toward children is certainly important for LaHaye and many premillennialists, as most people in the U.S. come to their religious beliefs before the age of thirteen and hold them relatively steadily through adulthood.[24]

Considering how powerful the ideas of premillennial dispensationalism play within the adult community, when looking at the psychological affects on children, the implications may be especially troubling. Writing in the *National Catholic Reporter*, Teresa Malcolm tells a startling and illuminating story of a Protestant friend who told of her of childhood nightmares about the Rapture. It is a story of fear and paranoia. "In her church, sermons on the subject were quite common: Someday without warning, Christ would snatch away to heaven all the true Christians, leaving behind unfortunates who would have to endure the seven-year Tribulation under the reign of the Antichrist," she writes. "One night when she was about 8 years old, my friend woke up to find her parents gone, and she was convinced that they had been 'Raptured' and she had been left behind. What a relief to discover they had briefly stepped out of the house."[25]

In a scene during the Rapture in the first novel, Left Behind, all the kids playing soccer at a Christian missionary school in Indonesia are taken to heaven except one unfortunate child. Due to his guilt-ridden sense of remorse he promptly commits suicide.[26] The despair of not being among the Raptured was so great for this fictional character that he had to kill himself, lending itself to the cultishness of the theology. Throughout the novels suicide post-Rapture is quite prevalent. Imagine if a child in real life such as the one described by Malcolm above had read these books, and instead of waiting to find out if the Rapture had really come and gone, took their own life.

Apocalypse, Now? And Now? And Now ...?

Left Behind: The Movie, which follows the first novel fairly close-ly, sold over three million copies on video in 2000 and was named the Video Software Dealers Association's Best Selling Title of the Year by an Independent Studio. During the first week of video sales it was the bestselling title in America, edging out *Toy Story 2* and *The Green Mile*. In late 2002, the second film, *Left Behind II: Tribulation Force*, was released. Academy Award winner Pam Wallace, who won the award for the screenplay for the Harrison Ford movie *Witness*, penned the adaptation of the second Left Behind book for Canadian film company Cloud Ten Pictures, the producer of the movies. By distributing to Wal-Mart, Sam's Club, Costco, and Christian outlets like Family Christian, Parable and Lifeway stores, LaHaye and Cloud Ten hoped to maximize their efforts. Unfortunately for them, even with an Academy Award–winning screenwriter on board, the novels didn't transfer very well to the screen and video sales couldn't compare with the wild success of the book series—the storyline gets fuzzy and the huge web of conspiracy background can't eas-ily be woven into the plot of a ninety-minute movie.[27]

When the Left Behind films and television series didn't do as well as LaHaye expected, he filed a suit against Cloud Ten Pictures, claiming the film company had breached its contract by making a film of lower quality promised. This was mainly seen as an attempt to get leverage and try to force them to relinquish the rights to the Left Behind children's series, which Cloud Ten was developing for television. The federal judge overseeing the case dismissed all claims brought by LaHaye against the compa-ny. In early 2003, Cloud Ten launched a television series in Canada, also on DVD and video in both Canada and the U.S., based on the Left Behind novels.

As well as the Left Behind movies and other premillennial-ist fictions, films like *The Omega Code*, and Arnold Schwarzenegger's *End of Days* helped add to the mare's nest of millennial fever pre-2000. The Rapture narrative–subscribing *Omega Code*, funded by the Trinity Broadcasting Network, was promoted by twenty-four hundred pastors, and End Times author Hal Lindsey (also of LaHaye's Pre-Trib network) was hired on as a prophecy consultant for the film. Due to this massive church promotion, in October 1999, *The Omega Code* was one of the top ten grossing movies of the month.[28]

One film genre which has done fairly well in evangelical circles, and that is alluded to in LaHaye's books, is something called the post-Rapture film. These are videos theoretically to be played by those "left behind," and can be found in the Left Behind novels and movies, and advertised along with them. At one point in both the first Left Behind novel and the first movie, newly left behind pastor Bruce Barnes shows the rest of the Tribulation Force, the group established to battle the Antichrist, a post-Rapture video that had been given to him by his own pastor, now among those believing Christians Raptured to heaven. Versions of this post-Rapture subgenre circulate through Christian book clubs and bookstores, with the most popular one being Cloud Ten CEO's Peter Lalonde's *Left Behind*, selling over two hundred thousand copies. This was not related to the LaHaye book or the LaHaye movie, though Lalonde who has made other apocalyptic films as well, later helped bring the LaHaye version of the books to the screen. A separate video was released with LaHaye and Jenkins Left Behind books called *Have You Been Left Behind?* to take advantage of the prominent segment of the book where the character Rayford watches a post-Rapture video and in the movie where Barnes shows the Trib-Force the same video.

Marketing for the LaHaye version of the video is intent on striking at the anxiety among this community of believers who fear they may be left behind, or at least know someone who might. The cover of the video reads: "If you find this tape, play it immediately. Your future depends on it!" Once the film is over, the video explains: "Every Christian needs to keep a copy of this video accessible in his or her home for those left behind."[29] At one point in the first Left Behind book, the authors even seem to be plugging their own Rapture video, the one that was left for those un-Raptured to view at Bruce's church, the same one that is plugged at the end of the Left Behind movies and at the back of the books themselves.

Here is some of that passage from the first Left Behind book where the former, and now Raptured, Pastor Vernon Billings is speaking to Rayford:

"Hello," came the pleasant voice of the pastor Rayford had met several times. As he spoke he sat on the edge of the desk in the very office Rayford had just visited. "My name is Vernon Billings, and I'm pastor of the New Hope Village Church of Mount Prospect, Illinois. As you watch this tape, I can only imagine the fear and despair you face, for this is being recorded for viewing only after the disappearance of God's people from the earth.

"That you are watching indicates that you have been left behind. You are no doubt stunned, shocked, afraid, and remorseful. I would like you to consider what I have to say here as instructions for life following Christ's rapture of his church. That is what has happened. Anyone you know or knew of who had placed his or her trust in Christ alone for salvation has been taken to heaven by Christ."[30]

Following this, the video has the pastor read a passage from 1 Corinthians 15:51–57, which Rayford finds after flipping through his own Bible that "though it was slightly different in [his wife's] translation, the meaning was the same." With a slight brush of the hand, the theological argument over the meaning of this passage from Paul, the one premillennialists point to as the verse that signifies the Rapture, is set aside—the passage that is open to a multitude of translations and interpretations and is the main basis of premillennialist theology, which makes them fixate so much on the Book of Revelation. Of course, in the post-Rapture videos, none of this debate comes up.

For centuries, however, these debates have had a profound influence on how the final book of the Bible has been read. Dispensational premillennialism is merely the latest in a long line of readings of this book.

WARS AND RUMORS OF WARS

If there is one quote from the Bible that has often been used to stir millennialist feeling, it may be the "wars and rumors of wars" passage in which Jesus speaks about the End and his coming millennial reign. Jenkins uses this quote from Matthew 24:6—"You will hear of wars and rumors of wars"—in an interview that ties into September 11 into proof we are living in the End Times. "Clearly, that's what we saw [on 9/11], and yet Jesus went on to say that that would not be the end, but rather the beginning of the end. . . . He could wait one more day, and to us it could seem like a thousand years, because scripture also says that to Him, a thousand years is as a day."[1]

While anticipation of a Second Coming of the Messiah and a millennial reign of Christ has been central to Christianity since it began, the idea of the Rapture came about very late. In the nineteenth century, Anglican priest John Nelson Darby constructed a theological interpretation around the book of the Revelation, crafting it into the complex organized vision that became known as dispensational premillennialism. Based on the theories of a twelfth-century monk, Joachim of Fiore, Darby developed the idea of "ages" of the church: three progressively more spiritual epochs Christianity was to "evolve" through. These dispensations were later used by the modern premillennialists to build their theories.[2] The closed and self-referential nature of the theories developed by major premillennialist theologians today—mainly through the dogmatic and centralizing nature of the LaHayeguided Pre-Trib Research Center—helps to keep these discussions "on message" and later to disseminate them to the larger public through the Christian publishing industry.

The term "premillennialism" is used here instead of the full title, as it makes more sense when discussing the political manifestations of the movement—premillennialism as a prelude to the millennial reign of Christ, a period of tribulation between what believers say will eventually occur between the Rapture and the second coming of Jesus Christ for his reign of a thousand years. The Darbian premillennialist philosophy, while relying on broad interpretation, professes that it is simply based on Biblical truth. The idea for Darby's Rapture, or the mass immigration of all true believers to heaven to immortal life before Tribulation, comes from a single passage of Paul's New Testament account where he says "the Lord shall descend from heaven with a shout" which comes just before the believers are "caught up . . . in the clouds, to meet with the Lord in the air." Whether this is actually what Paul wrote or how literally he meant it is largely a matter of debate. "Darby did not search for mystical meaning in the Bible, which he saw as a document that told the literal truth," writes Karen Armstrong. "[For Darby] the prophets and the author of the Book of Revelation were not speaking symbolically but making precise predictions which would shortly come to pass exactly as they had been foretold."[3]

Between 1859 and 1877, Darby ventured to America six times to proclaim his new theological concepts after having failed to convince his native British of their value. There, Protestant fundamentalists of various stripes began to blend these ideas into their own readings of eschatology. Premillennialism is now the most widely held view, though other views on the dispensations—mid-Tribulational and post-Tribulational—also developed, as well as arguments over whether Rapture would be partial (the most devout taken away) and prewrath (Rapture three-fourths of the way through the time of tribulation). It would be in the increasingly embattled Protestant fundamentalist America of the 1920s, fresh from the embarrassing portrayal of fundamentalists during the John Scopes "Monkey Trial," where the Darbian theology would find its proper home and the premillennial reading, which promises the greatest mass salvation to faithful believers, would take the most prominent position. Evangelical historian

Randall Balmer points out that the premillennialist "theology of despair" effected the early-twentieth-century evangelical movement enormously. Through the mental evangelical "retreat from the political arena" early in the century after the blows to prohibition and creationism, to fundamentalist architecture taking on a utilitarian, functional and "utterly artless" quality, this phase marked a physical retreat from the world, which reflected thoughts of the imminent return of Christ.[4] Later, in the late twentieth century, the Darbian theology would be conjoined with rightwing conspiracy fantasies as well as the American narrative myths of exceptionalism, the New Jerusalem, and the Shining City on a Hill, making for a new, resurgent form of evangelical fundamentalism and political activism.

One of the most successful ways dispensational premillennialism has made its way into American religious culture has been through the Scofield Reference Bible, first published by Cyrus Scofield in 1909. The publishing house Oxford University Press, hardly a fundamentalist mouthpiece, made a fortune off the book when it became an early bestseller, and now publishes a version called the Oxford Scofield Study Bible. Using Darby's ideas of "dispensations" or ages, Scofield attempted to date the Biblical events chronologically, hanging much of his claims on Archbishop James Ussher's theory that 4004 BC was the date of Creation. Ussher, a Protestant theologian and Archbishop of the Church of Ireland in the seventeenth century, was also staunchly anti-Catholic and resented the allegorical symbolism the mother Church relied upon. The eschatological and "timeline" frameworks borrowed from Scofield were also to play a major role in how American fundamentalists would understand creationism and later give people like Henry Morris of the LaHaye-founded Institute for Creation Research texts to back the claims they have made about "scientific creationism." Scofield's extensive and complex notes on the Revelation are a direct line to what has become the predominant view of the final book of the Bible among fundamentalist Protestants, displacing the older Calvinist interpretation of this book that was closer to the allegorical and symbolic views Catholicism has long held.

"We owe a great debt to the Baptists, Plymouth Brethren, many independent Churches, the Scofield Bible, and independent Christian publishing houses for the present general acceptance of a belief in both the 'Rapture' and the imminent return of Christ," writes LaHaye in his Pre-Trib Research Center newsletter. He then follows this remark with a contradiction: "The interesting thing is that when the common people read the Bible, they tend to take it literally unless some allegorist or symbolizer has tampered with their mind." The contradiction here is that dispensational premillennialists, while claiming a literal reading of the simple intent of scripture, go to great, and often dubious lengths, to interpret passages in the Bible to conform to their theories, as in the case with Rapture, basing them on what isn't readily apparent from a "simple literal reading" of those passages.

Authors such as LaHaye claim they base both their plotlines and their politics on is the literal reading of the last book of the Bible. Most widely known as the Book of Revelation, or by its Greek title—The Apocalypse or Apokalypsis from the verb *apokalypto* meaning "to reveal"—this book was the most significant resource for Darby and his latter day premillennialists for crafting their eschatological narrative. Yet in their literal interpretation, they fail to recognize, or at least make aware to those they preach to, how much debate there was in the early church over the significance, authenticity, and authority of the Revelation; not to mention that this debate still continues to this day. That the Revelation has come in and out of favor and been translated through a variety of languages is hardly acknowledged as problematic in premillennialist texts, even though they claim their teachings are based on the literal text. That the book is there in the Bible, in English, is proof enough for absolutists that it is the literal word of God. The Revelation, a book that was almost left out of what is now known to be the Bible, has arguably become the most prominent lens through which premillennialist Christians view the world today.[5]

Since the Revelation does borrow so much from the Old Testament prophetic books, the image of God in the premillennialist Left Behind series is much the same as the image in the Old Testament—a vengeful and destructive God, not the forgiving and redeeming savior Jesus depicted in the Gospels of the New Testament. This is one of the powerful concepts of premillennialist fixation on Revelation, that God will not be merciful or forgiving, that those who deny "the truth" as they portray it will not only face damnation in the netherworld, but also damnation through Tribulation on earth. Here is a scene of what is in store from *Soul Harvest*, where one of the Tribulation judgments is raining blood from the sky:

> Balls of fire dropped into the trees that bordered the backyard. They burst into flames as one, their branches sending a giant orange mushroom into the air. The trees cooled as quickly as they had ignited.
> "Here comes the blood," Tsion said, and suddenly Hattie sat straight up. She stared out the window as blood poured from the skies. She struggled to kneel on the bed so she could see farther. The parched yard was wet with melted hail and now red with blood.
> Lightning cracked and thunder rolled. Softball-sized hailstones drummed the roof, rolling and filling the yard. Tsion shouted, "Praise the Lord God Almighty, maker of heaven and earth! What you see before you is a picture of Isaiah 1:18: 'Though your sins are like scarlet, they shall be as white as the snow; though they are red like crimson, they shall be as wool.'"[6]

This construction is a return to the hellfire and brimstone of the Old Testament and an abandonment of the redemption through Jesus Christ preached in the New Testament. Remarkably, the interpretation of Isaiah 1:18 as possibly signifying Christ's redemption of sin is turned around in the above passage to place it in the literal context of an actual event as relative to a future understanding of Revelation events. In a passage from the eighth novel, *The Mark*, Jewish biblical scholar turned dispensational premillennialist Tsion Ben-Judah is delivering one of his Internet sermons which readers are told millions are reading:

> God goes to extreme measures to compress the decision-making time for men and women before the coming of Christ to set up his earthly kingdom.
> Despite that this is clearly the most awful time in history, I still say it is also a merciful act of God to give as many souls as possible an opportunity to put their faith in Christ. Oh, people, we are the army of God with a massive job to do in a short time. May we do it with willingness and eagerness, and the courage that comes only from him. There are countless lost souls in need of saving, and we have the truth.

> It may be hard to recognize God's mercy when his
> wrath is also intensifying. Woe to those who believe the
> lie that God is only "love." Yes, he is love. And his gift of
> Jesus as the sacrifice for our sin is the greatest evidence of
> this. But the Bible also says God is "holy, holy, holy." He
> is righteous and a God of justice, and it is not in his
> nature to allow sin to go unpunished or unpaid for.[7]

There are countless other justifications given for the pre-eminence of a vengeful and wrathful God over that of the teachings of Jesus throughout the novels. Early in the Left Behind series, Bruce Barnes, the pastor of the new church and head of the Tribulation Force—the only one left behind from his Raptured congregation—argues that his conceptions of God as a forgiving God had led him to be lazy in his faith; believing this way was the easiest and simplest path. Through the voice of the authors, Barnes gets defensive when he tells his congregation that he hasn't "become a wild-eyed madman, a cultist, or anything other than what I have been since I realized I had missed the 'Rapture.'"[8] But delivering a long, breathless sermon about the Four Horsemen of the Apocalypse and the Seven Judgments—railing against acceptance of mainline symbolism over fundamentalist literalism, and identifying Carpathia as the Antichrist incarnate—doesn't make him less of a wild-eyed madman or cultist. "The millenniums-old account reads as fresh to me as tomorrow's newspaper," Bruce says, ending his sermon. A few pages later he states, "You will never hear peace promised from this pulpit," and further on, "I will tell you only what the Scriptures say, and to follow the news."[9]

Revelation Revolution

Before going further into the Left Behind books themselves, it is important to look at the history of the Book of Revelation as well as its interpretation and uses over time. During the two centuries immediately before and after Christ—a time of increasing persecution by the Roman authorities—eschatological or prophetic narratives were primarily a Jewish preoccupation. As Jews became Christians, early Christian leaders adopted the literary style to suit their needs, using it to act out their apocalyptic fantasies on their own persecutors and to keep wayward believers in

line—or so goes most of the mainline and mainstream interpretations of the final book of the Bible.

"In Apocalypse, most Biblical scholars now agree, John of
Patmos is actually describing a situation that, through archeolo-
gy and textual analysis, we are more or less able to piece together," writes Tom Bissell in *Harper's Magazine*. "Some churches are
'falling asleep,' others are behaving licentiously and a great beast
(probably Nero Caesar, whose name adds up to 666 when
Hebrew letters are given numerical values; this is called germa-
tria) doth loom astride the scattered Christians' beleaguered
world. Apocalypse is an angry, fatherly chastisement that combines the 'cosmic battle' scenario familiar throughout the ancient
world with a more newly minted Christian persecution narrative. In other words, Apocalypse makes us privy not to the future
but to John of Patmos's recent past and immediate present—a
trick of perspective, often used by biblical authors, called *vaticinia
ex eventu*, history disguised as prophecy."[10]

Relatively little is known about John of Patmos, the supposed
author of the Revelation who was writing to the "seven churches
which are in Asia" at the end of the first century AD There is
debate over whether he was "banished to Patmos" or had gone to
Patmos "in order to hear the word of God" in solitude, a retreat
to seek revelation. Some scholars during the second century
attributed the text to a writer by the name of Cerinthus, and several Christian sects sprung up, namely the Alogi, around 200 AD,
in rejection of the doctrines in the book. The Bishop of
Alexandria, Dionysius, who believed the writer was one who had
taken the ideas of Cerinthus, but not that man himself, had a few
harsh words about the book, stating "this is the doctrine of
Cerinthus, that there will be an early reign of Christ, as he was a
lover of the body he dreamed that he would revel in the gratifica-
tion of the sensual appetite." During the fourth and fifth centuries, the Apocalypse, or the Revelation, was mostly excluded
from the list of sacred books in the Eastern churches.[11]

Comparing the Apocalypse to the Gospel of John, which
some scholars thought might have been written by the same
John, the figure of Jesus is treated in a strikingly different way. In
that Gospel, Jesus was seen as the "life and light of the world, the
fullness of grace and truth," while the character of the Revelation
Jesus is described as a militant "conqueror of Satan and his king-

dom." This and the grammatical defects of Revelation, when compared to the Gospel of John, are pointed to as reasons to believe the John of Patmos was not the John of the Gospel. Scholars for centuries have traced much of the language of the Revelation back to the more prophetic books of the Bible, principally Daniel, Ezekiel, Zachariah, and Joel, as well as from the earlier books of Exodus, Genesis, and a smattering of others— but mainly from Daniel. This conscious mining of the older books of the Bible is why the Revelation often appears to line up so neatly with the rest of the prophetic books.

Whether this was constructed as part of a "divine revelation" or simply a timely regurgitation and reinterpretation of an old Jewish myth applied to the persecution of the early Christian church is still under debate. The historical condition of the Jews during the writing of Daniel, persecuted under the reign of Antiochus Epiphanes, was similar to the persecution of Christians under the reign of Domitian, when the Revelation was written. The purpose of the Revelation to John, heavily drawing on Daniel as well as on Jesus's discourse on the Mount of Olives, was to burgeon the faith of early Christian believers with a sense of hope instilled in the idea that the imminent return of a militant Christ would wipe out their evil satanic foes.[12] From the beginning the Revelation is an extremely political book, meant to keep the mass of faithful in line during a "time of Tribulation" and lead them to an all-encompassing, activist faith. Read allegorically, the message transcends the specific time and can be applied to individual Tribulations faced by Christians today; taken literally, as an absolute guide to future events, it maintains the role of buoying a faithful community, as well as delivers a militantly active political narrative meant to spur literal believers to await, or if that fails, attain, the millennial promise.

Early versions of the Revelation spread into Christian communities throughout the region of Asia Minor, North Africa, Italy, and Greece—namely to churches in the regions that the author was writing to. In the first years after the death of Jesus Christ, it was widely believed that his return would be during the lifetime of those believers, and as that time waned, along came the Revelation to John to keep the idea of imminent return alive. The wane continued as the imminent return failed to become reality and the Church began to move into a more stable and static arena that embraced the Matthew passage 24:36—"But the day and the hour no one knoweth, no, not the angels of heaven, but the Father alone"—as a foil against imminency.

While early Christian scholars such as Clement and Origen did not doubt the authenticity of Revelation, they mostly interpreted the passages as allegorical and shied away from the literal millennialist overtones the book contains. St. Augustine, who LaHaye regards as an abomination, was the most important proponent of the allegorical interpretation. LaHaye, in his book *Are We Living in the End Times?*, refers to Augustine as a "Greek humanist" and basically a pagan for "spiritualizing scripture"— thus not interpreting scripture literally, but metaphorically. St. Augustine was probably the most influential early Church leader in moving away from the millennialist beliefs and into the stable, static arena of a historic Church. He argued that the foundation of the Church itself was the millennial kingdom, and that tone thousand wasn't a set number, but an allegorical one meant to signify an indefinite period. "St. Augustine, writing in the late 300s and early 400s, interpreted the reference to a 'thousand years' in Revelation 20 as a metaphor for the age of the Church," writes Carl E. Olsen, a convert from fundamentalism to Catholicism and now a Catholic theologian, in the magazine *Catholic Faith*. Olsen is the author of *Will Catholics Be 'Left Behind'?*, which looks at the series through a Catholic perspective: "This would become the accepted belief of the Church, going unchallenged for many centuries."

One of the forerunners to LaHaye, and one of the first to introduce premillennialist narratives and the ideas of Darby to mainstream readers, was his associate at the Pre-Trib Research Center Hal Lindsey, author of *The Late Great Planet Earth*, the bestselling book of the 1970s. "Lindsey's book was a systematic interpretation of current events in terms of fulfilling the prophecies of Revelation—and, obviously, the belief that we are fast approaching the final events. This was the kind of thing that Augustine formally and explicitly banned, and that, for at least six centuries after Augustine, churchmen were careful never to record in writing," said Richard Landes, director of the Center for Millennial Studies at Boston University, on PBS's Frontline program "Apocalypse!" in early 2004.[13]

"None of the Church Fathers believed in a secret removal of true believers prior to the Tribulation." writes Olsen.

> On the contrary, they taught that the Church would undergo a period of intense tribulation, without any Rapture of believers, prior to the Second Coming. Darby's idea of a "secret" "Rapture" would have been both foreign and repulsive to the early Christians, as it was bothersome to many of Darby's Protestant allies.[14]

Most recently, mainline churches have been attempting to fight back against the premillennialist theology as represented in the Left Behind novels. In 2001, an overwhelming resolution was passed at the General Assembly of the Presbyterian Church to declare the theology in the Left Behind series "not in accord" with the church's reading of the New Testament book of the Revelation. Late in 2000, the Missouri Synod of the Lutheran Church officially noted that the books contained "very serious errors about what the Bible really teaches" and published a critical analysis of it on its web site. Roman Catholic bishops in Chicago condemned the series as "anti-Catholic" in 2003 and sent out a statement to all the dioceses in the state saying the theology about the Second Coming was not in accord with Catholic beliefs on the Revelation, which don't fall in line with the dispensational rapture theology. Olsen refers to LaHaye as a "rabid anti-Catholic" because of LaHaye's earlier nonfiction references to the Church as "apostate, false, not Christian" and full of "Babylonian mysticism," as well as the long-standing fundamentalist belief that Catholics worship idols.[15]

Mainstream Baptist theologians have also been very critical of the "beam me up theology" of the Left Behind series and dispensational premillennialism in general as a "massive misunderstanding" of scripture. British theological scholar N.T. Wright wrote in the August 2001 issue of *Bible Review* that the success of the books "appears puzzling, even bizarre" when looked at by observers from across the pond. One evangelical scholar, Ben Witherington III of Asbury Theological Seminary, comments that the views of the Revelation propagated by the premillennialists misread the return of Christ. "The idea that John of Patmos, the author of Revelation, intended his message to be understood only by a late 20th-century or 21st-century Western

Christian audience is not only arrogant—it flies in the face of what John himself writes in Revelation (chapters 2–3). Here John states quite clearly that his intended audience was Christians in western Asia Minor at the end of the first century A.D."[16] It is here were John of Patmos specifically addresses those seven ancient communities of Ephesus, Smyrna, Pergamum, Thyatira, Sardis, Philadelphia, and Laodicea.

According to the Barna Research Group, which regularly polls the Christian community in the United States, the theological gap between Protestants and Catholics is quite wide—with Protestant groups twice as likely to believe the accuracy of the Bible, twice as ready to attempt to proselytize, twice as likely to believe in Christ's infallibility, twice as likely to believe in Satan as an actual being and not allegorically, and nearly five times more likely to reject the idea of faith through good works—one of the core tenets of Catholic spirituality, and one roundly rejected by LaHaye in the Left Behind novels and his other writings.[17]

Though ideas of the Rapture may be marginal and largely a product of the past 150 years, expectance of the Second Coming has been remarkably central to many significant events throughout Western history. In anticipation of the Second Coming, in the late 500s AD, Pope Gregory I dispatched monks to the British Isles in order to convert the English ruler Augustine, a man who became the first Archbishop of Canterbury and later a saint. Crusaders were urged on to retake Jerusalem from whichever Antichrists controlled it in hopes the millennial reign would soon come. Christopher Columbus felt his journey would bring about the return of Christ by spreading the word of God to all nations. Jews were brought back to England by Oliver Cromwell after the English Civil War with the thought that this would speed up prophecy. Later English Jewry was urged to resettle in Israel, largely based on biblical readings and the help of some Christians hoping for the End of History and the Kingdom of God.

Early Marxists were influenced by more communalist millennial groups such as some radical followers of Saint Francis, who wanted to abolish property and any institutions not under the guidance of the Church, and once finished, live in a perfect communal society. There were groups like the sixteenth-century Anabaptists who took over the town of Leiden in the Netherlands and abolished money, banned all books but the

Bible, and instituted polygamy. Their leader, in stark similarity to David Koresh and other would be messiahs, proclaimed himself the king and messiah. The Puritan settlement in Massachusetts saw itself as a theocratic colony that would be the model for the New Jerusalem, the precursor to establishing the millennial society on earth.[18]

In American history one of the greatest upsurges in apocalyptic feeling came from self-taught preacher William Miller, who forecasted numerous dates of the Second Coming throughout the early nineteenth century as the time of the end, gaining thousands of followers until those predictions culminated in the Great Disappointment of October 1844. Though most of that movement fell away, an ardent following founded the Seventh-Day Adventist movement, which doesn't make the same date setting mistakes as Miller anymore. Joseph Smith's Latter-Day Saints, or Mormons, also started with a heavy feeling of millennial fever. He had set the date of the Second Coming for 1890, but as we know, the guest didn't show. Since those failed predictions Mormons have moved away from specific predictions of the end into a much more stable belief system. Prior to the Revolutionary War, many colonists portrayed the British as the Antichrist system and the stamp act as "the Mark of the Beast" foretold in the Revelation.[19]

Today, the apocalyptic fervor of the Revelation is as alive as ever. How it has been manipulated for political means and mixed with far-right conspiracy theory is important for understanding LaHaye, as well as understanding how his use of these premillennialist narratives have helped spur the resurgent political activism of the religious right.

POLYESTER REVOLUTIONARIES

> The paranoid spokesman sees the fate of conspiracy in apocalyptic terms—he traffics in the birth and death of whole worlds, whole political orders, whole systems of human values . . . He is always manning the barricades of civilization. He constantly lives at a turning point. Like religious millenialists he expresses the anxiety of those who are living through the last days and his is sometimes disposed to set a date for the apocalypse.
> —Richard Hofstadter, "The Paranoid Style of American Politics."

Jerry Falwell perhaps best described Tim Lahaye's political influence: "His impact subliminally is probably greater than it ever has been, such that if you were to ask him he would tell you that he's no longer crusading, he's evangelizing" said Falwell in the *Los Angeles Times* in early 2004. "Once his converts get in our churches, we pastors have a tendency to tell them how to vote."[1]

A quarter century before this statement by his friend Falwell, before he came to national prominence as perhaps the single most "subliminally" influential leader on the religious right, LaHaye wrote of how he perceived the political and social struggle of the righteous against the forces of immoral secularism in his 1979 book *Battle for the Mind*. "There are millions of us— and only a handful of them," he wrote, going on to describe the eventual triumph of his brand of believers over what he sees as a cabal of secular humanists who have taken over American society through conspiracy.[2] Tim LaHaye can be seen as something of a Pied Piper of premillennialism, drawing upon the outline he has divined from Revelation and the prophetic books of the Bible, as well as other texts such as those of nineteenth-century British preacher John Darby, the man who popularized the phrase "Rapture of the Church" and the theology of dispensational premillennialism. Over the past thirty years LaHaye has been busy building an empire of his own. From his home in Rancho Mirage, California, he has been central to constructing some of the most powerful organizations in the conservative rightwing universe—the Moral Majority, Concerned Women for America, the Council for National Policy, the Institute for Creation Research, and a handful of others. LaHaye has been at the forefront in the battles against abortion rights, for putting Christian prayer and the teaching of creationism in public schools, to paint gay rights as part of a conspiratorial "homosexual agenda," to hold back women's equal rights, to secure the relationship between far-right Israeli parties and Christian groups in the U.S., to erode the lines between church and state, and to create a centralized lobbying force at the heart of the network of the most conservative think tanks, foundations and organizations in this country—the Council for National Policy.

In his famous 1964 *Harper's Magazine* essay, "The Paranoid Style of American Politics," Richard Hofstadter argued for the thesis that American politics has often been an "arena of angry minds" who have constructed paranoid narratives to achieve political aims, usually based on picking and choosing readily available facts and entwining them with powerful myths and suspicions.[3] Though writing in 1964 during the height of the Goldwater movement, he could have just as easily been writing about how entwined the anger of the conspiratorial extreme rightwing and the anger of the biblically literalist religious right toward secular society would become. What Hofstadter knew when writing this essay, which is important when examining the premillennialist movement, is that the paranoid style of American politics wouldn't be relevant if it was only confined to the minds of lunatics or the deranged. Conspiracy, rumor, and innuendo play as equally to the bigotries of the average man as they do to the minds of the deranged.

When millions of people believe in a narrative myth that encompasses their apocalyptic biblical worldview together with the historical rightwing conspiracy narrative, it is a phenomenon that has moved beyond the framework of localized subsections of evangelical fundamentalism into the realm of a mass ideology. The more the ideology grows; the more literature that becomes available; the more authors with reputable sounding PhDs from the self-contained universities and institutions such as those established by Falwell, Pat Robertson, and LaHaye back those theories up, the more the ideology spreads. Hofstadter says it best when describing how relentlessly these movements mine pieces of prior evidence to prove their cases to themselves and to their audience: "The entire rightwing movement of our time is a parade of experts, study groups, monographs, footnotes, and bibliographies." When people look to others to verify their beliefs and find a community that holds similar beliefs, the more those beliefs begin to make sense. The more churches that disseminate these views, the more the alternative media of fundamentalism builds, the more the narrative moves into the mainstream, the more people become involved in holding the tent up, the further the movement grows off itself. Thus the books, the movies, the sustained effort to define itself against anything outside the fundamentalist worldview.

Humanists, argued LaHaye, have been taking America "down a path of moral degeneracy" that would lead the country to become a "socialist state similar to Russia."[4] For LaHaye the worldwide conspiracy consists of groups such as the Illuminati; the Trilateral Commission; the American Civil Liberties Union (ACLU); the National Association for the Advancement of Colored People (NAACP); National Organization for Women (NOW); Planned Parenthood; the U.N.; the U.S. State Department; the "major TV networks, high-profile newspapers and newsmagazines"; major center-left foundations like Rockefeller, Ford and Carnegie; "the left-wing of the Democratic party"; as well as Harvard, Yale and "2,000 other colleges and universities"—all of these for LaHaye are out to turn America over to the hands of Satan. This is the message delivered through the Left Behind books and his institutions. Much of the genius of LaHaye and the paranoid rightwing is that it can couch such a wide range of groups into simplified language, the strict

division of black and white, with us or against us type of rhetoric—everything that they don't sanction is suspect, everything
outside their sphere of influence is part of an evil conspiracy that
must be destroyed. It is the language of revolution. It is language
that would make Trotsky and Lenin, former paranoid revolu-
tionaries of the left, quite proud.

While LaHaye has wanted to make people think the United
States is headed down the Antichrist path via a widespread secular humanist conspiracy these last thirty years, the numbers show
that this notion is highly exaggerated. Protestants, including liberal, mainline, and fundamentalist denominations make up 52
percent of the population. Roman Catholics account for another
24 percent of the population, Mormons 2 percent, Jews 1 percent,
and Muslims 1 percent. A further 10 percent of the population
believes in any number of other faiths (Hindu, Buddhist, Taoist,
animist, etc.), and only around 10 percent consider themselves
full-blown atheists.[5]

In 2004, 77 percent of American adults identified themselves
as Christian. On top of that, nearly 40 percent of the adult population in the U.S. described themselves as either evangelical or
nonevangelical born-again Christian.[6] LaHaye specifically targets this segment of society in his rhetoric, in the Left Behind
books and outside of it, fostering a sense of embattlement and
persecution along the way.

"I feel the largest army of any minority in this country is the
Christian army," Tim LaHaye wrote in the *Christian Inquirer* in
1984, just a few years into the founding of the Moral Majority
and Council for National Policy. "We have been intimidated into
silence by the so-called separation of church and state issue. I
should say, by the ACLU's interpretation of the separation of
church and state. And by the idea that so many ministers think
Christians shouldn't get involved in politics."[7]

But these hypothetical ministers have not been the only people reluctant to break down those walls of separation that
LaHaye believes have been erected through the action of twentieth-century secularists. A 2002 report by the Pew Forum on
Religion and Public Life found that 70 percent of Americans
believed churches should not endorse candidates, with Catholics
and mainline Protestants rejecting church political endorsements
by more than three to one. Nearly half of evangelicals voiced the

same concerns, but it is the other half, which LaHaye speaks to, that counts politically—they are much more engaged, active, and likely to man the political and spiritual barricades than moderates. In the past few years legislation supported by LaHaye and other members of the political Christian right has surfaced, which would allow churches to endorse candidates without changes in the tax-exempt status of those institutions. As 501(c)(3) tax-exempt organizations, they can do virtually everything to address policy concerns but endorse candidates or distribute campaign literature in church. In actuality, the legislation may not even be needed for the continued politicizing of "faith." It is estimated that around 40 percent of the votes cast for President George W. Bush in the 2000 elections came from evangelical Christians.[8] Polling data from the 2004 election shows a slight increase in that number, though the results are inconclusive due to the fact that different questions were asked in 2000 compared to 2004.

Tim LaHaye's recent bestselling nonfiction book *Mind Siege,* co-authored along with David Noebel, shows best where his current political thinking lies, and where he hopes his activism turns into reality. In this book LaHaye argues for a model society based on biblical values, a society where church and state are indistinguishable, where decency codes do away with things like free speech, and where abortion and homosexuality are equated with and punished as harshly as crimes such as pedophilia and prostitution. It also calls for religious litmus tests for public officials—"No humanist is fit to hold public office"— limiting the government to only biblical literalists.[9]

"I find LaHaye's politics distasteful—and I speak as an evangelical," Randall Balmer, author of *Encyclopedia of Evangelicalism* and noted scholar of Protestant Christianity wrote to me. "A politically liberal evangelical—one who finds it unfortunate (to say the least) that the Religious Right has defaulted on the noble heritage of 19th century evangelical activism."

Like the attitude expressed by Balmer, the larger community of mainline Protestant denominations are diverse and largely independent of political manipulation. Within this line, however, LaHaye has become representative of a narrow but powerful segment of Protestant evangelical fundamentalist belief, a group whose ideas have spilled over into many areas of American soci-

ety, politics, culture, and religion. Largely, this has been through
the successful efforts of LaHaye and others on the fundamentalist end of Christianity in America to define themselves as what
"true Christian" means in the country while shutting out a
diverse range of Christian beliefs. In the political arena, LaHaye
is representative of how these ideas have become a strong under-
current of the hardline conservative political machine that has
helped organize church communities into voting blocs in
America electoral politics. LaHaye has been central in influenc-
ing the direction of the political side of that movement, through
his writings, his activism, and his network-building that reaches
from the church to the White House via the organizing machinery of the Republican Party.

Although LaHaye is but one part of a large and diverse conservative movement ranging from extreme right to moderate
centrist, this book will make clear the central role he has played
in the rise of the conservative movement over the last thirty years,
in particular in the advancement of the rhetoric of "social values"
and "moral values" as specifically a monopoly of fundamentalist
Christianity. LaHaye's influence is widespread in Protestant religious communities, in conservative activist circles, on domestic
issues such as how people view abortion and evolution, and in
foreign policy, namely toward Israel and Iraq. Larry Eskridge of
the Institute for the Study of American Evangelicals called
LaHaye "the most influential American evangelical of the last 25
years," adding that "no one individual has played a more central
organizing role in the religious right than Tim LaHaye."[10]

Eskridge's comment has more to do with the institutions
LaHaye has built than the Left Behind books that have made
him famous, and LaHaye is intent on playing that role as long as
he can. Now in his early eighties, he has been among the most
important figures of the past thirty years in the "battle for the
minds" of American society, with a legacy that stretches from the
domestic to the international. On November 9, 2004, just the
week after the Bush administration won its election to a second
term, Jerry Falwell announced the "21st century resurrection of
the Moral Majority" by launching the Faith and Values
Coalition, with Tim LaHaye getting the nod as board chairman.[11]
But the newest incarnation of the Moral Majority is only the latest surge of political activity for LaHaye. From his early organi-

zations in Southern California in the late 1970s, LaHaye came to the fore of the conservative movement and the Religious Right just as Ronald Reagan was coming to prominence nationally.

The March of the Pied Piper

Tim LaHaye was born on April 27, 1926, the son of Frank LaHaye, an auto worker at Ford Motor Company, who was himself the son of French Canadian immigrants. Tim grew up in impoverished, Depression-era Detroit, selling newspapers on the street for extra spending money, later moving with his family to rural Farmington, Michigan. He was nine when his thirty-four-year-old father died—a psychological and spiritual trauma he would endure for the rest of his life.[12] LaHaye was inconsolable, until the minister at the funeral said: "'This is not the end of Frank LaHaye because he accepted Jesus. The day will come when the Lord will shout from heaven and descend, and the dead in Christ will rise first and then we'll be caught up together to meet him in the air.'" "All of a sudden, there was hope in my heart I'd see my father again," LaHaye said in an interview with the *Christian Science Monitor*.[13]

In the early 1940s, LaHaye went to night school and attended a Bible institute in Chicago. In 1944 he joined the Air Force and served as a machine-gunner aboard a bomber in the European theater until the end of the war. From there, LaHaye went on to begin his public ministry as a pastor in a small South Carolina church, and he undertook further study at Bob Jones University, the famously anti-Catholic Christian fundamentalist college. At Bob Jones, LaHaye met his future wife Beverly Jean Ratcliffe, who had also been raised in Detroit. After graduating, Tim served for a time as a Baptist pastor in Pumpkintown, South Carolina.

In 1958, the LaHayes moved to San Diego, which was at the time a magnet for neo-Nazis, McCarthyites, and the John Birch Society. These extremist groups, well-known for their paranoia and conspiratorial philosophies, had a profound effect on LaHaye's own brand of Protestant American religion. A similar mixture of far-right conspiracy and the intricate prophecy of premillennialist theology had gained prominence through a network of newsletters and radio programs such as those of Billy James Hargis, Paul Rader, and other important premillennialist preachers at this time. As one of the first radio-revivalists, Rader—who believed radio at the time was not only a "a new witnessing medium" directed by the hand of God but also a showing of how His providence blesses Protestant evangelical entrepreneurship—led the way for many premillennialists to follow in their own evangelical broadcasting empires of today.[14] The recently deceased Hargis, a popular premillennialist radio host and activist in the 1960s, passed on his torch to his right-hand man Noebel, who continues his activism together with LaHaye as the co-author of *Mind Siege*.

During the early years of LaHaye's development in California, as he built his empire of churches through his duties as pastor at Scott Memorial Baptist Church, he also spoke at John Birch Society training sessions and associated with its most influential leaders.[15] In his 1992 book, *No Fear of the Storm*, which was reissued in 1998 with a new marketing title *Rapture Under Attack*, LaHaye speaks openly about the influence the John Birch Society had on him. Here is LaHaye from the book speaking on the power behind the power that he thinks runs history, thus turning the past two hundred years into a big lie:

> I myself have been a 45-year student of the satanically-inspired, centuries-old conspiracy to use government, education, and media to destroy every vestige of Christianity within our society and establish a new world order. Having read at least fifty books on the *Illuminati*, I am convinced that it exists and can be blamed for many of man's inhumane actions against his fellow man during the past two hundred years.[16]

In this book he also reveals much about his own brand of paranoid reasoning by telling a story of how when he wanted to expand his church complex in the mid-1970s, the city council in San Diego nixed it because they wanted to preserve the wildlife habitat surrounding the area, which "made him realize that men and women largely hostile to the church controlled our city."[17]

Despite this small defeat, in a little over a decade LaHaye had started three churches and the twelve elementary and secondary schools of Christian Unified Schools of San Diego, as well as Christian Heritage College,and the Institute for Creation Research—an anti-evolution think tank on the same grounds as

this college. An unsuccessful effort by California state senator
Joseph Briggs in the late 1970s to ban gay educators from teaching
in public schools increasingly brought Tim LaHaye into the spot-
light in his adopted state as a "pro-family" campaigner and later
as co-organizer. Along with Briggs's 1978 senate run, campaign
director Lou Sheldon of the Traditional Values Coalition helped
get political support for the ban. Governor of California Ronald
Reagan opposed Briggs's initiative on the grounds that false
charges brought against teachers suspected of being gay would
lead to a witch hunt in the state schools and place a stranglehold
on the public education system.[18] LaHaye's positions on the issue
bordered on open-ended incitement as he pondered the death
penalty for homosexuals in his 1978 book, *The Unhappy Gays*—
"Who is really being cruel and inhuman—those whose leniency
allows homosexuality to spread to millions of victims . . . or those
who practiced Old Testament capital punishment?"[19]

When laws and court decisions began supporting the
acceptance of abortion and when school prayer became forbidden
in public schools, LaHaye grouped together Southern California
churches into a political block and in 1979 founded Californians
for Biblical Morality, an offshoot of the Traditional Values
Coalition, to lobby in Sacramento.[20] While on a preaching tour in
Southern California during the late 1970s, Reverend Jerry
Falwell met LaHaye and saw how he had organized hundreds of
churches into a political bloc. "In many ways, it was the genesis
of the Christian right," journalist Robert Dreyfuss writes in a
recent expose on LaHaye in *Rolling Stone*. This had a profound
influence on Falwell leaving the old "separatism" of Protestant
evangelicals behind and entering the world of Christian right
political activism. "More than any other person," Falwell said,
"Tim LaHaye challenged me to begin thinking through my
involvement in the political process."[21]

It's not that Falwell had never been close to the idea of polit-
ical evangelicalism before, however. In 1972, his associate Dr.
Elmer Towns from Thomas Road Baptist Church—where
Falwell began his own empire—published a book called
Capturing a Town for Christ, which outlined the political evangel-
ical blueprint for local stealth activism. Elmer Towns would later
go on to become a member of LaHaye's Pre-Trib Research
Center (a premillennialist prophecy group formed in the early

nineties to keep their theology "on message") and active premillennialism advocate, as would the dean of Falwell's Thomas
Road Bible Institute, Harold Willmington. Both have played an
instrumental part in combining LaHaye's political agenda with
premillennial theology.

That late 1970s genesis of political evangelicalism coincided
with an upsurge of conservative activism inside Washington, D.C.,
which saw the advantage of joining forces with an increasingly
activist fundamentalism. In the final years of the 1970s, conservative activists Howard Phillips, Richard Viguerie, Paul Weyrich,
and Ed McAteer met with Falwell to urge him to lead this very
public Christian organization to pressure the Republican Party, as
well as to break as much of the Catholic vote away from the
Democrats as possible by using the abortion issue as the wedge.
After his success in California, LaHaye joined with Falwell to help
create this new Moral Majority in 1979, a group which became
hugely influential in the 1980s, raising the agenda of traditional
values into the limelight and lashing out against feminism, abortion, homosexuality, pornography, and drugs. LaHaye joined the
board of directors along with a handful of other fundamentalist
preachers from across the country, taking a supporting role in the
nationwide organization while retaining a lead function in his
own activist empire in California. The movement's publication
Moral Majority Report swelled to a circulation of close to five hundred thousand in less than a year due to the already well established organizational structure of churches led by members of the
board of directors such as LaHaye. The Moral Majority soon
developed a trinity organizational structure being used by other
conservative movement organizations—the tax-exempt Moral
Majority Foundation; the political lobbying Moral Majority, Inc.;
and the Moral Majority Political Action Committee to raise funds
for conservative candidates—a structure also used by LaHaye to
form his own national institutions, the Council for National Policy
and Concerned Women for America.[22]

As evangelism spread rapidly through the South during the
1970s, the Moral Majority was there to ride the crest into the
1980s. In that decade the Southern Baptist Convention had
grown by 16 percent, and the Assemblies of God a remarkable 70
percent. Over the same time period the more liberal northeastern
denominations, the United Presbyterian Church and the

Episcopal Church, lost 21 and 15 percent of their congregations respectively.[23] Long perceived as a threat by fundamentalists, liberal ecumenical denominations had already gone into a steady nosedive. Despite this, fundamentalists continued the rhetoric that claimed these liberal denominations were taking over to spread their "One World" ecumenical religiosity. A new conservative ecumenicalism stepped up to overtake it with the Moral Majority at the fore.

"If the new group was to make a significant impact, it needed the support of like-minded Roman Catholics, Pentecostals, Mormons, Jews and secularists, since only 15 to 20 percent of the population of the United States were evangelical Protestants," writes Karen Armstrong in her 2000 book, *The Battle for God*. The Moral Majority—open to many faiths, along with the relatively moderate and nonspecific faith typified by Reagan—tried to successfully blend the more religious and secular factions on the right in the first years of the 1980s. In actuality, notes Armstrong, though moral support was offered from many congregations, the movement remained mostly white Protestant and in fact turned off many "Jews, black Baptists, and [Catholic] Pentecostals" because of the racism of prominent leaders and supporters such as "committed opponent of the civil rights movement" Jesse Helms.[24]

Nevertheless, the Morality Majority gained supporters along with national prominence and increasing media scrutiny. Over a year's time, thirty evening news programs featured Moral Majority, over a hundred mainstream magazine articles covered the group, and around seventy national newspaper articles appeared about it. That intense coverage and sometimes outright hostility led LaHaye to remark that a vast conspiracy sought destruction of the organization.[25] Tens of millions of conservative Christian voters joined the Moral Majority to form a new and powerful constituent of the Republican Party, and together they served as a core constituency of Ronald Reagan's 1980 election campaign. In an interview with *Church and State* magazine in 1985, LaHaye asserted that Reagan's election in 1980 and reelection four years later had been engineered by God, not by a group of Republican organizers such as himself and Falwell.[26]

Continuing on his empire-building success, LaHaye founded the Council for National Policy (CNP) in 1981 and served as its first president. Developed with LaHaye by conservative fundraisers T. Cullen Davis and Nelson Bunker Hunt, the latter a former council member of the John Birch Society, in a few short years this organization, with a $1 million annual budget, would become the "primary coordinating body" of the religious right.[27] The Council for National Policy functions as a policy factory and funding octopus of a few hundred of the most far-right elite Christian activists, wealthy donors, evangelical ministers, and conservative think tank and foundation leaders in the country. Currently the CNP continues to hold meetings three times a year in rotating, often lavish, locations. Members are forbidden to talk about what is discussed in the meetings without the expressed consent of other members—something of a cross between the Council on Foreign Relations and the World Economic Forum in miniature. Conservative activist Grover Norquist of Americans for Tax Reform, sometimes called the V.I. Lenin of the anti-tax movement, is one of the most prominent members of the group today and holds a position on the board of directors along with conservative organizer Howard Phillips.[28] Leading Christian right activist James Dobson of Focus on the Family and the Eagle Forum's Phyllis Schlafly, "the Madame of the conservative movement," co-chaired the Council for National Policy's Committee on the Family during the middle to late 1990s.

Two years after the CNP was developed, LaHaye became the president and chairman of American Coalition for Traditional Values, bringing along luminaries like Jimmy Swaggart, Jim Bakker, Bill Bright, Paul Crouch, James Dobson, Falwell, D. James Kennedy, and Jack Van Impe. Created in 1983 with funding from televangelist ministries, ACTV was part of the larger strategy hatched along with the Moral Majority, the Christian Coalition, and a wide swath of Christian groups for winning the battles for the "mind, the family, and the public schools" in the run-up to the Reagan campaign for reelection.[29] Charged by the Reagan-Bush election committee to serve as a liaison to the evangelical community and continue the evangelical voter drive, LaHaye brought a group of three hundred ministers to the White House in July 1984 for a meeting with Reagan, George H.W. Bush, and their top aides.[30] Funded by a $1 million grant from Joe Rodgers, a White House fundraiser who later became the ambassador to France, a network of thousands of churches supervised by 350 field directors handed out voting guides and registration-drive training manuals.

Claiming to represent 45 million Christians, ACTV presented 1984 vice presidential candidate Geraldine Ferraro, the chairman of the Democratic platform committee, with a list of ten moral concerns they felt the Democrats should adopt—knowing full well they would be rejected—while at the same time presenting the same list to Trent Lott, then chairman of the Republican platform committee. Not so surprisingly, the Democrats rejected the platform and the Republicans accepted it. ACTV was a pivotal player in the 1984 election, successfully bending one barrier in the separation of church and state by enlisting pastor representatives in all 435 congressional districts in the country to register voters.[31] Claims have been made by LaHaye that ACTV's efforts brought somewhere around 2 million new voters out for Reagan. LaHaye talks about his fears before the 1984 election, saying it was the "most important election of our lifetime," not because of abortion, home-schooling, school prayer, or other policies one could imagine LaHaye would be worried about, but because the control over the media was at stake, insinuating that the media were controlled by whoever is in the White House. "The first thing they would do if a liberal administration gets back in would be to move to cut off the electric church—both radio and TV," LaHaye warned. "So I would expect the leftist leadership to do those two things and by 1988 socialism would be so dominant in our country that it would be irreversible."

The political watershed came in that 1984 election, with Reagan squashing Mondale and the entrenchment of the links the pro-corporate wing of the conservative movement had formed with the Religious right—largely through groups such as the Council for National Policy. Free-market capitalism ideologues had now informally joined with the forces of theocratic fundamentalism, mining narratives of rightwing conspiracy theory as well as the rhetorical proto-myths of Christian-American nationalism—the Shining City on the Hill, the New Jerusalem, and Manifest Destiny.

Linda Kintz, a scholar studying the media of the Christian Right, argues that what unites the clarity and vision of the Religious right and its extensions into the conservative movement is the circular symbolic resonance of a "superrationality"—

a "combination of emotion and rationality that makes empirical facts seem irrelevant." That is, like many mass movements, its worldview is self-perpetuating. This passion and clarity ties diverse groups together into a circular logic of the movement, a Christian-American nationalism where all parts are one extension of the other.

"Nestled within each other like Russian dolls," Kintz writes,

> the elements of this symbolic structure rise from the womb to the heavens, uniting God as Creator, the family, a divinely inspired Declaration of Independence and U.S. Constitution, a nation defined as God's unique experiment in human history, a belief that the unregulated free market is inherent in human nature, a belief that the United States has a God-given responsibility to spread free-market capitalism to the rest of the world. At both the beginning and the end of this clear narrative, God's judgment seals a circular logic of God, family, nation, and global duty within a Judeo-Christian Book of the World made coherent from top to bottom, from beginning to end.[32]

Though tremendous gains had been made for fundamentalists in helping to construct this American movement of Christian nationalism since he began his political activism, the situation did not remain without controversy for LaHaye. In the mid-1980s, he began to be examined not only by long time critics, but by those within his own circles as well. Connections to Reverend Sun Myung Moon and the Unification Church started to sprout up in news articles, and when Moon became involved in legal troubles due to tax evasion, LaHaye defended the self-proclaimed messiah. When reports surfaced that LaHaye's pet projects had received massive amounts of funding from Moon aide Bi Ho Park for relocation costs for ACTV's headquarters, many of his associates tried to distance themselves from him, ultimately leading to the dissolution of the ACTV.[33] Even the *Christian Inquirer* reported on the growing influence of Moon in the network of conservative organizations after it became known that anti-Communist CAUSA, the Confederation of Associations for the Unity of the Societies of the Americas, which had strong ties to members of the Council for National Policy, was entirely funded through the business interests of Moon's Unification

Church. "The alarming fact is that more and more conservatives are accepting Rev. Moon and his cult operations," wrote the *Christian Inquirer* editorial board, "though not his *church,* which claims he is a prophet and maybe even a second messiah."[34]

But it wasn't until 1988 that LaHaye felt the real heat. The LaHayes broke with most of their evangelical associates by supporting the race of Republican Jack Kemp, even using the CWA to distribute letters to gain support for Kemp, while George H.W. Bush, who eventually won the nomination, was supported by Falwell.[35] While LaHaye worked for the presidential nomination of Jack Kemp, media reports surfaced about his past anti-Catholic remarks and he was dropped from Kemp's team.[36] Around this time it was also reported that throughout the 1970s LaHaye's churches in San Diego had sponsored an anti-Catholic group called Mission to Catholics, whose literature claimed Pope Paul VI, the pope who led the Roman Catholic Church during the reforms of the Second Vatican Council, was "archpriest of Satan, a deceiver, and an Antichrist, who has, like Judas, gone to his own place."[37]

As Dreyfuss writes in his *Rolling Stone* piece, LaHaye had become so politically poisonous that he even gave then–vice president Bush a fright when he showed up a year later at the elder Bush's home during a campaign event. At the time not many Republicans bent on mining the Christian right wanted anything to do with LaHaye.

During the period after his involvement with Moon surfaced, LaHaye continued to write and publish, often using the CWA Bulletin as a platform to speak to the issues of the day. One of his targets at the time was Vice President George H.W. Bush, who would go on to become the Republican nominee and later president. LaHaye claims Bush "attacked" and "chided" Christians at the National Religious Broadcasters Convention when he said that there was no reason for a minority of conservative Christians with a growing media empire to attempt to suppress the reading of books like *The Diary of Anne Frank* and *The Adventures of Huckleberry Finn* in public schools.[38]

So for much of the early 1990s, LaHaye contented himself with staying out of the limelight, shuttling back and forth between his San Diego area stronghold and a small Baptist church in Rockville, Maryland. Little is know about this time, though the sting he had received from these setbacks does seem to have added to the persecution mentality he maintains, as well as the increasing paranoid vision which manifests itself in the premillennialist ideology of the Left Behind books. In the end, it wasn't any of LaHaye's diatribes against secular humanism that would prove most successful in reaching his audience, but the Left Behind series. Far from being marginalized as a political liability, LaHaye has ridden this success back to prominence and has received something of "rock star status" on the social conservative right, according to Grover Norquist.[39] That status has been turned into political and cultural capital for LaHaye and the fundamentalists he represents.

GOD'S OWN MEDIA

Though he jokes the "six-foot-four and gorgeous" pilot Rayford Steele is the character most like him in the Left Behind novels, writer Larry Jenkins says he identifies most with Buck Williams, the world-renowned journalist and writer who works for the Global News Network, a caricature of real-world CNN, which becomes the personal broadcasting network for the Antichrist character Nicolae Carpathia. Williams eventually goes underground along with the rest of the Tribulation Force to start his internet publication called *The Truth*; its sole purpose is to counter the propaganda of the Global Community.[1] Buck's character purposefully becomes the embodiment of the distrust of mainstream media, something which resonates wildly in conservative American culture.

Throughout the series journalists are portrayed as cynical, miserable, and negative, with no humor or personality. Some of this assumes the form of anti-intellectualism, or strong populism, as is the case where Buck's Ivy League degree is disparaged by the authors. Here are a few passages from that section in the first book, *Left Behind*:

> The Holy Land attack had been a watershed event in his [Buck's] life. He had stared mortality in the face and had to acknowledge that something otherworldly—yes, supernatural, something directly from God almighty— had been thrust upon those dusty hills in the form of a fire in the sky. And he had known beyond a doubt for

the first time in his life that unexplainable things out
there could not be dissected and evaluated scientifically
from a detached Ivy League perspective.[2]

Other times the characterization takes on the manifestation
of broad and simplistic strokes of criticism, such as the ominous
remark that the media are "dedicated" to covering "around the
clock mayhem," as if the media were leading the mayhem, and
not the other way around. Before his conversion, Buck is taken
through a series of encounters that lead him to believe all that he
has known and worked for his whole life has been a sham. Buck's
proximity to Carpathia and the characters who facilitate the conspiracy of Carpathia's rise to power, as well as how the other characters of the Tribulation Force come to believe in that conspiracy,
gives the reader an omniscient view of just what is about to tran-
spire—that Buck will soon convert. For being one of the world's
top journalists, Buck seems easily accepting of everything
Carpathia says and does. As Buck begins to wonder if there "really is something to this Rapture thing," the authors have already
started the ball rolling for his leap of faith off the secular train
wreck readers all know is coming.[3]

After his conversion in the second half of the first book,
Buck wonders "what kind of despicable subhuman creature" he
had become before knowing the truth and for failing to believe
the way the authors intended him to believe. Buck reflecting on
his past, as well as the miracle which saved Israel from being
obliterated by the Russians:

> In the lonely darkness he came to the painful realization
> that he had long ago compartmentalized this most basic
> of human needs that had rendered it a nonissue. What
> did it say about him, what kind of despicable subhuman
> creature had he become, that even the stark evidence of
> the Israel miracle—for it could be nothing less—had
> not thawed his spirit's receptiveness to God?[4]

That Buck sees his pre-conversion self as a "despicable subhuman creature" effects the reader by identifying all those not
converted to the line of premillennialist belief as "despicable subhuman" creatures. Vast assumptions must be made by the reader
to see Buck's former self as inherently bad, evil, or despicably

subhuman. One has to wonder what purpose other than creating a divide between those who believe they are "human" and the "others" who are not. From "barbarians" to "Jews" to "aliens," the past is littered with the corpses of those painted as despicably subhuman for one intention or another.

In *Tribulation Force* Buck vows to become a "good journalist now with God in his life" just after he has explained how his studies, intellectual pursuits, and status as a journalist somehow made him an unbeliever. Here the authors assume that being a journalist equates with a lack of faith or belief, buoying the readers' fears about a mainstream media alien to their concerns. Essentially LaHaye is saying that journalists as a group should serve faith and belief, preferably in his ideological framework of far-right conspiracy and premillennial theology. Buck becomes just what the authors suspect him of being in the first place, a conscious propagandist for a narrow segment of belief. After his conversion, Buck comments that everything pastor Bruce Barnes had been teaching the Tribulation Force about Carpathia was occurring on CNN, just as "black and white" as it was in the Bible. At one point this same notion occurs to Rayford Steele, who, after he becomes a believer, "suddenly [finds] himself believing without question the most ludicrous news accounts, as long as they were corroborated by Scripture." In *Nicolae*, the reader finds out that "Scripture had come to life" and that the judgments written in the Revelation had come true.[5]

Carpathia and the global system later buy up all the media, including most of what conservatives consider the liberal mainstream media, possibly a LaHaye fantasy in reverse. Carpathia also happens to buy up the Christian Broadcasting Network, Family Radio Network, and Trinity Broadcasting Network as well, something only dropped into one line.[6] This media conglomeration under the Antichrist pushes Buck and the Tribulation Force group to the Internet where they publish *The Truth*, the only place, Buck later claims, that people could get news with "objective substance" anymore, now that Carpathia owns the world's media. This website mirrors LaHaye's own Pre-Trib Research Center website, where he frequently writes on prophecy and politics. Buck complains about all the "pedigreed know-it-alls" they put before the cameras of Carpathia-owned media, thereby completing his internal transformation from Ivy

League–educated, world-renowned journalist to a reactionary, anti-intellectual tool for the Tribulation Force. Much of this rhetoric feeds into the right's belief in a "mainstream media" controlled by the "liberal elite," itself a reflection of fundamentalists' feeling have that they are shut out of that mainstream media.

From Fiction to Reality—The Construction of a Parallel Universe of "Christian" Media

Much of the purpose of these fictional attacks are to back real-world attacks on "the media" in order to sow distrust, and once doing so, to push people toward a growing "Christian" media empire.[7] In March 2000, writing in *Tim LaHaye's Perspective*, a Pre-Trib Research Center publication, LaHaye claimed that "the Clinton dominated FCC" had "arrogantly attacked all Christian TV" by its four-to-one ruling in the *Cornerstone* case. The case had been filed by WQED (TV) in Pittsburgh, which was attempting to circumvent debt obligations by turning over its broadcasting license to Cornerstone, a religious broadcaster. Due do its position in the spectrum, WQED is required to broadcast a set amount of children's educational programming, a requirement that does not change when the liscense is sold to another broadcaster. Cornerstone claimed its religious programming was educational, but the FCC found this failed to meet the minimum standards of the license. LaHaye complained that the decision was an "anti-Christian" and "un-American" action, comparing what he sees as the FCC giving air time to "smut and filth masquerading as *entertainment*" and that this action proves "liberals hate Christians."[8]

LaHaye continued by saying that an all powerful *they* got the message when the FCC ruling was flipped to a four-to-one vote in favor of the Christian broadcasters, after his activists rose up and swamped the FCC switchboards with phone calls. This case was an example of the anti-Christian attitude, he says, of liberals, who do not want "anything Christian on *their* air waves"; if Christians did not get out and vote in the 2000 election they would "effectively lose the freedoms they enjoyed." This echoes his similar statements about the media in 1984, striking fear to energize his activist political fundamentalists—fear that turns out to be unfounded. In this case, even though they won the ruling, Cornerstone eventually pulled out of acquiring the airtime because it couldn't even meet the minimum standards of educational programming. LaHaye's preoccupation with media control goes at least as far back as his book *Battle for the Mind*, and here again he uses the threat of the loss of freedom and a variety of scare language, while not disclosing that the issue wasn't about "Christian" programming, but "educational" programming. Certainly Christian programming can be educational, but in this case, Cornerstone failed to meet those standards.

Though while LaHaye did correctly forecast that the 2000 race would be decided by a very fine margin, he did miscalculate, assuming it would be decided by "how many *responsible* Christians go to the polls," not by how the Supreme Court would rule. The grand assumption here is that all Christians are Republicans, an act of division which LaHaye and company have been working to fulfill since they became involved in politics. What has dismayed LaHaye, and others in the aggressive politically religious camp time and again is that the larger Christian community isn't always as activist as they would hope. The approximately 4 million Christian voters that President Bush's political strategist Karl Rove had expected to come to the polls in the 2000 election didn't show.

"The next President will appoint three members to the FCC, and even more important, three or four Supreme Court justices," LaHaye wrote just before the 2000 elections. As of early 2005, two of those hoped for Supreme Court justices have appeared. As for the FCC, four of the five commissioners were appointed by the Bush administration, while the lone holdover from the Clinton presidency was Michael Powell, son of former secretary of state Colin Powell, not one of the feared liberals LaHaye mongers about.

During the months leading up to the 2004 election, the Bush White House kept in regular contact with the leadership of the Christian right through weekly conference calls led by Tim Goeglein, Bush's liaison to the conservative community. "We have direct access," Reverend Ted Haggard, senior pastor of the giant New Life Church in Colorado Springs, Colorado, told the *Wall Street Journal*. "I can call [Goeglein]; he'll take my concern to the president and get back to me in 24 hours."[9] Much of this outreach to churches can be seen as an attempt by Republican political leaders to reach individual voters through their churches, politicizing these congregations to a degree that is difficult to measure. As if directly appealing to church leaders wasn't enough, feeding into the notion that "real Christians" are Republican, there has been an increasingly active use of the "Christian" media by Republicans. As the conservative Christian media empire has expanded over the past thirty years, tapping into it has become increasingly central in how Republicans connect with those conservative voters, with both Christians and conservatives pulling each other further toward the right on social and political issues.

Using the Christian media empire has been a natural progression for political activists of the conservative movement. The two have grown together, largely with the help of those connections made through the LaHaye-founded Council for National Policy. Between 1970 and 1980, the audience for evangelical television and radio programs grew from around 11 million to 61 million viewers. By 1980, Robertson's *700 Club* and Falwell's *Old Time Gospel Hour* broadcasted each week to nearly 15 million people, and the Christian Broadcast Network had become the fifth largest cable network in America with its 30 million subscribers.[10]

Christian radio has become the most popular radio genre in the country over the last twenty years, followed by country and adult contemporary programming. Fewer than ten years ago there were around twelve hundred full-time Christian radio stations in the U.S. and by 2004 that had jumped to around eighteen hundred. Used as a medium for political activism, radio is one of the most effective means for the conservative Christian activists to join forces with pervasive conservative radio broadcasting celebrities such as Rush Limbaugh, Neil Bortz, Michael Savage, and Sean Hannity. By contrast, in 2003 there were 750 National Public Radio stations in the U.S. and its territories. Over the last decade many of those have been targeted by conservatives for dismantling through purchase. Along with calls for the abolition of the Corporation for Public Broadcasting as a whole, the assault on public interest broadcasting has been taken up by activists in Christian and corporate media bent on filling the gaps these closings create.

Today, more Americans experience the Christian faith through radio, television, and books than do so by attending church, predominantly Protestant versions of the faith.[11] In 2002, six out of ten Americans attended church at least once a month while a slightly larger percentage—two out of three—tuned into Christian media on the radio, TV, or through books at least once a month. Leading this group were evangelicals, 96 percent of whom consumed Christian-specific media. According to Barna Research Group, an evangelical Christian polling and research agency, in 2002 over half of American adults listened to Christian radio each month—or almost 110 million listeners.[12] A smaller group of about 43 percent of Americans tuned into Christian television at least once a month, and one out of three adults had read a Christian fiction or nonfiction book other than the Bible in the past month, according to the 2002 data.

Compared to the reading habits of Americans as a whole, it would seem that Christian readers are leading the group of book readers in the country. A National Endowment for the Arts report released in 2004, *Reading at Risk,* found just over half of all American adults had read a book in the past year, and less than half had read what the NEA defines as literature. Most alarmingly, the numbers of eighteen-to-twenty-four-year-olds who had read a book in the last year had dropped significantly in the past decade, from 53.3 percent to 42.8 percent, which was nearly 30 percent below 1982.[13] In April 2004, the American Library Association documented deep cuts in federal, state, and local funding of public libraries, as much as 50 percent in the budgets of libraries in fort-one states.

Christian right activists often use the nonprofit foundations they have built to give greater reach to their own books, radio, and television shows. In January 2002, Tim's wife Beverly LaHaye, founder and chairman of Concerned Women for America, and Janice Crouse, the same organization's executive director and a senior fellow at the Beverly LaHaye Institute, had their book *A Different Kind of Strength* selected as the "Inspirational Book of the Month" by the Conservative Book Club. The Conservative Book Club has been prominent in disseminating many of the books put out by rightwing and Christian right organizations, nonprofits, and think tanks. These promotions included an updated version of the 1982 book called

The Homosexual Network, reworked and packaged into a title called *Gays, AIDS and You*. This updated version was commissioned and coordinated by conservative activist Paul Weyrich's Free Congress Foundation (FCF), disseminated in the late eighties, and given a boost by the Conservative Book Club.[14]

Even before the book was compiled, Weyrich sent out calls for prominent members of the FCF-connected network of rightwing organizations to endorse the book—Beverly LaHaye provided a star endorsement and allowed the FCF to place a letter in CWA's magazine with order forms for $18.75 action kits to "Fight the Gay Lobby." James Dobson, Pat Robertson, Jerry Falwell, and others all worked to promote the book and the Conservative Book Club gave it a seal of approval. *Gays, AIDS and You* helped "popularize many of the myths and slogans later circulated in public homophobic campaigns" writes Chip Berlet, a long time chronicler of the religious right. Berlet traces the rhetoric of this book from the page to physical attacks and harassment on gays and lesbians in the nineties. "The concerted rightwing media campaigns to frame gays and lesbians as undeserving outlaws helped create an atmosphere conducive to these attacks."[15]

Between 1980 and 2002, the Christian entertainment industry—publishing, music, and spin-off products—grew from $1 billion to $4.2 billion in revenue generated per year. The Left Behind series has been the pinnacle achievement of this industry over the past ten years—an avalanche of audio books, books on CD, books on cassette, a kids series of more than twenty volumes, a graphic novel series of up to forty comic books, movies, videos, a worship album, clothes, teddy bears, maps, and movie soundtracks. And this doesn't even count the over 60 million Left Behind books sold. Compared with the porn industry, which brings in somewhere between $10 billion and $14 billion a year, Christian media is but a mere molehill in the shadow of its silicon brethren. But then Jenna Jameson and Larry Flint aren't establishing foundations, think tanks, and nonprofit organizations in attempt to restructure American society as "One Nation Under Porn." Nor do they hold weekly conference calls with the White House.

While porn has been doing quite well in its own rights, what some have termed "Christian pornography"—the apocalyptic genre in which the Left Behind novels fit—has soared on the waves of fear caused by the millennium and the September 11 attacks. In a poll taken after September 11, a staggering 59 percent of Americans believed that the events of the *Revelation* will come to fruition and 25 percent believed that those attacks were foretold by their Bibles. After the attacks, a survey by the Evangelical Christian Association of five hundred bookstores showed the increase in sales of books about prophecy rose 71 percent in the eight weeks after September 11. Sales of the Left Behind series doubled from the nearly half-million copies sold a month before the terrorist attacks. For the first time ever, two Christian titles headed the annual charts of the *Publishers Weekly* bestseller lists for fiction and nonfiction in 2001 with LaHaye's *Desecration* and Bruce Wilkinson's *The Prayer of Jabez* leading the charge.[16] Early 2004 saw the release of Mel Gibson's *Passion of the Christ*, which scored over $260 million dollars during the first three weeks running.

The Nineties Deregulation Feast

Much of the rise of Christian broadcasting media can be attributed to the nineties media deregulation. The 1996 Telecommunications Act helped open the door for deregulation and a vast feast by formerly unknown entities to gobble up. On the television side of the deregulation, a corporate give-out fueled by the act helped people like Christian broadcasting owner Dr. Garth W. Coonce in Marion, Illinois, earn millions of dollars auctioning off portions of their electromagnetic spectrum or digital television space. Under that 1996 act, television broadcasters were allowed to expand by six megahertz of spectrum for free. When digital television failed to take off, this government gift became what the National Association of Broadcasters estimated to be between $37 to $70 billion dollars in assets the broadcasters could later turn around and sell. Writing in *American Prospect*, Brendan Koerner reported that Bernstein Investment Research later estimated that the figure could be something more like $367 billion, due largely to the demand for spectrum space from wireless telecommunications companies. Senator John McCain of Arizona called this grab "one of the greatest scams in American history."[17]

Coonce's main evangelical broadcasting outlets Tri-State Christian TV and Radiant Life Ministries joined Spectrum

Clearing Alliance, an association of around twenty broadcasters that populate the channel 60 to 69 segment of UHF—home to televangelists, home shopping networks, and family friendly television—and together they could cash in on the spectrum auction to a tune of millions, if not billions, of dollars according to some estimates, though the end figures are not yet calculated. Another member of the alliance is the nation's largest Christian television broadcast network, Trinity Broadcasting Network, which made around $285 million in profits over the past five years and funded the movie studio that produced the apocalyptic film *Omega Code*.[18] Owned by husband and wife team Paul and Jan Crouch, close associates of Tim and Beverly LaHaye, Trinity has become one of the most influential Christian media broadcasters in the nation.

The lawyer for the alliance representing Coonce and the other broadcasters, Colby M. May of the American Center for Law and Justice, has been one of the leading activists of Christian right nonprofit organizations and churches in their fight against IRS interference in their free-speech rights. As 501(c)(3) organizations, these groups can't give legislative or presidential candidate endorsements or engage in political activity outside that clearly delineated by law. Along with the LaHayes, the Crouches and a gaggle of other familiar names, May was a leading proponent of HR 235, the Houses of Worship Free Speech Restoration Act, which would allow politicking and political endorsements directly from the pulpit, roll back IRS codes and further erode church-state separation.

John Whitehead, a lawyer and ardent defender of the idea that the First Amendment of the Constitution has been misread by secular humanists twisting Jefferson's ideas, argues that the amendment was established to protect the church from the state. This is also the argument that Whitehead's organization, the Rutherford Institute puts out as it trains evangelical lawyers to fight directly against these "misreadings."[19]

Going back to my landlord David, Crouch's Trinity Broadcasting Network, and Coonce's Tri-State Christian TV and Radiant Life were among his favorites of the Christian television channels he watched almost continuously. He had insulated himself within this bubble of reality where it essentially became his only reality. A large part of the momentum in the rise of the Christian media has been due to a ready and willing ability to harness societal fears and anxieties—fears of terrorism; fears of crime, drugs and moral degradation; fears of federal government power, fears of secular society encroaching on their lives—that also go hand in hand with the concerns of the larger and diverse conservative movement.

Such media dissemination, through books, radio, television, and now the Internet, is perhaps the most important example of the scaffolding of future and present action on which LaHaye builds his mixture of conspiracy and Revelation. LaHaye, as well as evangelists like Jerry Falwell and Pat Robertson, are part of the carefully constructed and now vast political and social movement—not conspiracy, a *movement*—which Protestant fundamentalists have helped weave into the fabric of the yet broader conservative movement in this country. At the heart of this movement lies the apocalyptic-conspiracy narrative that has been manipulated and used since the combining of the Johns—John Darby, John Birch, and John of Patmos.

A BATTLE FOR THE MIND

LaHaye's 1979 book *Battle for the Mind* portrays secular humanism as a harbinger of the Great Tribulation so prominent in the Left Behind novels, the seven-year period of death and destruction premillennialists claim will occur before Christ's return. There are two ways to avoid the Great Tribulation in this ideology, and they both involve conversion to the premillennialist line of Protestant fundamentalism. First, those who lead the life of a believer and accept Jesus as their personal savior will be saved from this trial by fire due to the mass-Rapture of the believing church; second, one may be saved by creating a utopian society based on biblical values and instituting the millennial reign on Earth prior to the Rapture. In nearly everything LaHaye writes, the "total" salvation of "society" that relies on the imminent return of Christ is favored above the "pragmatic" salvation of the "individual" which accepts a more static relation to faith.

"Since moral conditions have become worse in direct proportion to humanism's influence, which has moved our country from a biblically based society to an amoral 'democratic' society during the past forty years, one would think that humanists would realize the futility of their position," LaHaye writes in *Battle for the Mind*. "To the contrary, they treacherously refuse to face the reality of their failures, blaming them instead on traditional religion or ignorance or capitalism or religious superstitions."[1] LaHaye often attempts to recall that mythical golden age, some bygone era "forty years" ago, back before World War II, back into the Depression, prohibition, the Civil War, slavery, to the genocide of the American Indians, to the American Revolution, and finally back to the to the mythical golden age of the Puritan era. For those who believe the mythical idea of the founding of America as part of God's plan for the world, the most golden age of all is centered around the Puritan era—before the creation of the democratic United States of America.

It was in *Battle for the Mind* that LaHaye began to take up the premillennialist flag from Hal Lindsey and construct it on his own terms, delivering it to his wide audience, reading the "secular humanist conspiracy" to take over the country as a tribulation before the Great Tribulation.[2] In essence, this was the first battle cry—if this "secular humanist conspiracy" was not stopped it would destroy the country. This construction of a tribulation before the tribulation acts exactly as the Great Tribulation in its seriousness and its psychology on the mass of believers. It is an urge to action, now and forever—for all that is left now and in the future is tribulation. Prayer, saving souls, living biblically, and saving the nation en masse—is all a Christian can really do, according to LaHaye. The Great Tribulation "is predestined and will surely come to pass," LaHaye writes.

> But the pre-tribulation tribulation—that is, the tribulation that will engulf this country if liberal humanists are permitted to take total control of our government—is neither predestined nor necessary. But it will deluge the entire land in the next few years, unless Christians are willing to become much more assertive in defense of morality and decency than they have been during the past three decades.[3]

This is essentially why the Left Behind series can be read both as a fictional account about the hypothetical prophecies of a future Great Tribulation and as an account of current political preoccupations, fantasies, hopes, fears, and paranoias, of the Christian right. Of *The Battle for the Mind*, LaHaye later wrote, "That book, published in 1980, was written as a clarion call to ministers and Christian leaders to become more assertive and activist. I was trying to get the 100,000 ministers in America to recognize that if we don't lead the army of 45 million Christians to become assertive and activist in preserving moral values we are going to lose this country."[4]

It is no accident that many of the groups that are demonized by LaHaye in the Left Behind books and by other premillennialists are the same ones railed at by much of the rest of the Christian right and the conservative movement, as well as by most fringe rightwing conspiracy groups. In his 1987 book, *Faith of Our Founding Fathers: A Comprehensive Study of America's Christian Foundations*, LaHaye accuses secular humanists of the "deliberate rape of history" in relying on moral and cultural relativism, rather than the accepted American myths and Puritan foundations.[5] Deploying broad strokes and hovering intimations of "evil," LaHaye and his followers make it easy for groups and organizations like the United Nations, liberals, Europeans, Russia, Muslims, Iraq, the monolithic "media"; dead horses like freemasons, mysterious international bankers, Communists, socialists, and humanists; and just about anyone outside their sphere of reasoning to be dragged into the circle and dismissed. Embedded in much of this is the more dangerous and divisive xenophobia which harkens back to strains of old time anti-Catholicism, anti-Semitism, and nineteenth-century nativism.

Through his organizing a network of evangelical churches, building a wide array of conservative contacts, and helping to construct a Christian media empire, LaHaye has shown a remarkable genius for couching political propaganda in simple language that melds conspiracy and religious belief with concepts on what it means to be American. Formerly, his apocalyptic-conspiracy narrative was restrained to a small segment of Protestant fundamentalism. Now that LaHaye's ideas are making their way into mainstream culture through the vehicle of the Left Behind series, his ideas deserve close scrutiny.

LaHaye and his writings are not a singular phenomenon; there are hundreds of other books on the shelves just like these that describe events of the End Times. That many of them are written by friends and acquaintances of LaHaye who belong to the Pre-Trib Research Center gives credence to the idea that this is part of a highly centralized, conscious effort on the part of premillennialists to stay on message and deliver it most effectively to a wide population. In the 1970s, Hal Lindsey's *Late Great Planet Earth*, the forerunner to this type of popular prophecy, was the bestselling book of that decade, though it has since been debunked by the collision of prophecy and history; the Left Behind series took on that mantle for the ten years straddling the millennium. Scholars of evangelical fundamentalism believe it is plausible that many, if not most evangelical Christians in America share a conception of the End Times with LaHaye. In 2004, Protestant fundamentalists accounted for an estimated 25 million Americans, yet the theology of the End Times events, Rapture, and Revelation reach a much wider audience. Somewhere between 40 and 59 percent of all Americans believe what is written in the Revelation will occur in the future, depending on what polls you read.[6]

"Other popular novelists, Stephen King among them, are often just as Apocalyptic as LaHaye and Jenkins without inspiring dire warnings that America is about to embrace fascist theocracy," writes Jeremy Lott in *Reason* magazine. "True, King and company don't take their apocalypses seriously. On the other hand, the end of the world has been a popular subgenre for many years. Exactly what has drawn readers to so many secular total destruction fantasies is a question that's hard to answer, but that answer is unlikely to be compassion for humanity."[7]

Often the Left Behind books are portrayed simply as fiction and fantasy—like Star Wars, or the Lord of the Rings, or books by Stephen King or perhaps Dean Koontz. In appearance they are similar to a great degree. In how they affect readers they are as diverse as the numbers sold. Yet, behind this there is something as equally important to understand. Usually when purchasing a book of fiction there isn't much worry about what may lie behind it or what one may be funding through its purchase. The Left Behind books are something else—they are thinly veiled works of political propaganda using a good-versus-evil narrative set in the very near future, containing real places and real peoples; nonfiction polemics masquerading as fiction; and fundraisers for yet more explicit ventures into political activism. Jenkins himself doesn't argue the fact that the books are purposefully written with propaganda in mind, though it's likely that most fans of the novels are not aware of this and itis possible they would not in fact care.

"We have never denied that Left Behind is propaganda. We do have a message, and I maintain that most novelists do and don't shrink from it," said Jenkins.[8] In defending this position, he compares the intent with the pro-choice messages in John Irving's *The Cider House Rules* without noting that Irving's book does not portray the apocalyptic destruction of the human race in a good-versus-evil framework, nor the fact that Irving is not a leading political activist such as the man behind the Left Behind series, Tim LaHaye.

The success of the Left Behind series and other books in the apocalyptic-thriller genre has often be attributed to a reading public that hungers to devour such beliefs as a confirmation of its own paranoia, escapist fantasies, and age-old bigotries. A *Newsweek* poll in 1999 found that 40 percent of Americans thought the world would end as described in the Revelation.[9] A research poll commissioned prior to the September 11 attacks in 2001 by Tyndale House, publishers of the Left Behind series, found that 40 percent of Americans believed that the world would end due to supernatural intervention by the hand of God.[10] Considering a reading public that already had an appetite for psychological thrillers, religious self-help manuals, current event polemics, and violent epics, it really isn't so incomprehensible that Hal Lindsey's book *The Late Great Planet Earth* became the best-selling book of the 1970s. It still sells somewhere between ten and twenty thousand copies a year. Nor is it surprising that, building on Lindsey's success, books like the Left Behind series became so profitable and widespread in the nineties and into this century. What is remarkable is how politically and socially influential people like LaHaye and Lindsey have become. How did Hal Lindsey, a former fast-living tugboat captain on the Mississippi River who found God and went to the Dallas Theological Seminary, come to serve as a consultant to the Reagan administration and the Israeli government on Middle Eastern affairs? How did LaHaye become a frequent contact with the Reagan administration in its outreach to the evangelical vote? That these people could get the ear of the president on matters of such importance only increases their respectability within the community of readers.

It's hard to recall the last time a novel or series of novels influenced so many people in America or had an effect on American society as these books have. It is a truism of the postmodern landscape that books do not have the massive power they once had to spark social movements. But for those who believe in Rapture theology, there is none of that postmodern skepticism about a murky and slippery truth. What LaHaye and Jenkins appeal to is a rejection of that modern skepticism, a "with us or against us," good-versus-evil, black and white reality, with morals clearly delineated—or at least clearly defined—through the prism of their interpretation of prophecy. In the final book, *Glorious Appearing*, just after millions of "nonbelievers" (from the premillennialist version of the Revelation) have been slaughtered for not believing in Jesus as Messiah, the authors have the avenging Jesus draw the line quite clearly:

> "Every spirit that confesses that I came in the flesh is of God, and every spirit that does not confess that I came in the flesh is not of God. And this is the spirit of the Antichrist."[11]
>
> Rayford heard Carpathia raging, cursing.
>
> And Jesus said, "A mighty king arose who ruled with great dominion, and did according to his will. But his kingdom shall be broken up and divided toward the four winds of heaven, but not among his posterity nor according to his dominion with which he ruled; for his kingdom shall be uprooted.
>
> "Now is the appointed time. The king of this world did according to his own will: he exalted and magnified himself above every god, spoke blasphemies against the God of gods, and prospered until now. But what has been determined shall be done."
>
> The great army was in pandemonium, tens of thousands at a time screaming in terror and pain and dying in the open air. Their blood poured from them in great waves, combining to make a river that quickly became a swamp.
>
> "He regarded neither true God nor any god," Jesus continued as the soldiers fell and the blood rose, "for he exalted himself above them all."[12]

ANTICHRISTS AMONG US

> The enemy is clearly delineated: he is a perfect model of
> malice, a kind of amoral superman—sinister, ubiqui-
> tous, powerful, cruel, sensual, luxury loving. . . . He
> makes crisises, starts runs on banks, causes depressions,
> manufactures disasters, and then enjoys and profits
> from the misery he has produced.
> —Richard Hofstadter, "The Paranoid Style of
> American Politics"

Though the word "Antichrist" does not appear in the Book of
Revelation, the notion of an Antichrist figure has long been
associated with the book. Throughout history, the possible ascen-
sion of an Antichrist has been used in attempts to stir believing
masses to action against perceived enemies. A number of popes
(including John Paul II), Stalin, Hitler, and Napoleon have all suf-
fered the label—even the unfortunate spot on Gorbachev's head
singled him out as being marked by the Beast. Yasser Arafat,
Jimmy Carter, David Rockefeller, Nero Caesar, Saddam Hussein,
John F. Kennedy, Bill Gates, Henry Kissinger, Benito Mussolini,
Ronald Reagan, and Pat Robertson have all been rumored to be
the Antichrist. Peace activist and folk singer Pete Seeger somehow also showed up on the Antichrist radar.[1] Martin Luther used
the Book of Revelation to portray the papacy as "Antichrist"
(while that papacy called him the same name) to spur the development of the Reformation. The idea of the papacy as Antichrist
flourished throughout Protestantism, and in America, the land

where Protestant fundamentalism holds its strongest base, it still shows itself through books like *Left Behind*. That during the Reformation, the Catholic power center in Rome was depicted as the home of the Antichrist and "Babylon" by Protestants looking to divide and break from the Roman Catholic Church is evidence of some of the powerful revolutionary influence this type of apocalyptic rhetoric has on social movements.

Saladin was once the Antichrist for crusading Christians trying to take Jerusalem by force in the twelfth century. Later, the entire Ottoman Empire represented the Antichrist for many Christians in Europe. Islam has often held a place in Christian popular culture as Antichrist, and modern figures such as Saddam Hussein and Osama Bin Laden have taken the lead in how many Christians perceive the Islamic world—not as the moderate religion of a billion people, but as a radical and destructive evil out to destroy Christianity and Judaism. Couching foreign policy issues in the rhetoric of Antichrist could currently be having an equally influential impact on American relations in the Middle East.[2] A group called Jews for Jesus once ran a full-page newspaper ad during the early-nineties Gulf War saying Saddam represented "the spirit of the Antichrist about which the Bible warns us." Judaism and the establishment of a greater Israel is for premillennialist Christian Zionists—or Christians who believe that Jews must return to Israel and create a "Greater Israel" to fulfill prophecy—an important step toward the fulfillment of what they see as written in Revelation. That this establishment will lead to the destruction or conversion of Judaism is hardly acknowledged, and that this view is inherently anti-Semitic is brushed off as propaganda by premillennialists or as misreading their intentions.

"Given the influence of fundamentalist Christians in the Republican Party, and the role conservative Christian activists have begun to play in forming U.S. policy toward Israel and its neighbors, foreign policy students in the United States and abroad are increasingly searching to understand their influential world view," writes foreign policy analyst Walter Russell Mead in *Foreign Affairs* in the fall of 2003. "The Left Behind books will help. . . . Those wanting to familiarize themselves with the overall end-time scenario that has gripped the imagination of tens of millions of American voters would do well do start here . . . inter-

ested parties can also go to the series Web site, where they will
encounter one of the greatest orgies of religious marketing since
itinerant indulgence sellers infuriated Marin Luther."[3]

Antichrist figure Nicolae Carpathia, often portrayed as an
Aryan figure with Robert Redford's good looks and peacenik
philosophies who likes to use Communistic code phrases like
"the greater good," is the embodiment of this "Antichrist" rhetoric in the Left Behind books. Early in the first book Carpathia is
painted as a pacifist, as Israeli scientist Chaim Rosenzweig
describes him, with the qualifier that "I am a bit of a pacifist
myself, you know. Not unrealistically . . . ," a qualifier that belief
in peace is tantamount to being the Antichrist on one hand, and
on the other painting yearning for peace as unrealistic and back-
wards. In its intent, pacifists are either not to be trusted because
they would be duped by an Antichrist set to take over the world,
or pitied as self-deluded for the same reason. Remember, there
will be "no peace until Jesus comes" for premillennialists.

Carpathia lays down the timeline for many conspiracy-
minded premillennialists in a speech at the United Nations in
which he outlines the birth of the global system: the U.N. (whose
building in New York he says is as sacred as any in the Holy
Land), the World Bank, and the International Monetary Fund.
Along with these global constructions, the founding of the state
of Israel in 1948, for prophecy watchers who have constructed
connections with these events to the Book of Revelations, has set
that clock ticking. Carpathia then pronounces the names of every
country in the United Nations, which automatically seems to
give him the opportunity to head the organization—he reads off
every name of every nation on earth—and with an authorial
flourish, Jenkins has journalists cheering for Carpathia as he
delivers the speech. That Carpathia was previously a low-level
bureaucrat in Romania doesn't seem to make much difference to
a large and important organization such as the United Nations as
much as his ability to say its constituent countries' names correctly. Later, in the first prequel, *The Rising*, it's discovered that
Carpathia was constructed as part of an evil conspiracy of "international bankers"—in fact, the authors have him being born out
of wedlock, a test-tube baby fertilized by the sperm of two homosexual men.

Again playing to the more conspiratorial-minded, Carpathia later says it was actually George H.W. Bush's "New World Order" speech that made one world government resonate "deep within my young heart," one world government being another premillennialist preoccupation. Further in the book Carpathia addresses that old ecumenical bugaboo, the World Council of Churches, about millenarianism, eschatology, the Last Judgment, and the Second Coming of Christ. The man only just became head of the U.N. days before, and here he is giving a sermon to the World Council of Churches. Much of this is later brushed aside by the authors, who explain it away by using Carpathia's mind controlling powers invoked throughout the books as an excuse for how billions of people shut off their brains for several years. These absurdities would seem just the random imaginings of the author's attempt to make the Left Behind better fit the genre. But to premillenialists, this litany of events—and LaHaye reiterates these issues in his nonfiction books—signal just how far the "secular humanist conspiracy" has come.[4]

In order to conform to the prophetic scheme, one that fits in nicely with current events, in the first book, the authors have Carpathia insist that the United Nations be moved from New York (which he calls the "capital of the world") to Iraq, the highly charged "New Babylon." Carpathia wants to rebuild Babylon, rebuild the Temple in Jerusalem, and start a one-world religion based in Rome. In the third book, Carpathia says "how anyone can still insist on taking the Bible literally and interpreting its prophecies in that light is beyond me," and in the eighth book that the Bible "is the playbook for those that oppose me." Midway through the series, Carpathia even gives a critique of premillennialism where he defends the mainstream allegorical reading of the Revelation. The authors have Carpathia supporting taxation, abortion, euthanasia, disarmament, and universal healthcare, as well as promoting the theory of evolution (in the final scenes of the book, Jesus rebukes "evolution" telling Satan that "for all your lies about having evolved, you are a created being"). In an apparent use of Clinton-era liberal language, Carpathia describes what he has created as one big happy "global village." That Carpathia later identifies himself with Lucifer and Hitler simply adds nails to his metaphorical coffin.[5]

At least once in every book the litany of evil is regurgitated—one world currency, one world government, one world language, one system of religion. Carpathia wants to "govern life from the womb to the tomb." A seven-year pact is hatched early in the books between "U.N. members and Israel" (there is never a mention of any Palestinians in the novels) to guarantee "its borders and [promise] peace"; this, coming from Carpathia, drips with insidiousness. In reality, premillenialists arm-in-arm with the furthest of the rightwing in Israel wants the nation to keep control of the Palestinian lands and even expand to its biblical dominion.

Prejudices like the fundamentalist perception that Catholics worship icons are demonstrated through the author's use of Carpathia's new religion, Carpathianism, as statues and all manner of "graven images" are constructed around the new leader. Installed as head of this new religion is Carpathia's lapdog Leon Fortunato (a man absurdly concerned with official titles); in being named spiritual leader of the new religion, he is crowned at the Sistine Chapel. To really know how bad a man Carpathia is, wait until the *Glorious Appearing* where he turns over the Cradle of Jesus (part of the Stables of Solomon on the Temple Mount site) to be used as the septic tank. Earlier in the series, he rides a pig into Jerusalem a la Jesus on a mule, but with certain nonkosher ramifications—the pig is later sacrificed with way more authorial joy than expected from people who would like to convert Jews to Christianity.[6] At one point Hattie Durham confronts the evil duo in Jerusalem and is fatally burned by Fortunato's new-found fireball powers, a martyrdom in which Chloe (Rayford's daughter) takes great envy:

> Rayford tried to dismiss an intruding thought but he couldn't. "Chloe, are you envious?"
> "Of Hattie?"
> "Yeah."
> "Of course I am. More than I can say."
> [. . .]
> "Dad, am I a scoundrel?"
> "Nah. I know how you feel. At least I think I do. But most people see you as a hero, hon."
> "That's not the point. That's not why I'm envious."
> "What then?"
> "She was there, Dad! Front lines. Doing the job."

"The Tribulation backs up much of the American far-right agenda right now," writes Gorenberg of the Left Behind books and the power of premillennialism. "The line between today and Tribulation is blurry; we live with one foot in the time of the End and tomorrows evil gives force to today's urgent activism." Not only have the Tribulation and the politics of Antichrist backed up recent far-right agenda in America, they have backed the resurgence of activist fundamentalism for the past thirty years, its roots found in the blending on far-right conspiracy theories and premillennialism between the years of the McCarthy Red Scare era and into the Goldwater versus Johnson presidential race in 1964.

New Europe, Old Antichrist

It is important to realize how much the embrace of fundamentalist and conservative regimes abroad engaged in their own battles against secular society has influenced U.S. foreign policy. The United States backed conservative dictatorial regimes throughout the world during the cold war, especially during the Reagan administration. In Central and South America, the battle against Catholic liberation theology and its close relations to Marxist ideologies led the U.S. to support the more conservative Catholic ruling classes, the military, and corporate industry. In the Middle East they treaded a fine line between supporting top heavy monarchies and military dictatorships by playing fundamentalists off Arab Nationalists in Egypt, Iran and Iraq, Syria, Saudi Arabia, Pakistan, and eventually using the virulent Muslim fundamentalists directly in Afghanistan against the Soviet invasion. Oil consumption, arms sales, real politik strategies of supporting stability in one country and instability in another, as well as the special prominence given to Israel are the main reasons this occurred. Europe, which had been covered by the umbrella of NATO protection and massive investment, prospered as a "socialist" secular paradise—one of the many reasons (as well as historical American exceptionalism) fundamentalist conservatives in the U.S. see Europe as the epitome of the Antichrist caricature.

There has long been a premillennialist fascination with Russia being the instigator of an attack against Israel, which author Hal Lindsey used so specifically, and LaHaye to a lesser degree. This comes from Scofield's annotations about an attack from "the north." In the opening pages of the first Left Behind book, Russia and "other northern forces" attack Israel because Nobel Prize–winning Dr. Rosenzweig has developed a miracle formula to "make the desert bloom" turning the "Miracle of the Desert" from an allegorical to a reality. The massive Russo-European attack is repulsed by the "Miracle of the Israeli Defense Force" with little damage to Israel but the entire destruction of that invasion—all witnessed by *Global Weekly* journalist Buck Williams.[7]

Though LaHaye and most others now drop Russia out of this—since the Soviet empire and anti-Christ Communism are now a fading memory—their thoughts have turned to those "northern powers" that put the secular paradise of the European Union smack in the sights of today's premillennialist fantasy. Yet, even if the prophecy never comes to pass, the aim of fighting against the mostly secular Europe is still worthy in the eyes of the premillennialists, just as fighting the anti-religious Soviet Union was during the second half of the twentieth century. Terry James of the Pre-Trib Research Center and Todd Strandberg at RaptureReady.com have taken up the flag of anti-European feeling.[8] In a seven-page essay they explain why the European Union is the Antichrist's playground, complete with plenty of references to the prophetic books of the Bible. "The European Union is on the march as never before, despite its family feuding on occasion," they warn. They then insinuate that the opposition to the U.S. invasion of Iraq from Germany, France, and Belgium is somehow part of the Antichrist's plan, elaborating in detail by using historic fact and vague prophecy forecasts. The writers then dissect the Road Map to Peace between the Palestinians and Israel, labeling the E.U., Russia, and the U.N. as the Antichrist triumvirate poised against Israel. The writers go further in admonishing President Bush for even making simple steps toward peace. "America's part in pushing Israel toward the table of false peace is troubling," they write. "President George W. Bush, who in many other ways has proved himself a stalwart friend of Israel, has declared that nation must bring to the table the idea that a Palestinian state will be created. The future state must, the U.S. as well as the EU and others of the Quartet demand, be formed out of land of the West Bank (Judea and Samaria). This, the usually fiercely combative and defensive minded Israeli Prime Minister

Ariel Sharon has amazingly agreed to consider."[9] Also, on the website are the writings of another author calling the EU the seed of Antichrist, one David Breese, a member of the Council for National Policy, LaHaye's Pre-Trib Research Center, as well president and founder of Christian Destiny and advisor to the Rev. Moon lobby Christian Voice.[10]

The website RaptureReady, started by premillennialist writer Todd Strandberg, features a Rapture Index showing the latest numbers that correspond to how soon the Rapture may occur. He calls it the "Dow Jones industrial average of end-times activity," and specifically says the function is to get people to convert to Christianity before the Rapture occurs.[11] For example, any date with a rating over 145 on the Rapture Index signifies it is time to "fasten your safety belts" according to the website. A 182 rating was the record high on September 23, 2001, just after the September 11 attacks, with by biblical passages such as Isaiah 30:25 ("in the day of great slaughter, when the towers fall") and Revelation 18:10 ("though mighty city, Babylon! In one hour has thy judgment come") to buoy the claims of imminent return. Just before the presidential elections of 2004, the index stood at 156, still in the "safety belt" area of maximum believer energy. The site is run by Exodus Design Studios, which also maintains a number of other prominent rapture sites.

On November 3, 2004, a look at the ratings that track current happenings and correlates them to the prophetic calendar revealed that number thirty-three—the "Beast Government"— scored high. The site says that because "there is a growing belief that the EU is going to have a difficult time ratifying its Constitution." Number thirty-four—the signs of an Antichrist— was on the rise, since the "EU is looking for a new president." Some of this shows the intense naivety of people who don't know that the presidency of the European Council, the most powerful body of the EU, changes every six months through a rotating "presidency" that thrusts the prime minister of whatever country that happens to hold the position at the time into the leadership spot of the EU.

As evidence for that creeping Antichristism, premillenialists point to a mysterious one-world government, one world economic system, a one world religion, and the coming of the Antichrist—with Europe at the fore. Sadly, most Europeans are unaware that this increasingly influential segment of American society believes the EU will be central in bringing the Antichrist to leadership. As evidence of this, premillennialists such as Hindson point to the "New Europe," or the EU and European Unification, as fulfilling the prophecy of a revived Roman Empire. "The key players in the New Europe will be England, Germany and Russia," Hindson says darkly. "The unification or cooperation of these three superstates could determine the issue of who controls the world in the future. Already Chancellor Helmut Kohn of the reunified Germany is calling for Germany to *take a bigger role . . .* in the community of nations."

Writing in September 1999, LaHaye buttresses Hindson's assertion, that the Antichrist philosophy already controls Europe. An alien philosophy has taken over the United States as well, he tells us, antithetical to the Bible; "flying under the banner of *liberalism*" it is really "atheistic socialism at its best and Marxism at worst."[12] This could have great influence on future generations of Americans and how they perceive Europe. But this is remarkably nothing new in American, largely Protestant fundamentalist, mythology toward primarily Catholic "Old Europe." Seen as essentially a debauched and evil place, this strain of thought about Europe has been with America from the time the Pilgrims landed to claim their New Jerusalem. Yet never has this segment of American society been as powerful as now.

EARLY PROPAGANDA

Hofstadter traces many of the initial paranoid styles in American politics to a book called *Proofs of a Conspiracy Against All Religions and Governments of Europe, Carried on in Secret Meetings of Free Masons, Illuminati, and Reading Societies*—a book by Scottish scientist John Robison, which led to the panic over the "Illuminati" in 1797. The book, as Hofstadter states, attributed the French Revolution to the Illuminati, who Robison thought promoted a libertine, anti-Christian, woman corrupting, sensual, anti-property philosophy. This led to a widespread paranoia about Continental Illuminism infesting the American democracy through Jeffersonian political ideals. Other extensions of this through the twentieth century and into the John Birch movement include the anti-Masonic movements of the 1820s and 1830s, as well as the anti-Catholic conspiracies of the 1830s, when larger numbers of Catholics began immigrating to America from Europe.

Much like the white supremacist militia movement novel *The Turner Diaries*, the Left Behind series presents an America where most figures in mainstream public and political life are something to be distrusted, to be feared—either as agents or as unwitting participants in the schemes of the Antichrist. They become part of a system set against the biblically inspired worldview that is imagined as a subtext of the novels, a utopian paradise in one instance ruled by Aryan Christians, and in the other ruled by a triumphant American nationalist–style Christianity.

After the Second Coming in the Left Behind series, there are no more Jews, no Catholics, no mainline Protestants, no more Muslims, no Hindus, no Buddhists—there are only believers in the final premillenialist solution. There is no role for democratic institutions in these books and there is no role for democracy. After all, what brought about this mess anyway if it wasn't democracy? How did these leaders of government become so corrupt that they would be dupes or pawns in the system of the Antichrist, if not for the democracy that brought them to power? While the Left Behind novels aren't full-blown conspiracy tomes in the mode of *The Turner Diaries*, they do encapsulate most of the ardent conspiracy theories of the radical right. By toning down the conspiracy politics to such an extent that they become simply part of the background of a fictional world, the authors reach a more widespread audience than something that would be overtly political. In essence it is a form of guerilla proselytizing.

If there is one book that could claim status as a precursor to the conspiracy theories widespread throughout far-right literature in the latter half of the twentieth century, it is *None Dare Call It Treason* by John Stormer. This book essentially plays out the same complex Communist and secular humanist conspiracy theory LaHaye uses today, and in the years following the 1964 election, it was widely used as a recruiting tool for the John Birch Society. Like the paranoid literature that Hofstadter points to in his critiques, Stormer's book goes to great lengths to look legitimate, with its "heroic strivings for evidence"—weighing in with some eight hundred footnotes and documentations—deployed in an attempt to prove that much of the leadership of the U.S. had been taken over by Communists or Communist sympathizers, that the Illuminati had been a part of this, and that the U.S. was rapidly careening toward becoming a socialist state on par with the USSR. The year was 1964 and the Republican candidate Goldwater was running against Lyndon Johnson for the presidency of the United States. Though Goldwater eventually lost, some see his campaign as the birth of the modern conservative movement. It was during this campaign that around 4 million copies of the Stormer book were printed and distributed at party precincts and party headquarters, as well as among men's groups and professional associations. The book went on to sell around 7 million copies and was reissued in 1990 with extended texts by Stormer. That Goldwater's support base was portrayed as a reactionary mob by the media of the time isn't entirely inaccurate—a large segment was made up by John Birch Society–style conspiracy theorists, who helped quite greatly through the distribution of *None Dare Call It Treason*. While there were many commentaries at the time about the book, there is only one lengthy and objective analysis that refutes the distortions and falsifications of the facts: *None Dare Call It Reason* by a political science professor at California State College, Fullerton, Julian Foster.[1] Who would be interested in publishing such a book and disseminating it at Republican rallies for Goldwater, asks Foster rhetorically. The book had been published by Liberty Bell Press, a back-alley political press functioning as Stormer's personal publisher that operated out of Florissant, Missouri, in the 1960s and 1970s.

An early John Birch Society book comparable to *The Turner Diaries* is *The John Franklin Letters*, which argued a patriotic underground army would have to be formed to overthrow the U.S. government. Through the sixties and seventies the publisher of that book, Western Islands Press, also published the newsletter *The Birch Log* for the society. This strongly anti-labor pamphlet called for a repeal of income tax, called for the U.S. to get out of the U.N, and talked up Communist conspiracy and one-world government fears. Even today, the John Birch Society remains active below the radar. Based in Appleton, Wisconsin, the organization is now headed by John F. McManus, author of the conspiracy book *The Insiders*. The group still publishes *American Opinion* magazine and a newsletter called the *JBS Bulletin* and hosts its own website.[2] The organization has a college in Appleton, Robert Welch University, which has started a distance education program recently. Heading the history courses for this program is Thomas E. Woods Jr., author of the best-selling *Politically Incorrect Guide to American History* (Regenery 2004) and one of the founders of a group called League of the South, which "advocates the secession and subsequent independence of the Southern States from this forced union and the formation of a Southern republic," and refers to the federal government as an "alien occupier."[3] Along with other premillennialists and adherents of various rightwing movements, LaHaye was profoundly influenced by his involvement.

Many of these paranoid movements have emulated the very conspiracies they believed were armed against them. "The [devoutly anti-Catholic] Ku Klux Klan imitated Catholicism to the point of donning priestly vestments, developing an elaborate ritual and an equally elaborate hierarchy," writes Hofstadter.

> The John Birch Society emulates Communist cells and quasi-secret operation through "front" groups and preaches a ruthless prosecution of the ideological war along lines very similar to those it finds in the Communist enemy. Spokesmen of the various funda-mentalist anti-Communist "crusades" openly express their admiration for the dedication and discipline the Communist cause calls forth.

This tactic is often taken from the expression by Mao Tse-tung— "Give me just two or three men in a village and I will take the village"—and has popped up throughout rightwing conspiracy literature with much admiration. The 1968 book *How to Win an Election* by conservative political operative Stephen C. Shadegg cites Mao's adage as influential in how he helped run the Goldwater campaign.

A large number of publications throughout the last sixty years have been used by premillennialists to promote their message. More often than not in the enclosed world of this subculture, ideas have a way of repeating themselves through publications competing for the attention of the flock. Among the apocalyptic-conspiracy publications that circulated throughout the middle of the twentieth century, some tended to take on a more militant air than others. Some leaned more toward conspiracy, and others toward prophecy, but what marks these is that they always contained a little of each. Nearly all of them were concerned with Israel and the Middle East in some way, some with an anti-Semitic position and others with an eye on conversion of Jews. Many of these influenced the philosophy LaHaye brought with him from Bob Jones University to California, where he began to encounter the conspiracy narrative of the John Birch Society, melding that with his premillennialist worldview.

The Sword of the Lord

John R. Rice's *The Sword of the Lord* was one of the most widely available premillennialist publications of the past century. Launched in 1934, *The Sword of the Lord*, published out of Wheaton, Illinois, became one of the largest circulating independent religious weeklies in the world, with subscribers in every U.S. state and more than 100 countries by the time of Rice's death in 1980. As the author, Rice had a tremendous impact on fundamentalist premillennial thought during his lifetime. His radio show, *Voice of Revival* was broadcast in twenty-nine states.

A June 30, 1961, copy of *The Sword of the Lord* defines a premillennialist as:

> [Someone] who believes that we are living in an age when God is calling his people for His name, and when that calling is completed, Christ will return. He believes that the world itself will go on from bad to worse until its terrible condition will necessitate the intervention of God, even as the sin of the days of Noah necessitated the judgment of the flood.

It continues along, in much of the same way as the plot of most premillennialist ideology—that we are in the dispensation before the Tribulation and that the Messiah will come only after the "Man of Sin," or the Antichrist, is defeated at the battle of Armageddon, after which he will be bound for a thousand years (Rev. 20:1–3). Symbolically for the premillennialists, secularism and nonpremillennialism is the center of this Antichrist philosophy—necessitating an all out battle against these forces in order to win the keys to the kingdom.

The editorial advisory board for *The Sword of the Lord* comprised some of the most prominent premillennial Protestant preachers and publishers of the last fifty years—Dr. Billy Graham, Dr. Bob Jones, Dr. Bob Jones Jr., Dr. Bob Schuler, Dr. Louis Talbot, Mr. Pat Zondervan, and Mr. Bernie Zondervan. While not openly conspiratorial in tone, there was a strong anti-Catholic message in the publication, not surprising considering the position of many fundamentalist Protestants. In the September 16, 1960, edition, for example, a headline asks "Kennedy for President?" and offers a free pamphlet—really a forty-page booklet—concerning whether a Catholic should be president of the United States. Lastly and also unsurprisingly, the publication displayed in articles and advertisements an overarching fascination with trying to convert Jews to Protestant Christianity.[4]

Alarming Cry

On the front page of the Spring 1959 edition of *Alarming Cry* there is a picture of eleven somber evangelical scholars responsible for revising the Scofield Reference Bible. Among these was Dr. John Walvood, long an influential premillennialist and currently a member of LaHaye's Pre-Trib Research Center.[5] *Alarming Cry* is one of many premillennialist pamphlets that have circulated throughout the past century since Darby developed the "theology of premillennialism" and Moody popularized the Scofield Reference Bible and premillenialist belief in America. It is mainly after World War II—after the Soviet advance into Eastern Europe, the Red Chinese grip on China, and the founding of the United Nations—that these took on a heavy anti-Communist and John Birch–style conspiratorial tone as well.

Browsing through a few issues, one finds fears about the United Nations flag and a pledge of allegiance to that flag ("How can there come peace of blessing from a league with a murderous record such as blight the history of this anti-god, anti-freedom land of Communist intrigue and slaughter!"); paranoia over the World Council of Churches and modernist ecumenical movements; early Hollywood bashing detailing Errol Flynn's sexual excesses; and warnings (from 1968) that "one year from now some of you who are reading his article may be on your way to a new political concentration camp located in central Alaska" set up by "one-worlders" of the *Bobby Kennedy type,* mixed with advertisements for mail-order Bible courses, pictures of bake sales, and P.O. box numbers to write for premillennialist or conspiracy books. There is a comic strip in one issue of *Alarming Cry,* located below an article on how prayer can save America, in which a young man foisting a copy of his student paper on his friends asks if they have read the article "Have You Been Brainwashed on Evolution?"—to which one girl responds "We've been taught that we evolved from lower life, which evolved from dead matter . . . it just doesn't add up."

Citizens Intelligence Digest

Similar graphics could be found in *Citizens Intelligence Digest*, published out of Bakersfield, California leading up to the Goldwater run. The first volume shows a map of the United States with the title "The War Against America" above it, while images of clouds with the words "Nuclear Blackmail" and "Psychological Warfare" hover over Canada. A Soviet hammer and sickle flies ominously over the globe and arrows of fire with the words "economic war" and "political war" come from the unseen foe in the north, "subversion" and "international social-ism" from Mexico and Cuba in the south. The figure of a patri-otic firefighter races across the heartland trying to put out fires of "vice, riots, uncensored propaganda, treason" and the hose he is hauling called "The Constitution" is being cut in half by an axe labeled "Leftist organizations." In the midst of all this sits the "apathetic American citizen" in front of his TV, being told that "the threat is only external" with the disclaimer in brackets "[propaganda]."

Page eight is an even more paranoid vision of America. The picture displays an average American housewife disheveled on the ground and reaching out to her little boy, who is being led away by a U.N. soldier through a barbed wire gate to an await-ing U.N. truck full of other little American children ready to be hauled away to their doom. Below this it reads: WHAT WILL YOU TELL YOUR CHILDREN?

> Will you tell them you were too busy making money or playing golf or going fishing to be interested in any patri-otic movements, or to read the truth they published at great personal sacrifice? Or that you were brainwashed by an avalanche of propaganda, lies and deception? . . . What will you say if you are forced to take your children to the embarkation point and see them, perhaps for the last time, being shipped off for indoctrination in some foreign land? . . . Look at your children. If they are asleep, walk in and look at them—peaceful, innocent, and trusting. What are you doing to prevent the possibil-ity of such a terrifying event from occurring?[6]

Flag of Truth

The *Flag of Truth*, another premillennialist publication from the early sixties, shows a picture entitled "Can this happen to America?" A beautiful girl who has fainted or has somehow fallen asleep in the woods is gazed at lustily by a swarthy Che Guevara–type man in a black beret. The words surrounding the picture are much more interesting really—

> Your DAUGHTER will be sent to REMOTE REGIONS as a teacher; not to really teach but to be dragged into a LIFE OF PROMISCUITY. . . . The Socialist Party has a death grip on the Democratic Party. . . . Look at Socialist Doctrine of Minority cramming Communistic Civil Rights down upon the big Majority. Register, pay your poll tax and be ready to vote . . . A right vote is the only way to oppose socialism. . . . PROTECT HELPLESS GIRLS! . . . Corruption and licentiousness are essential elements of the Communist state!

Below all this is a P.O. box address in Miami, Florida where one can write for more information and send a donation to the Cuban Anti-Castro Movimente. It seems a bit strange that an "anti-Castro" group in Miami would be advertising against the civil rights movement in America in a premillennialist publication, but since logically many premillennialists were also tapping into the populist far-right theories such as developed by the John Birch Society and the Goldwater movement, there is an overlap here. It is much the same type of overlap seen today between how LaHaye has joined forces with such conservative activists like Grover Norquist through institutions such as the Council for National Policy. But instead of being located far out in the hinterland as these groups were before, now they are firmly entrenched in the insider machinery of Washington, D.C.[7] An August 1964 edition of the *Flag of Truth* newsletter has a picture of George Washington with a statement about Jews attributed to him, which certainly won't be found in history textbooks:

> They work more effectively against us than the enemies' armies. They are a hundred times more dangerous to our liberties and the great cause we are engaged in. It is much to be lamented that each State, long ago has not

> hunted them down as pests to society and the greatest
> enemies we have to the happiness of America.

The opposite page is full of slander against Jews, claiming that the Jews of Israel are not really the Jews. This idea is similar to much of the Anglo-Israel strain of conspiracy-religiosity that sparks such white supremacist millennial groups as Christian Identity, and in subtler fashion, is contained in the Left Behind books.[8]

Humbard Christian Report

Humbard Christian Report, out of Youngstown, Ohio, when it wasn't saying that UFOs were invading the U.S. and that computers were tools of the Antichrist, started one of many balls rolling against a separate land for the Palestinians in an editorial about "The Future of Israel" on April 5, 1974. "The late David Ben Gurion once referred to the establishment of Israel as one of the greatest miracles of modern times," writes Ray Brubaker, now a Pre-Trib Research Center member.

> He noted that in order to achieve peace with the Arabs
> there must be the surrender of territories now under
> control of Israel. However, from our observation, this is
> not the will of the Almighty. By covenant, God gave
> Abraham the land described from the river of Egypt
> unto the great river of Euphrates (Gen 15:18).

In backing his claims, Brubaker references Hal Lindsey's *Late Great Planet Earth* and a host of other premillennialists, and specifically charged scripture passages to support his case. Brubaker again states, in an article called "The Middle East Conflict!" that the "Palestinian problem" is of utmost importance and warns against a "peace deal" between Israel and her neighbors because this signifies the rise of the Antichrist. It isn't just coincidence that many of these publications with similar stories also had advertisements for "Holy Land Adventures" and tours of the biblical lands, as the September 8, 1974, edition of the *Humbard* does. Readers simply had to fork over a $25 registration fee, a $100 confirmation fee, and $620 for the rest of the complete tour for a chartered trip to the Holy Land with Reverend

Clement Humbard himself.[9] From the November 29, 1974, article "Topics for Tribulation" comes this:

> Today's news headlines read like a page from the
> "Rapture Journal" of Topics for Tribulation! There's the
> "gold" crisis with the price of precious metal going at an
> all time high. Surely if heaven's streets are paved with
> gold—heaven's getting worth more all the time. . . . That
> the Great Tribulation is just around the corner is evi-
> dent because of several developments—including the
> money crisis.

The anonymous author goes on to assert famine, massive sickness,
global destruction, nuclear war, and nearly every other imagina-
ble misfortune will soon strike the earth, then states "There will
be no peace on earth until the PRINCE OF PEACE comes."

Christian Crusade

Finally there was *Christian Crusade*, published by Evangelist Billy
James Hargis out of Tulsa, Oklahoma, to promote his radio broadcasts as well as books by such people as David A. Noebel, his former aide to Hargis. Noebel, currently one of LaHaye's Pre-Trib
members and co-author of the book *Mind Siege* with LaHaye, is
also head of the prominent Summit Ministries, which was first created as a Christian training center outside Colorado Springs,
Colorado—Manitou Springs. Noebel's base in Manitou Springs
had long been used as a "Christian anti-Communist" summer
camp, and now houses schools that argue that secular humanism
has taken the place of communism as the anti-Christian philosophy most dangerous to fundamentalists. Manitou Springs features
in many of the premillennialist journals of the sixties and seventies.
A letter from Hargis to subscribers on July 31, 1970, says the purpose of the camps was for "training dedicated Christian young
people to defend America and biblical morality and counteract the
Communist revolution on college and high school campuses across
America." One of Hargis's favorite targets was Reverend Martin
Luther King, who he called a Communist "deceiver" with all the
Antichrist flair of those words.[10] Hargis, who died in November
2004, had largely dropped from the public eye after a sex scandal
hit his American Christian College in Tulsa, Oklaohma, in the

seventies. A *Time* magazine report surfaced saying Hargis had had sex with a number of students of both sexes at the campus— charges admitted to, then denied and later blamed on a "Communist" smear campaign.[11]

Though Hargis came to prominence before LaHaye, he cuts a strikingly similar figure and it is obvious LaHaye absorbed much of his rhetoric. Hargis writing about the "Corrupt Liberal Establishment" in the lead-up to the 1968 election is mimicked in LaHaye's writing about the corrupt liberal establishment in all the elections of his own lifetime. It is the language of the perpetually embattled, but one that always points to future victory. "God's victory over Antichrist liberalism is evidenced by happenings at home and abroad," writes Hargis. "Liberalism is corrupt, satanic, destructive, the form and substance of Marxism. . . . God is giving America, I believe, one last chance to reverse the trend toward atheism, immorality, and anarchy and an opportunity to return to the New Testament Christianity and constitutional concepts . . . the feeling of victory is in the air for Christian conservatism."

Hargis, writing against Johnson's "Great Society"—under a piece titled "Wars and Rumors of Wars"—explains that the "Bible makes it clear that not until the Prince of Peace comes to reign on this earth will there be an end to bigotry and poverty. Of course, the politicians disagree with the Bible." Similar arguments against "socialist medicine" frame his debates about Medicare and any federal aid to education as "socialist" and Communist inspired. His arguments against alleviating poverty quote Jesus on one hand as saying, "For ye will have the poor with you always," then trail off into bigotry—"Let's face it. There are some people who want to be poor, who won't work, who won't accept responsibility. They enjoy poverty."[12]

There is little coincidence that prior to Hargis's writing against the evils of progressive income tax during the Johnson administration, the IRS had been investigating *Christian Crusade* for possibly violating its tax exempt status through the political lobbying efforts of its parent organization, Christian Echoes Ministry.

In the Left Behind books, promoters of social justice such as Franklin D. Roosevelt, John F. Kennedy, Martin Luther King, and even Abraham Lincoln are connected to the "Antichrist" nature of Nicolae Carpathia in another sleight of hand move by the authors—Carpathia embodies many of their good aspects early on in the books. Later, when Carpathia is a full-blown Satan, these aspects no longer look so redeeming, thus the title "The Great Deciever" for the Antichrist or Satan, or Lucifer. All of the aforementioned play into the conspiracy notions developed in the Left Behind books and in rightwing conspiracy in general. Here is a passage from the first book where Buck Williams is being swept up in Carpathia's aura of social promise:

> He wanted to believe a person could come along once in a generation who could capture the imagination of the world. Could Carpathia be another Lincoln, a Roosevelt, or the embodiment of Camelot that Kennedy had appeared to some?[13]

On September 22, 1966, the U.S. Treasury Department revoked *Christian Crusade*'s tax-exempt status on the grounds that—"1. [Christian Echoes Ministry] are not operated exclusively for religious, educational or charitable purposes within the meaning of section 501(c)(3) and 170(c) of the Code; 2. A substantial part of your activities is attempting to influence legislation, contrary to the prohibition contained in section 501(c) and (3); 3. There was direct and indirect intervention in political campaigns on behalf of candidates for public office."[14] Later the IRS imposed a fine of over $60,000 on *Christian Crusade*, which Hargis paid off with loans from sympathizers. What is striking when looking at this case today is how lax the IRS has become on enforcing the 501(c)(3) and 170 codes—many on both the left and the right that could be considered religious, educational, or charitable also now have lobbying arms, political action committees, which function as subsidiaries of the tax-exempt parent organization. Noebel argued in a 1966 edition of *Christian Crusade* against this ruling, claiming that the only specific legislation *Christian Crusade* was guilty of promoting was voluntary prayer and Bible reading in the public schools. What *Christian Crusade* refused to admit was that a substantial portion of the material in their publication and on Hargis's radio broadcasts had become political instead of educational, charitable, or religious. In mid-2004, the IRS began investigating around four hundred non-profit entities, part of a booming sector of the economy that spends around $875 billion per year and employs nearly 12 million people. One of the difficult aspects of policing nonprofits is that 70 percent of them have budgets under $500,000.

As an example of the "educational" output from a December 1966 edition of *Christian Crusade*, David Noebel's book *Rhythm, Riots and Revolution* could be ordered for just $1—"the unvarnished facts about the American Reds' use of music to destroy our youth, morally and patriotically, " including a massive 650 footnotes and nearly 100 pages of appendices to back up those claims. Just next to that ad is an article about how the President Lyndon Johnson was "reigning and prospering and is executing Liberal, vindictive political judgment and injustice in the earth" not with his Vietnam policies, but his "anti-Christ" polices, which put simply means the Great Society programs. Another version of Noebel's book called *Marxist Minstrels* has long been actively promoted through John Birch Society publications, and was once a John Birch "notable book."[15] In another issue of *Christian Crusade*, Noebel writes about how the Communists were hypnotizing youth through the music of the Beatles. Much of this is similar to the 1991 book Noebel wrote called *Understanding the Times*. This nearly nine-hundred-page textbook lays out the philosophy of a battle against "secular society" and is now used in 850 Christian schools by over fifteen thousand students.[16]

As well as being avidly anti-Communist, *Christian Crusade* had racist subtexts, and a heavy disdain for federal education, socialized medicine, and the idea of "world peace" as an instrument of Communist propaganda.[17] Noebel is now president of American Christian College, Inc., of Summit Ministries based in Manitou Springs, Colorado. Up to 1988, Noebel's conferences hosted an average of about 350 students per year. But after Focus on the Family's Dr. James Dobson sent his own son through the program and featured Summit on his radio show, the "camp style" meetings developed into a full blown anti-secularist factory. Currently, Summit churns out an average of thirteen hundred graduates from its eight two-week seminars each year. In 1991, Noebel started a year-long program for Christian high school seniors, with the textbook *Understanding the Times* as a major portion of the curriculum. About thirty-five hundred seniors graduate from this program each year. More programs have been developed to train pastors, teachers, parents, and lay people, and a number of spin-off seminars have been established in Canada, South Africa, and New Zealand.

From Word to Action

Christian Crusade, as well as the above, are just a few of dozens of apocalyptic-conspiracy publications that circulated widely, beginning after World War I and culminating during the sixties. It was after this time, as the religious conservative movement began to go mainstream in the seventies, that the literature began to go mainstream along with the ascendance of a Christian media built upon the success of people like Hargis. The 1968 election, in which Nixon beat Humphrey by just over eight hundred thousand in the popular vote (Nixon won handily in the electoral college with 301 to Humphrey's 191, and George Wallace's 46), marks the beginning of what some observers call the "conservative backlash." George Wallace's defection, along with the defection of many southern white Democrats, from the Democratic Party was essentially the first step in the seismic voting shift that occurred as the civil rights and anti-war movements were alienating many Americans. It was at this time that the narrative from the conspiratorial right—which recognized these not as social movements, but as Communist or humanist or atheist plots—began to filter into the mainstream culture through this nexus of John Birch and fundamentalist church.

Hofstadter compares the fears of the American rightwing of the sixties to those in early America—the old conspiracy theories were used politically to battle ideas coming from below, whereas the rightwing movements of the sixties placed their narrative in the frame of reference that they'd already lost to these forces and had been dispossessed. Instead of holding off that which they feared, the rightwing had watched wicked ideas had take over every aspect of society, and it was now time to battle from within and create a resurgent or "reconstructive" ideology. He writes that "events since 1939 have given the contemporary rightwing paranoid a vast theatre for his imagination, full of rich and proliferating detail, replete with realistic cues and undeniable proofs of the validity of his suspicions."

Hofstadter believes that paranoid rightwing thought can be reduced to three elements:

- A sustained and realized conspiracy that reached its climax under Roosevelt's New Deal and aimed to undermine free market capitalism, bring the economy under the direction of the federal government, and usher in communism and socialism. The beginning of this was the income-tax amendment to the Constitution in 1913.

- The political leadership of America has been infiltrated by a network of Communists bent on selling out American national interests.

- America is infused with a network of Communist agents, a network which encompasses everything from education, religion, the press, and mass media in an effort to paralyze the resistance of loyal Americans.

Hofstadter writes this in the sixties, a few years after the McCarthyist Red Scare and well into the establishment of the John Birch Society, a group which centralized Communist conspiracy as its dogma of existence. Others such as Reconstructionist pioneer R. J. Rushdoony, founder of the Chalcedon Foundation, have been seen by some within the movement as having formed many of the core ideas that led to the rise of the Christian right. Before his death in 2001, he summed up much of the ideology of the Reconstructionist movement:

> [As] a reaction against the chaos of modernism, Fundamentalist Christianity is a Revolution against Socialism, Marxism and Enlightenment . . . against contempt for God and Law . . . against the assault on Biblical Morality.[18]

Rushdoony, also a former member of the LaHaye founded Council for National Policy, was one of the leaders of the Christian Reconstructionist movement, a strain of Protestant political theology that wants the U.S. to base its government on a biblical worldview—in essence to create an American theocracy. His book *Institutes of Biblical Law*, published in 1973, an overtly racist and extremist tract defending segregation and slavery, missed most of the mainstream but circulated widely among hard-line fundamentalists. A publication from the seventies called *Applied Christianity*, out of Buena Park, California, and distributed by the Christian Freedom Foundation, mixed an anti-tax message with biblical morality using the writings of future millennialist profiteer Gary North, Henry Morris of the LaHaye-founded Institute for Creation Researc,h and Rushdoony. Rushdoony has at times advocated the public execution for women who've undergone abortions as well as the doctors who performed them, along with a whole host of others— gays, heretics, and adulterers to name but a few.[19] Though there is an inherent dilemma between premillennialism and Reconstructionism—with the latter an ultraconservative Presbyterian brand of Calvinism believing in postmillennialism, or that God's Kingdom first has to be established on earth before he will return—both serve each other's purposes in exactly the same way: gaining believers and gaining power.

Another evangelical hardliner, Francis Schaeffer, also had an important influence on the LaHaye's views of a secular humanist conspiracy wrapped in an apocalyptic and theocratic narrative. Author of the late-seventies books *How Should We Then Live?* and *What Happened to the Human Race?*, Schaeffer argued that society was being destroyed by secular humanism, that such must be confronted, and that Christians had the duty to take control over the godless secular society. His 1981 book *The Manifesto*, which sold three hundred thousand copies during Reagan's first year in office, suggested that the way to ignite the battle against secular society was to make abortion the central issue of contention. It's little coincidence that the Council for National Policy started that year and other LaHaye organizations like the Moral Majority and CWA were founded around this time as well, with abortion as their central focus. Schaeffer was one of the people who urged Falwell to use his broadcasting for political aims earlier in the seventies, and he and LaHaye stand arm-in-arm in framing the fundamentalist "battle for the mind" against secular society.[20]

"The Bible teaches us that in the last days mens' hearts will fail them for fear," LaHaye writes. "To those who criticize fear as a motivator, I say fear has gotten a bad rap," says Jenkins. "I believe that people who die without Christ will go to hell, that if they are alive at the 'Rapture,' they will be left behind. That is something to fear."[21]

Prophecy Profiteering

As evidence of the wide reach of paranoia mixed with profit, around the turn of the millennium Christian magazines began featuring advertisements for "Rapture insurance policies" for family members Left Behind, as well as gold bullion and mineral investment schemes, a favorite of premillennialist profiteers. An associate of LaHaye who cashed in on Y2K was fundamentalist economics "guru" Gary North, who had been claiming Y2K would lead to the "breakdown of Western society" into the autumn of 1999. At the same time, he was urging investors to pull their money out of the markets and buy precious minerals through his newsletters and seminar tapes. As far back as 1983, North was publishing the *Remnant Review* and warning of government plans to introduce a new currency, tapping into "one currency" paranoia. It's somewhat fitting that North might desire a biblical version of economics for America—his PhD dissertation was "History of Economic Thought in Puritan New England." North is connected to LaHaye through the Council for National Policy, which he was a member of in the developing years of the 1980s.[22]

During those same years, Donald S. McAlvany, of Denver, Colorado, was especially interested in Africa and precious metals. He produced a bulletin called *African Intelligence Digest*, which argued that freeing blacks in South Africa would deliver that country to the U.S.S.R. But aside from ideological reasons for opposing the freedom of blacks in South Africa, McAlvany also had economic interests there. The *McAlvany Intelligence Advisor,* which gave precious metals analysis to investors, was published from the same office as the *African Intelligence Digest*. In the same building was a company called Gold, Silver, and Rare Coin Brokerage. The *Intelligence Advisor* magazine mixed conservative politics, political activism, conspiracy theory, fear, staunch patriotism, and of course, End Times investment advice.[23]

McAlvany, a former Prophecy Club speaker, was also once director of conservative activist Howard Phillips's organization, Conservative Caucus. The Conservative Caucus lobbied against taxation, government spending, federal subsidies, and was anti-U.N., anti-busing, anti-National Council of Churches; it also argued for more spending for the military and energy independence. In 1985 national director Phillips issued the "Conservative Manifesto" to members through the *Conservative Caucus*, published by his Policy Analysis, Inc., which outlined many of the above concerns. The group published a "Senate Issues Handbook" with ratings of congressmen, especially singling out everyone's favorite liberal to bash, Senator Edward Kennedy. The *Conservative Caucus* was also instrumental in the National Campaign to Defeat SALT II. In the late 1990s, McAlvany cashed in on the Y2K scare with his *Y2K Tidal Wave: Year 2000 Economic Survival* guide, which is still available at Armageddon Books. The McAlvany *Intelligence Advisor* also regularly promoted conspiracy books such as Larry Abraham's *Call It Conspiracy*—an updated rendering of John Stormer's *None Dare Call It Treason* John Birch Society manifesto from the 60s.[24] The book features a prologue by Council for National Policy member and Y2K profiteer Gary North.

To understand this type of paranoia profiteering on the rightwing it is essential to understand William R. Kennedy is and why he is so important to LaHaye and James Dobson. As of this writing, Kennedy is serving out a twenty-year federal prison sentence after being convicted by jury on one count of racketeering, nine counts of aiding and abetting mail fraud, and seven counts of aiding and abetting money laundering. These convictions stem from a federal investigation into Western Monetary Consultants, Inc., a company which he presided over in the 1980s in Denver, Colorado. Between 1980 and 1985, Western Monetary Consultants went from $1 million in sales a year to $87 million—but by 1988 the business had filed Chapter 11 bankruptcy. Like many of the Y2K money-making scams and prophecy investment brokerages, Kennedy lured investors by using fear—fear of apocalypse, fear of wars and rumors of wars, fears of global upheaval. The indictment in 1992 by a federal grand jury found him guilty of a massive Ponzi scheme to defraud precious metal investors, and after sending the ruling to the Tenth Circuit Court of Appeals in 1995, Kennedy was convicted of all charges relating to the case. The government's case was the result of a five year investigation, after which it filed a 109-count indictment against Kennedy. Through this scheme Kennedy diverted investor funds to his favorite rightwing organizations, including the *Conservative Digest* of which he was the publisher; monies were also traced to off-shore accounts in the Grand Cayman Islands. Kennedy, who had been one of the early members of the Council for National Policy while all this was going on, was a student of James Dobson when he was young and had once run for Congress in Colorado.[25]

In 2004, LaHaye, Dobson, and Christian right activists sent a petition to President Bush asking him to commute Kennedy's sentence based on allegations that his case was mishandled by prosecutors. There is a website established to help garner support for Kennedy's release called Justice For Kennedy (www.justiceforkennedy.com) on which LaHaye and Dobson feature prominently. On the website LaHaye, who calls Kennedy a "political prisoner," has been saying Kennedy has now "found faith." But it's not that faith or LaHaye were anything new to Kennedy—they'd known each other for years. According to a lawyer involved with the case, the LaHayes put up property to back a bail bond for Kennedy when the initial charges were brought. That lawyer also claims his clients are still owed over $2 million from an unpaid judgment stemming from litigation brought forth in the Northern District of California, which led to the federal investigation. "[Kennedy] has always claimed that his business was just 'growing out of control,'" this lawyer said. "But in fact, he was selling short and this was proven in court. Many people paid a dear price for his lavish lifestyle. There is no doubt that Kennedy was stealing from his clients and using the money to fund his political causes and buy influence with the Reagan Administration."

One of the gambits used to raise money for these precious metals schemes was something called War College Seminars, where Kennedy and a man named Sam Zakhem would hawk their silver and gold along with their doom and gloom prophecy messages. Zakhem, once a prominent conservative in Colorado, spoke at a number of these conferences. In 1992, at the time he was running for Congress from Colorado, Zakhem was indicted on twelve counts for failing to register as a foreign agent, tax evasion, and for taking millions of dollars from the government of Kuwait in order to lobby in the U.S. for military intervention against Iraq in the First Gulf War. After three years the case fell apart, with Zakhem being acquitted on two counts, and the rest of the charges being dropped when the lead prosecutor left his position and his successor decided not to pursue the case.[26]

Zakhem, an immigrant from Lebanon, had served in the Colorado House of Representatives in the late 1970s where, among many things, he had sponsored bills to give creationism equal time in Colorado public schools and strong anti-abortion legislation. The *Rocky Mountain Journal* called him "a posturing politician with a genius for transforming honest expressions of patriotism and morality into gross acts of political exhibition-ism." In 1986, Zakhem was appointed U.S. ambassador to Bahrain by the Reagan administration, a move criticized in for-eign policy circles due to his lack of experience. After returning from the Gulf, Zakhem joined up with Kennedy's new organi-zation, Coalition for America at Risk, and the Freedom Task Force to lobby for military intervention against Kuwait. The 1992 indictment against Zakhem and Kennedy, not officially connected with the Western Monatery Consultants C case, alleged that less than one-third of the $7.7 million that Kuwait had given to Freedom Task Force had gone to advertising, and that $1 million had been diverted to Zakhem's brother Khalil in Lebanon for "consulting fees."

Waiting for the End, American Style

There has always been one large problem for prophecy profi-teers in America—America doesn't exist in prophecy and America is not in the Bible. LaHaye tells his readers in an August 1999 newsletter that the reason the United States is not easily found in prophecy is because the "United States may soon surrender her national sovereignty in the name of *world peace* to the United Nations." This message is trumpeted quite clearly in the Left Behind series, or rather, that "corruption and betrayal" will implode the nation, adding that "all it would take is anoth-er eight years of liberalism in the White House and a liberal majority in the Congress, Senate, and Supreme Court—the election of 2000 will determine that!"[27]

In propagandist language, the above statement means that surrendering in any way to peace, dealing with the United Nations, or voting for liberals is tantamount to giving in to the

Antichrist. At some moments, the language of the Left Behind books and urges believers to fight against letting the events that would leave Americans out of prophecy occur. In other instances, such as in America's dealings with Israel, there is a great zeal to speed up the End Times scenarios in order to make prophecy come to life before their eyes. These two contradictions make sense in the larger picture for premillennialists—the mass salvation through the Rapture takes place through the combination of prophetic fulfillment, and through that pre-Rapture proselytizing, more will be saved in that Rapture. LaHaye brings these together to form a coherent worldview for the current time—one which draws upon past prophecy interpretation, one that paints a gloomy picture of the future for the unbeliever, and in the end one that attempts to fuel support for his political agenda. Here are his four scenarios for why the United States would be left on the sidelines of the End Times for LaHaye:

- The liberal media attacks on Christian values escalate, with the entertainment and education industries leading the way, collapsing the country in less than a decade and bringing anarchy.

- Church members who do not vote allow liberal secular humanists ("who are socialists at heart," adds LaHaye) to be elected into office, bringing on big government, big brother, and controlling the religious, economic, and educational lives of children.

- Control of the U.S. is turned over to the U.N. by liberal socialist politicians who use the resources of the nation to implement One World Government.

It is no wonder LaHaye delves so deeply in the black arts of propaganda. Politics is all tricks and conspiracies to him. "Many Americans are tricked by the media into voting for people that are completely in opposition to their own ideology," he says in a 1984 interview with the *Washington Times*. He also claims, "The purchase of the 1996 election of the United States for Bill Clinton by the Chinese Communists (which has been downplayed or ignored by our socialist Marxist loving media) had resulted in the most corrupt administration in American history." [28]

Behind this rhetoric is not only political power, but also a great opportunity to make the almighty dollar. Early in 1999, Jerry Falwell distributed a packet called "The Y2K Time Bomb" that included a video, "A Christian's Guide to the Millennium Bug," and a family readiness checklist. Apocalyptic filmmaker Pat Matrisciana also jumped into the Y2K and millennial apocalypse game with his movie *The Crash: The Coming Financial Collapse of America*. At the same time, Falwell claimed in a television broadcast that "Y2K is God's instrument to shake this nation, to humble this nation. He may be preparing to confound our language, to jam our communications, scatter our efforts, and judge us for our sin and rebellion for going against his lordship." A year and a half later, Falwell would be spouting similar rhetoric of national sin, blaming the September 11 attacks on gays, lesbians, liberals, and their ilk, who had brought God's wrath upon the nation. For years LaHaye has held the idea that secularism, humanism, and homosexuality in a nation equated eventual biblical destruction for that nation. Writing in *What Everyone Should Know About Homosexuality* in 1980, he states, "when sodomy fills the national cup of man's abomination to overflowing, God earmarks that nation for destruction."[29] Though homosexuality is not attacked outright in the series of twelve main Left Behind books, the first prequel, *The Rising*, pulls no punches by portraying the "creation" of Nicolae Carpathia as the product of the sperm of two homosexual Romanians, genetically manipulated and inserted into the egg of Carpathia's future mother. This sets up the entire series as quite homophobic as everything which flows from Carpathia after this point is evil.

"The literal interpretation of the Bible is the foundation stone of prophetic truth," LaHaye writes. "As a pastor for thirty-seven years I can tell you there is a difference in the lifestyle of those believers who live in the light of Christ's imminent return, for they do not want to *be ashamed before Him as His coming*. As we have seen, the lack of the *at any moment* awareness of our Lord's return often leads to a carnal life." [30]

Like the inconsistencies noted before, another shell game used by premillennialists is how they change their story when errors show themselves or when events don't work the way they've interpreted prophecy forecasts. Instead of giving up and losing believers, they simply say they were mistaken and construct new predictions. The case of multimillionaire Hal Lindsey is appropriate to illuminate. Most of his later works are simply updates of his *Late Great Planet Earth*, which alone has gone through over one hundred printings, republished with changes made to smooth out what went wrong and what didn't work anymore. Something like 20 million copies of that book have been sold since the seventies.[31]

Politics, paranoia, and precious metals for these profiteers go hand in hand with prophecy just as well. At a four-day Bible prophecy conference in Tampa, Florida in 1999—at which televangelist Jack Van Impe, author Hal Lindsay, and author Gary Kah spoke—$1.75 million in gold and silver coins as well as other precious minerals were bought by the attendees, according to one seller at the event who relayed the story to the *Los Angeles Times*.[32]

As the year 2000 approached and the millennial fever rose to new heights, the business of selling prophecy reached a zenith that has lasted into the first few years of the new millennium. Even after another year of waiting for the real millennial date to show, December 31, 2000—none of the big Y2K crashes, the Second Comings, the arrival of extraterrestrials that the Heaven's Gate cult thought would snatch them away to paradise, the Armageddons, or other massive catastrophes came to fruition.

A year before the turn of the century, LaHaye warned the Y2K bug might trigger a "financial meltdown" that would "make it possible for the Antichrist or his emissaries . . . to dominate the world commercially until it is destroyed." He wasn't alone in thinking something would happen—about 30 percent of Americans expected civil unrest, and another 26 percent thought natural disasters would occur around the millennium. One in ten people reported they were stockpiling food. Among Bible literalists, 40 percent thought the new millennium would bring the return of Christ—and LaHaye was keen to tap into that belief.[33]

The prophetic potential of September 11 to LaHaye reverberates with the significance he gives nearly any event—that it
will contribute to world government, world commerce, a one-
world religion, and more animosity toward Israel. On the last
point, premillennialists with an active role in Christian
Zionism, totally reject a two-state solution. By sending massive
amounts of money into the occupied territories, propping up
the rightwing Likud party with funding, helping settle the disputed territories with Jews from around the world, and discounting the existence of Palestinians at all, they further fuel
hate toward Jews and Israelis. The terrorist attacks on
September 11 helped lift sales of the Left Behind books after the
millennium failed to bring apocalypse. LaHaye writes at the
Pre-Trib Research Center website that the attacks clearly show
God's plan for America and that even the "skeptical scoffers"
are intellectually dishonest for their blindness.[34]

Instead of blaming the attackers, themselves bred on
Islamic fundamentalism and conspiracy theories, LaHaye sug-
gests that "what happened in New York and Washington, D.C.
is a larger symptom of the anti-God, Antichristian, spirit of
officialdom in America, Europe and the rest of the world."[35]
Destruction of the secular state is something LaHaye had been
calling for and hoping for since he became active in political circles.

"All through the 20th Century we allowed godless secularism to replace the Judeo-Christian values of our society," writes
premillennialist theologian Ed Hindson. "God has been deliberately and systematically removed from prominence in our
culture and in our intellectual lives."[36] Other analysis shows that
America is probably as religious as it has ever been. As Sara
Diamond, a former chronicler of the religious right notes in
Spiritual Warfare, "secular humanism" has become a catch-all
phrase or convenient label for virtually anything the Christian
right stands opposed to, a phrase in their lexicon for a human-
centered rather than God-centered philosophy, or basically anything outside of a literal fundamentalist understanding of what
religion is as well as its relationship to secular ideas, one which
can coexist and the other which shuns any forms of secularism.
Tim LaHaye stands at the head of this battle on the Christian
Right. In doing so he relies on a complex conspiracy theory that

links all his usual suspects to the impending downfall of civilization. While "Communism" used to be the most reliable threat for far-right conspiracy narratives like those developed by the John Birch Society, with the fall of Communism, and the role of Russia in narratives like Lindsey's largely gone, secular humanism and secular society in general has become the evil which must be vanquished.

Writing in his Perspective column at the Pre-Trib Research Center just after the 2000 New Year failed to bring the dreaded and much-hyped Y2K disaster, LaHaye warned that America would lose 40 percent of its population through Rapture, which would leave the nation so helpless that it would become a colony of Europe, from where it is said the Antichrist is said will rise. "The good news is the 'Rapture' is scheduled to take places before the *time of the end,*" he writes, summing up the premillennial dispensationalist theology in a few words. "Think about it, the largest population in history will not have an entire lifetime to make their decision for Christ."

Much of this rhetoric shows the conversion by fire—pre-fire or pre-Tribulation—tactics by premillennialist philosophy throughout the last century. By far the premillennial line of dispensationalism is the most geared toward political, social, and evangelical activism due to its "promise" of *mass* salvation *before* the Tribulation and the end of the world. The immediacy of Christ's return, the way current events are interpreted and followed like a biblical CNN, the active participation in bringing about the Reign of Christ on earth, the "winning of souls," and the hope of missing all the mayhem through Rapture is a seductive mantra for many who believe that these are perilous times to be living in. The seduction of a return to heaven en masse—militantly taking of heaven by force—is at the ideological base of premillennialism. It is largely an ideology empty of hope in humanity, drained of hope in individual salvation, or any notion of faith in modern reason or progress. The only viable option is through abandoning this wretched planet—this is the religious side of the premillennialist argument; the political side of it is a yearning to remake America into a biblical paradise based on the very powerful words of the Bible.

THE OCTOPUS

The significance of the LaHaye role in joining the forces of free-market ideologues with fundamentalists through his institutions, especially the Council for National Policy, is largely underacknowledged. In a sense, he is at the center of a larger social-conservative elite working to remake America in its image. LaHaye, through his political activism as well as his fictional accounts of the End Times, taps into an American nationalism mixed with apocalypticism quite naturally. "I think if Jerry and I were cut, we'd both bleed red, white, and blue," said LaHaye in an interview with CBS's *60 Minutes*. "We believe that God has raised up America to be a tool in these last days, to get the Gospel to the innermost parts of the Earth."[1] Much of this Christian-American nationalism mixed with biblical mythology comes from Ezekiel 40–48: "God dwells in the midst of His saints who enjoy complete happiness. The 'New Jerusalem' is the spouse of the lamb. The names of the Twelve Tribes and the 12 Apostles are written on its gates. God and the lamb are the sanctuary in this new city."

The image of America as a "New Jerusalem," with a manifest destiny and biblical promise plays heavily among the Christian right. For many this is not myth to provide meaning, but absolute for the building. "In the virgin wilderness of America, God was making His most significant attempt since Israel of people living in obedience to the laws of God, through faith in Jesus Christ," write Peter Marshall and David Manuel in

The Light and the Glory, one of the most popular books on the Christian right for claim these myths as their own. Tim LaHaye's belief, expanded upon in *The Battle for the Mind*, that the Ten Commandments and civil laws of the Old Testament "formed the basis of our Constitution" is but a branch of this philosophy.[2]

An article called "The Finances of Revolution" in 1969 outlined for conservatives how liberal foundations and organizations were using tax exempt laws to promote political and social upheaval in America. The following, from a study by the Committee for Responsive Philanthropy, echoes the desire of a conservative movement to remake America:

> [The] full spectrum of the conservative movement was described in a memo written in 1971—from Lewis Powell, just before he was appointed to the Supreme Court—to Eugene B. Sydnor Jr., at the U.S. Chamber of Commerce. Powell outlined what he saw as the liberal attack on the American free-enterprise system and how all sectors, both private and public, needed to fight back. He saw the biggest threat not coming from what he termed Communists or New Leftists, but rather from college campuses, the media, intellectual and literary journals, and the arts and sciences—what he deemed the "respectable elements of society." He called on American business to fight back against these dissenting voices to fund an organized, coordinated, long-range plan against the left that would be amply financed and implemented through united action and national organizations.[3]

Looking at today's rightwing and fundamentalist foundation landscape, it seems like the counterrevolution learned enough to eventually become what they were fighting against.[4] In 1986 the Arthur S. DeMoss Foundation published a booklet called *The Rebirth of America*, which outlines the concerns of the more biblically absolutist conservative movement. John Whitehead, Senator Jesse Helms, David Jeremiah, D. James Kennedy, Charles W. Colson, and Jerry Falwell each contributed essays to this text, laying out the philosophy of their Christian American nationalism.[5] Through the books three parts—a look back at early America and its myths, a look at the current nation adrift, and a look ahead to a bright future, an America reborn— *The Rebirth of America* mines those puritanical myths of

Americanism to to describe the America that ought to be remade—a society based on the absolutes of the Bible, government based on God, Judeo-Christian theism and law—from a nation that is currently adrift, under attack from "militant atheists and socialists."[6]

Over the past thirty years, religious right and conservative leaders have been building an extensive and effective network of foundations and think tanks such as the Council for National Policy to make these myths into reality. In 2001, over one thousand conservative foundations gave $1.8 billion dollars in grants for public affairs and societal benefit programs. The top five conservative foundations—Sarah Scaife Foundation, the Lynde and Harry Bradley Foundation, the John M. Olin Foundation, the Shelby Cullom Davis Foundation, and the Richard and Helen DeVos Foundation—gave over 50 percent of the conservative public policy funding granted. Richard DeVos, multimillionaire founder of Amway, is one of many Council for National Policy members who has either served on the board or has been an active member of these top five foundations. On the state level, the State Policy Network, founded partly through the help of the Coors' Castle Rock Foundation, has been influential in coordinating the growing number of state-based conservative public policy think tanks through media assistance, program planning, and connecting like-minded business leaders, politicians, and religious conservatives.

In a recent study by the National Committee for Responsive Philanthropy, which examined seventy-nine of the top conservative foundations, the average holdings for each was $89.5 million. Of those foundations examined, twenty-three individuals who serve as foundation board or staff were leaders of three or more foundations, nineteen of whom served on the boards or staffs of at least one nonprofit and one foundation. Conservative foundations have been able to skirt anti-lobbying legislation set in the Tax Reform Act of 1969 by giving block grants for operating support instead of specific program grants, thus allowing grantees to use funds to lobby without threatening the charitable status of their foundations. In 2001, general operating support granted by these foundations totaled around $94 million, $17 million more than specific program support grants. By far, the most money doled out went to funding organizations within the public policy arena—$115,900,000.

Between 1999 and 2001, most grants never went to organizations very far outside the beltway—more than one-third, or almost $110 million was spent in Washington, D.C., while another $33 million landed close by in Virginia. Rounding out the top six, funding was targeted at predominantly Democratic states—California, Delaware, New York, and Michigan saw about $65 million in conservative grants coming into their states. Higher education institutions, one of Lewis Powell's pillars to be transformed through conservative action, received the highest average grant size of $113,000. Of the lowest funded grantees were consumer rights activities, with an average grant award of $6,400.[7]

In the years between 1999 and 2001, the conservative foundations surveyed gave a total of over $17 million to organizations working against such issues as homosexuality, feminism, abortion, and those promoting family values and gun rights. Over $7 million went to groups focused on family values issues such as promoting traditional marriage—the largest grant of this type, over $3 million, went to James Dobson's nonprofit Focus on the Family.

Founded in 1977, the Focus on the Family has led much of the morality agenda from Colorado Springs, Colorado, under the leadership of James Dobson, a close associate of the LaHaye's through activist circles such as the Council for National Policy. The two share common enemies and make common cause in the effort to "disseminate the Gospel of Jesus Christ" and to help "preserve traditional values and the institution of the family." Dobson's daily talk show is broadcast to over 3,000 radio stations in North America, and over 3,300 in more than 116 countries around the world, reaching something close to 7.5 million listeners daily. The organization's ten magazines reach 2.3 million people a month, and countless more are reached through the group's books.[8] Focus on the Family is part of the Arlington Group—a collation of conservative organizations working to block civil unions for homosexuals—which includes the LaHaye's Concerned Women for America and the Dobson-founded Family Research Council. In his rhetoric, Dobson has compared abortion to the atrocities committed by the Nazis.

Following the reelection of Bush in 2004, Dobson used his position as a powerful unelected member of the moral elite to put pressure on the Bush administration and conservative Republicans in Congress. He tried to push Pennsylvania senator Arlen Specter out of his appointment to the Senate Judiciary Committee, one in which he would oversee Bush nominations to the Supreme Court. Specter, a moderate and independent minded Republican, had urged the Bush administration to carefully consider nominating judges that would try to overturn *Roe v. Wade*. They would likely not make it through the hearing process, even with Republican majorities in both houses. On the edition of ABC's *This Week* that aired the weekend afterward, Dobson called Specter "a problem" and said that "he must be derailed."[9]

Another branch on the LaHaye and Dobson family tree is David Noebel's Summit Ministries. This nonprofit creates and distributes course materials for Christian homeschooling, Sunday schools, Christian middle schools, churches, and soon Christian elementary schools. One pamphlet of Noebel's, published in the 1980s, *War, Peace and the Nuclear Age: A Balanced Christian Approach to the Nuclear Age* called for Strategic Defense Initiative implementation as well as further expenditures on nuclear arms.[10]

With assets of nearly $7 million and taking in about $2 million per year, Summit Ministries is one of the leading premillennialist and anti-secular educational institutions in the nation. Noebel's salary from Summit is a little over $100,000 a year. Income for Summit from student enrollment, adult conferences, the house journal, and professional speaking by Noebel in 2002 was over $900,000.

But these creations of Dobson and Noebel are only pieces of a larger network that LaHaye has had a central role in building, that comprising the Council for National Policy, and his wife's organization, Concerned Women for America.

The CNP

"Every Christian ought to be happy that we have someone in the White House who says he believes what we do"
—Jerry B. Jenkins commenting on President George W. Bush and his own "End Times" beliefs in Rolling Stone[11]

Central to the political marriage of fundamentalists with conservatives has been Council for National Policy. The CNP, founded by LaHaye in 1981, asks members who join not to reveal to the media who the other members are or talk about anything that has been discussed in their meetings. A few members do talk about it though, and one is Falwell. "My guess is that literally billions of dollars have been utilized through the Council for National Policy that would have otherwise not been available," he said in 2004.[12]

Members such as Joseph Coors of the Coors Brewing Company, Richard DeVos, the founder of Amway, and Texas oilman Nelson Bunker Hunt form a sort of bank for the CNP and the foundations they have links to, such as the Heritage Foundation. Footsoldier activists like Grover Norquist and Oliver North of Iran-Contra infamy round out the roster. The CNP serves not only as a "debate club"—as those on the right like to call their favorite punching bag, the United Nations—but also as a source of policy suggestions and spin. A number of members helped fund Oliver North's campaign of support for the Nicaraguan contras in the eighties, and when the axe fell on the whole Iran-Contra affair, they were instrumental in shaping public opinion about North through the conservative media empire that is linked through their foundations, think tanks and, institutions.[13]

LaHaye started the tax-exempt Council For National Policy as a policy-generating counterweight to the Council of Foreign Relations, a group he sees as essentially another vanguard of atheistic socialistic conspiracy. While it operates on a relatively small budget for most think tanks, the Council for National Policy brings together social conservatives with more free market–oriented conservatives. The CNP also serves as something of a launching pad for keeping the conservative movement "on message" as well as a shoulder-slapping boys club for discussions of domestic and foreign policy. The long arm of the CNP, the political action committee CNP Action, helps remind conservative lawmakers of the influence its membership wields and is virtually indistinguishable from its parent group other than by name.

Headquartered at 10329-A Democracy Lane in Fairfax, Virginia, and sharing the same office space and supplies with its taxable lobbying group, the CNP had an income of over $1.24 million, with nearly a third going to organizing the three conferences in 2002.[14] Almost $160,000 of that income went to the executive director Steve Baldwin, a former California assembly member for the Seventy-seventh District. The CNP's power does not come from the money it has as an organization, but from the money and influence the organizers wield. Take Baldwin, for example. In the 1990s, he was a key architect of a low-key "stealth strategy" used by Christian right groups to take over school board positions and local offices in California. After the six-year term limit curtailed his political activities in California, he left for the CNP in 2000. An article he wrote for the law review at Pat Robertson's Regent University, now widely circulated on the Christian right, called "Child Molestation and the Homosexual Movement," Baldwin uses the arguments of LaHaye and a discredited psychologist named Dr. Paul Cameron to link homosexuality and pedophilia.[15]

Also on the current board of directors is Becky Norton Dunlop, vice president of external relations at the Heritage Foundation, a prominent conservative domestic and foreign policy think tank that received over $28 million dollars in grants from conservative foundations between 1999 and 2001. Edwin J. Feulner, president of Heritage Foundation, has long been active with the CNP and has served on the boards of the Sarah Scaife Foundation, and as vice chairman of the Roe Foundation, in addition to being a trustee for the Intercollegiate Studies Institute. Board member Stewart W. Epperson is the chairman of the Christian radio network Salem Communications, which owns ninety-five stations nationwide and sixty of those in the top twenty-five markets. E. Peb Jackson, formerly president of Young Life out of Colorado Springs, as well as former executive with the Promise Keepers and Focus on the Family is another board member. Each week, newsletters go out the members to keep them abreast on the activities of the other members, and a journal containing key speeches made at the conferences is compiled yearly. These are all, however, not accessible to the public.

In the 1990s, allegations surfaced that the impeachment effort against Clinton was conceived at a June 1997 CNP meeting in Montreal.[16] While this is not certain, it is known that members of the CNP had been prominent in attacking Clinton via conspiracy theory videos and books. Pat Mastisciana, a member of the CNP, publisher of the conspiratorial newsletter *Citizen's Intelligence Digest*, head of Citizens for Honest Government and Jeremiah Films, a film company based out of Hemet, California, which specialized in apocalyptic Christian fundamentalist videos, documentaries, is one of them. In the 1990s Mastisciana produced the anti-Clinton conspiracy video *The Clinton Chronicles*, which played on wild theories about the death of Vince Foster. Falwell sold more than sixty thousand copies of the video through his media networks. In 1994 copies were distributed to the Republican members of the House of Representatives. Just a few years before, his films like *The Evolution Conspiracy* and *Halloween, Trick or Treat?* warned equally of the anti-god of Darwinian science and the pagan occultism of the satanic holiday. Back in 1989, his film *Gay Rights, Special Rights* argued that AIDS had spread due to a "homosexual cover-up."[17]

Though many foundations and institutions attempt to form consensus and shape public policy, few are as secretive and influential as the Council for National Policy. During the run-up to George W. Bush's presidential run, LaHaye and the CNP played a "quiet but pivotal role" in putting the president in the White House.[18] As Bush was starting his presidential campaign he visited a group of Christian activists called the Committee to Restore American Values, which is chaired by LaHaye and represented by a host of others connected through the CNP. This gathering of two dozen of the nation's most prominent fundamentalist leaders was skeptical of Bush's record as Texas governor, which they felt wasn't sufficiently evangelical. Behind closed doors that day LaHaye presented Bush, "with a lengthy questionnaire on issues such as abortion, judicial appointments, education, religious freedom, gun control, and the Middle East."

According to Paul Weyrich, before his meetings with CRAV, Bush was considered "not totally acceptable" yet he came out "not only acceptable but enthusiastically supported."[19] Bush was now backed by the high level evangelical support he needed to beat out his rivals in the primaries and go on to win the nomination of the Republican Party. Leading up to his election, Bush made a second pilgrimage to a LaHaye-founded institution and directly to the CNP. These two meetings were key to Bush getting not only moral support from evangelical leaders, but in opening up the infrastructure to the vast network of conservative foundations, think tanks, associated PACs and their well organized, grassroots money-raising efforts. Just before the republican convention in 2004, the CNP met in New York City to hammer out their agenda for the next four months.

THE OCTOPUS II: CONCERNED WOMEN FOR AMERICA

Around the same time as Moral Majority was founded, LaHaye helped start Concerned Women for America (CWA) along with his wife Beverley. Already a popular figure among evangelical women who knew her from lectures and writing on marriage, Beverley LaHaye used these inroads to launch her nationwide organization.[1] The CWA currently boasts a membership of six hundred thousand "Godly women." CWA was created by the LaHaye family as a bulwark against what they considered the feminist-socialist National Organization for Women (NOW). CWA membership inflation is used as propaganda—membership is indefinite for anyone who has ever paid the annual membership fee. Former National Organization for Women president Eleanor Smeal declared that if her organization used the same system, their membership would "be in the millions."[2]

With the success of the Family Life Seminars and as a way to cross-promote the endeavor, Tim and Beverley co-authored a Christian sex manual called *The Act of Marriage* in 1976—the book gave explicit sexual advice in a Christian setting and condemned the growing acceptance of abortion and homosexuality in the Baby Boom generation. From the ideas they developed in the Family Life Seminars and their stances against abortion, homosexuality, feminism, and other now well-known conservative bugaboos, the LaHayes turned their energy into activism, joining forces with Phyllis Schlafly of the Eagle Forum, to battle against the Equal Rights Amendment. CWA is also one of the greatest success stories of grassroots organizing in American history. Less than a decade after it was founded, the CWA budget was already $6 million and by 2003, IRS returns show CWA brought in over $11 million.[3]

Heading the newfound organization in the early 1980s, Beverly LaHaye warned her fellow godly women that the adoption of the ERA amendment would result in unisex restrooms, legalized homosexuality, sexual integration in prison facilities, abolition of sodomy and adultery laws, women being required to register for the draft, the loss of a woman's right to her husband's social security benefits, the loss of men's place as the required supporter of the family, the abolition of single-sex schools, churches having to hire homosexuals and women as clergy, and, finally abortion being established as a constitutional right. "I believe many of our social problems have been fomented by conscious agents of Communism," Beverly LaHaye says, echoing the conspiracy narratives of her husband and associates on the far right. "They have simply carried out Communist doctrine: divide the nation into warring classes in an effort to weaken us, sap our strength, and destroy us."[4]

Though she says she never meant to eclipse the influence of Schlafly's nationwide Republican women's clubs (the Eagle Forum), Beverly LaHaye eventually did so by tapping into the hitherto untouched base of women's Bible study groups at Christian churches with targeted CWA campaigns and her connections with the growing Christian media empire. While Beverley LaHaye—along with many evangelicals—takes the view that men must lead in the home, the organization under her leadership became one of the three most important groups on the Christian right during the 1980s along with the closely connected Moral Majority and Focus on the Family. Her husband Tim has long accused feminists of destroying the best of femininity and undermining men; Falwell argues that women are defying their "God-given roles," an argument that has resonated across the biblically conservative anti-feminist movement.

There's an advertisement for CWA in the *Christian Inquirer* under an article written by Tim in August 1983 that shows a picture of Beverly surrounded by the alarmist language of the persecuted. Here one gets an earful about the "feminist threat" and the "alarming" abortion rate, followed by a quote from Ephesians 5:16—"Making the most of your time, because the days are evil."

For the LaHayes and many of their supporters, the full page ad claims, God created family and "established definite guidelines for maintaining and developing it," outlining the goals of both "alerting and informing" concerned women about the "tide of immorality sweeping America." Like much of the LaHayes' and the Christian right's language in general over the last thirty years, anything counter to their argument is evil, immoral, and anti-God, which for them is also anti-American.[5]

Along with the CWA chapter activities, training seminars push these conservative women to act as campaign staff for local, state, and national candidates, thereby giving them the experience to run for office themselves.[6] Looking through CWA tax filings, it is also worth noting that the organization skirts federal restrictions on direct donations to political candidates by dispersing small sums of money of $50 or $25 to chapter leaders who then give the money to specifically targeted candidates in hotly contested races. Though this isn't a tactic only employed on the right, it does indicate how efficient some politically active nonprofit groups have become over the last few decades at using loopholes that allow them to retain their nonprofit privileges.

Moreover, by valorizing women's choice to stay at home to raise children, CWA can use that availability to mobilize these "traditional women" for political activism.[7] Sara Diamond states that in order "to mobilize female activists to wage 'spiritual warfare,' Christian right leaders perform a semantic sleight-of-hand. The trick is to insist that their form of women's activism, contrasted with that of the 'women's libbers,' is selfless and ordained by God."[8]

The LaHaye family's connections to other prominent evangelical organizations helped spread the word even further in the early years. As single entities their power is marginal and spread out, but entwined together in a web of organizations, the structure is a powerful force for social change. For example, the fact that many of the same organizations have much of the same leadership, or at least members of families or close associates in positions of power within them further enhances the web-like structure and ability to stay on message. In 1985, the list advisory board members for CWA sounded like a Council for National

Policy women's club—Kay Arthur, a premillennialist minister and one of two women members of Tim LaHaye's Pre-Trib Research Center; Dorothy Helms, wife of former hardline conservative U.S. senator from North Carolina Jesse Helms; Frances Swaggart, wife of televangelist Jimmy Swaggart who resigned from the Assemblies of God broadcasting program in 1988 after photos were leaked showing him consorting with a prostitute; Anne Kennedy, wife of D. James Kennedy, influential author and televangelist pastor of Coral Ridge Presbyterian Church in Fort Lauderdale, Florida, a fervent supporter of missile and laser defense contractor group High Frontier.[9]

In its own bulletins, CWA regularly promotes, at discounted prices, books by its members and affiliates. For example, in the November 1985 *CWA Bulletin*, three books by Tim LaHaye (*Battle for the Mind*, *Hidden Censors*, *The Unhappy Gays*) as well as Beverley's own *Who But a Woman?* were prominently displayed in an interior advertisement. Other titles in this "Shop Early for Christmas" ad include Pre-Trib Research Center writer David Jeremiah's *Before It's Too Late*, Connie Marshner's *The New Traditional Woman*, a cassette of family friend Pat Boone's antiabortion song *16,000 Faces*, as well as works by many other familiar names within the LaHaye circle. Based on their 2003 IRS filing, CWA income from sales of books amounted to $125,215 while royalties accounted for a more substantial $526,535. While none of this is damning in its own right, it does show the remarkable connectedness of many of these organizations and their publishing interests in an effort to get their word out.

Radio is another way. By the mid-1990s, Beverly LaHaye's radio broadcasts aired on over sixty stations and were listened to by an estimated five hundred thousand daily. On many Christian right radio networks, preaching the gospel is augmented by several hours of political broadcasting per day. Keeping with this, Beverly LaHaye has often ended her show by urging listeners to call their congressional representatives, send money to causes represented by CWA, and check out the local school libraries for books they found unsuitable. In 1993, listeners sent thirty thousand telegrams to Congress at Beverly LaHaye's insistence, a feat she claimed helped halt the passage of the pro-choice Freedom of Choice Act.[10] Over a decade ago, during a 1993 broadcast of her radio program *Beverly LaHaye Live,* conspiracy author Gary Kah

(*En Route to Global Occupation*) told of a "well organized move-
ment" to bring about a New World Order, and the role of then
first-term President Clinton in these plans. Later in an issue of the
CWA's *Family Voice*, Kah's book and an audiotape of his inter-
view with LaHaye were offered to readers for a $20 "donation."
At the 1993 CWA convention, Kah claimed that the Federal
Reserve, the Council of Foreign Relations, and the Trilateral
Commission were all part of the one-world conspiracy plan.

The thirty years of hammering on the terms "liberal" and
"media" has also garnered support from the corporate world
whose interests mesh with the interests of the anti-government
right—low taxation, small government, gender inequality, weak
unions, and less regulation both at home and abroad. A CWA
newsletter in 1987 contained an article by a legislative analyst
which argued against equal pay for women, saying it would
result in a "socialist economy where government officials and
judges would determine wages according to an arbitrary and
subjective point system."[11]

Beverly LaHaye's invocation of the apocalyptic narrative to
portray the dangers of feminism and the role of traditional
Christian women is quite similar to how this narrative used to
gain support for anti-Communist activism. "In the work of
Schlafly and LaHaye," speculates Kintz,

> an anti-Communist Cold War framework joins abso-
> lutist Christianity in such a way as to code ambiguity not
> only as subversive to a national security state but as a
> Satanic force that threatens Christian civilization itself.
> And this Christian anti-Communist framework
> exhibits another characteristic of war. If a nation thinks
> it is fighting for freedom . . . might it not be that it is, in
> fact, the fear of freedom, in particular the freedom of
> women by both men and women, that leads to war?[12]

What is important to highlight is that this narrative structure is equally effective for plugging any piece of the secular
humanist conspiracy theory—abortion, public schooling, drugs,
pornography, homosexuality—into the apocalyptic vision that
each one of these threats alone is a sign and symbol of the imminent end that must be triumphed over, either through fighting
back or through salvation through Rapture. These apocalyptic

narratives work equally well for framing threats abroad as part of these anti-Christian forces.

Writing about Beverly LaHaye in 1989, Sara Diamond remarks that "some analysts have focused almost exclusively on the social agenda of the movement, without recognizing that conservatism on the domestic front is used as a bridge to build support for anti-Communist military intervention abroad."[13] There is always the risk of a social movement becoming a mirror of exactly what that movement claims to be fighting against. In the case of Beverly LaHaye coming to organize the CWA, it is interesting to note that her ideas came from the anti-democratic forces that served as "conscious agents" intent on dividing their "nation into warring classes." In this case, it was the counterrevolutionary elements within elite Brazilian society during the 1960s.

In her 1984 book *Who But a Woman?* Beverly showed her disdain for elected government, and perhaps gives some clues into the psychology behind her and her husband's efforts to form their own groups such as the CNP and CWA, as well as their use of stealth strategy. Opening the book, she tells of a story she'd read in *Reader's Digest* about how "Communism" was defeated in Brazil in the 1960s.

"Several prominent businessmen began meeting informally in 1961 to halt Brazil's plunge into totalitarianism," wrote Beverly LaHaye, by forming the Institute for Economic and Social Research, which she describes as an "intelligence network." The purpose of this group was to out subversives in political leadership positions, set up media for disseminating misinformation about the opposition, and to form women's cell groups to establish prayer meetings, organize protest marches, and buy space on television and in newspapers to get out their anti-Communist message.[14] This Campaign of Women for Democracy organized a March for the Family with God Toward Freedom, drawing sixty thousand women under the banner "Family, Tradition, Property." In her description of these events in Brazil, she fails to mention that the democratically elected government of Joao Goulart was overthrown by a U.S.-backed military coup in 1964.

Linda Kintz writes about this subject: "At the time, priests and lay people were involved in Peasant Leagues in the

countryside. [The Peasant League's] work included literacy projects and health education, among other activities, and were part
of the social justice work of liberation theology." It was the "anti-
Communist" groups that LaHaye describes and a crackdown by
the Pope on progressive priests and bishops that helped the military overthrow the democratically elected government.[15] That
1964 coup led to twenty-one years of Brazilian military rule
under which the country's dictators ordered the kidnapping, torture, and murder of opposition leaders, labor leaders, and pro-
gressives; shut down the Congress; halted voting for mayors and
governors; censored all media; and possibly assassinated the ex-
president himself. In 2002, fresh inquiries into Operation Condor
(or Plan Condor), the joint operation conducted by dictators in
Brazil, Bolivia, Argentina, Uruguay, Paraguay, and Chile with
the reported aim of killing regime opponents, led to investiga-
tions into whether ex-Brazilian president Joao Goulart was murdered in his sleep while in exile in 1976.

What LaHaye learned about the "anti-Communist"
women's groups set up to topple the Goulart presidency in Brazil,
as well as the similar organizational tactics used by Schlafly to
defeat the ERA Amendment, led her to adapt similar strategies
for organizing CWA.

Individual activists are organized into prayer groups and
"phone trees" who voice their opinion via letter writing, telephoning, and now emailing the offices of government representatives. Chapters are made up of fifty individuals with a leader
and several prayer group leaders who organize telephoning, letter writing, and emailing. Each of these individual women
activists are also likely to also be involved in other nationwide
organizations such as the Christian Coalition, as well as local
school boards and churches, which further spreads the web of
influence and interconnectedness. Each individual acts as her
own political action committee—she can fax, email, and phone
lawmakers with the most important message of the day. In 1985,
before spam clogged government email inboxes, CWA flooded
one federal agency with ninety-seven thousand letters over a two
week period.[16]

Most recently, CWA has opposed such things as the U.N.
Genocide Convention, arguing that the treaty's definition of
genocide could affect "missionary activity." But back in

November 1986, Tim LaHaye wrote in the CWA newsletter about what he declared "genocide" against Christians in Nicaragua by Sandinista Communists, not mentioning that most of those Sandinista Communists were also Christian, mostly Catholic, and mostly bred on the Marxist-socialist liberation theology, which was prominent in left-wing Catholic circles in Central and South America.[17] There is really no context here in LaHaye's writings other than inflamatory language, which appropriately chimes with his, his wife's, and many members of the Council for National Policy involvement with the Contras in Nicaragua.

CWA began sponsoring a refugee camp in Costa Rica called Amor de La Libertad, in the 1980s, and in September 1987 Beverley went to Nicaragua on a "fact-finding mission" that was filmed for her activists back home. There "LaHaye met with Violeta Chamorro, editor of the U.S. funded *La Prensa* tabloid and pledged her support for the 'freedom fighters,'" writes Diamond. "LaHaye held a 'secret' meeting (though filmed in a way as to reveal participants' identities) with the Movement of Mothers of Political Prisoners—relatives of Contras jailed by the government. The pro-Contra mothers received $100,000 from the U.S. National Endowment for Democracy (NED) in 1987."[18] Diamond reports there was no effort by the CWA and other groups to view how the Sandinistas had also had sons and daughters disappeared, killed, and maimed in order to "manipulate ideological symbols and political debate" for the rightwing agenda abroad.

From the way the Iran-Contra affair was depicted by the CWA, one would think the Reagan administration's felonies were manufactured by the "liberal establishment."

"When I think of what our great President is being put through," writes Beverly LaHaye in a 1987 letter to CWA supporters, "how our conservative cause is being harmed by members of the liberal establishment who continue to hammer away at the Iran-Contra issue, I realize that we could be in danger of losing everything we've worked so hard to achieve over the last six years." "Since these are very dark days," LaHaye says later, "would you ask the Lord how much you should send? We need to remain strong as we face the difficult days which lie ahead . . . if you planned to send $100, why not find a way to send $150? If you were sending $25, please try to make it $35 or $40 . . . if it turns out that there was any wrong doing in the Iran-Contra controversy, no conservative Christian would ever support such conduct. Most certainly CWA does not endorse law-breaking or immorality."

By presenting a total dismissal of the Iran-Contra affair as simply a plot by the "liberal establishment" to roll back all that has been achieved under Reagan to supporters, a defensive Beverly LaHaye again uses the language of persecution, which her husband Tim routinely employs to rally the faithful. "Like the predators they really are," Beverly continues, "liberal politicians and members of the media are using every opportunity to try to destroy the presidency of Ronald Reagan. We must not let them succeed!"

In the wave of spin that washed over the nation, Oliver North was portrayed as "Ollie the Scapegoat" and a "Son of Liberty" by the conservatives, as the CWA newsletter of February 1987 headline testifies—"Colonel Oliver North, National Hero." "Ollie North is hated by the Left because of his effectiveness in getting things done," writes CWA staff member and attorney Albert Veldhuyzen in the same newsletter.[19] For this he became a rallying point for the "embattled" like Beverly LaHaye—he was so popular that he was invited to speak at the 1985 and 1986 CWA national conventions.

Considering where the CWA stands, and the people it represents, its positions on issues such as abortion, homosexuality, school prayer, homeschooling, and morality aren't all that surprising. Yet the group has also gone outside traditional family values activism to foster long and vocal support for programs such as the Strategic Defense Initiative (SDI), or "Star Wars," as many labeled it throughout the Reagan years. On the fifth anniversary of High Frontier, a private-sector group that promoted the development of SDI systems, Dr. D. James Kennedy was recognized for "his outstanding contribution to the defense of the nation"; essentially complimenting Kennedy for his efforts in sermonizing missile defense issues to his Coral Ridge Presbyterian Church in Fort Lauderdale and the television sermons he produces. One of his sermons reproduced in the *CWA Bulletin* outlines Kennedy's support for the SDI program and why all "God Fearing American Christians" should support such a scheme. This sermon does not go on to say what Kennedy's connections to the defense contracting industry are, such as High Frontiers, though it does go into lengthy discourse about how the Russian Communists and American liberals distort the facts of SDI's costs. In the same *CWA* issue is a long article by Heritage Foundation fellow John Kwapisz entitled "SDI: Protecting the Future of America's Families," which overplays a $60 billion Department of Defense estimate of SDI costs and totally discounts the $2 trillion number estimated at the time by a variety of experts.[20]

In June 2004, *Financial Times* columnist Ian Bremmer argued that one major problem with SDI is that no one knew then or now what the program would cost in the end. Originally the program was to be a $26 billion dollar research plan. Since 1985 the Pentagon figures that more than $80 billion has been spent on missile defense. The U.S. still doesn't have a functioning, or even well-tested prototype—the research is unending. The Bush administration budget for 2005 gives SDI $10 billion alone, more than what is spent in R&D on any other military program. The Pentagon's Missile Defense Agency estimates an additional $53 billion will have to be spent on the system up to 2009.[21]

The World Policy Institute estimated in 2000 that since the cold war started missile defense programs have cost $120 billion, and since 1940 the cost of building, deploying, maintaining, and cleaning up after the U.S. nuclear arsenal has cost $5.6 trillion.[22] Domestically, the Department of Energy claimed that between 2000 and 2070, from $151 billion to $195 billion would be needed to cleanup and close surplus American nuclear weapons facilities, or from $2.1 to $2.7 billion dollars per year. Possibility of contamination, accidents, and mishandling of these cold war byproducts seem much more inevitable than a ballistic missile strike on the U.S. mainland, mostly due to the massive retaliatory power the American military still wields.[23] Even more likely is the threat posed by loose nuclear material abroad falling into terrorist hands, something that is much more difficult to track than a ballistic missile launch, which can be detected almost immediately by satellite. The Bush administration budget to Congress sought $1.35 billion for international nonproliferation spending in 2005. That the proposed U.S. spending on international and domestic safekeeping and cleanup of nuclear weapons and materials comes out to between $3.45 billion and $4.05 billion annually—while the budget for 2005 and the next four years after is around $10 billion per year for missile defense—points to the argument that the priorities are not what they should be.

If there is anyone to blame for misleading the country regarding priorities when it comes to nuclear issues, it is the defense industry and its supporting cast of lobbyists, think tanks, and pressure groups. This is where groups such as CWA play their part. There is relatively less money to be made from research and development on the dismantling and cleanup of nuclear weapons at home and abroad than from government contracts for the continued development, even if they never work, of missile defense initiatives. Another moneymaker is in tactical nuclear weapons, otherwise known as low-yield, or "bunker busting" bombs, which have been pushed by the Bush administration during its first term. According to the White House, $6.8 billion had been requested in the Bush Department of Energy budget for 2005 spending on the "maintenance, modernization, development, and production" of nuclear weapons; they hoped for $30 billion over the next four years. This is even above cold war levels. Through the four and a half decade cold war, the annual budget for these costs was at an average of $4.2 billion, adjusted for inflation.[24]

Since taking office, the Bush Administration had an easier time delivering internationally for the CWA constituency than it has domestically.[25] The loud cry from the social conservative base of the Republican Party that taxpayer money should not go toward abortion, birth control, or other forms of reproductive rights saw its biggest gains abroad, largely from pressure and action by grassroots groups like CWA.[26] Within weeks after Bush's inauguration the U.N. Population Fund lost 12.5 percent of its budget and $3 million was cut from expenditures to the World Health Organization's Human Reproduction Program. The $3 million saved from the population fund was then diverted into the administration's domestic sex education program promoting abstinence. "The Bush Administration has been able to get away with [internationally] what would be appalling to most

moderate Republicans," said Jennifer Butler, the UN representative for the Presbyterian Church, of this evangelical coup abroad.

It is crucial to understand also that the CWA is not merely a
political lobbying group for a segment of society whose voice is
underrepresented in Washington—unlike many women's
groups its influence goes beyond pure lobbying for policies into
real domestic and international policy.

Members of key lobbying CWA organizations have been
given direct access to the U.N. as part of the official U.S. delega-
tions, including Janice Crouse—now a consultant on the payroll
for Concerned Women for America—and Jeanne Head of the
National Right to Life Committee. In mid-2001, Jeanne Head
represented the U.S. at the annual World Health Assembly, and
while the delegation would ordinarily include representatives of
the American Public Health Association and American Medical
Association, these groups were quietly left behind. A year later at
the U.N. Special Session on Children in New York, the U.S.
allied itself with regimes like Iran, Iraq, Libya, Sudan, and Syria
in restricting sex education information for adolescents and con-
traceptive and STD-prevention information for heterosexual
couples; excluding legal abortion from the terminology of reproductive health services; and opposing an agreement over language that would provide "services" to children who had been
victims of violence and war because "services" might be taken to
mean abortion for young people who were victims of rape in war
situations (though they also mean any services provided in a post-
conflict situation). In another remarkable feat of absurd theater,
the U.S. delegation blocked consensus that opposed capital punishment for adolescents, fearing that this international standard
could be applied in legal language domestically, which it now
has, by the U.S. Supreme Court.[27] At the mid–December 2002
Asian and Pacific Population Conference in Bangkok, the Bush
administration team again mystified the other delegates by insisting on natural family planning techniques over access to contra-
ceptives and that references to "reproductive health services" and
"reproductive rights" be stricken from the documents. In the end
the U.S. team was the lone dissenting vote along with abstentions
by Nepal and Sri Lanka (who were reportedly threatened with
USAID cuts if they didn't side with the U.S.) and then issued a
document at the end of the conference which stated its reserva-

tions about the agreement based on the fact that the U.S. "supports innocent life from conception to natural death"—that it does not support, promote, or endorse abortions abroad.[28]

Clair McCurdy, an archivist for the clinic defense and research division of Planned Parenthood, attended the 1995 CWA National Convention in Washington, D.C., in which around one thousand others participated. She documented a well-organized, grassroots movement—and one in which heavy security and uncritical media dominated, press passes were difficult to come by, and access to literature handed out at the meeting very limited. Workshops accentuated leadership activities in the attendees local areas, emphasizing that "religious women and men should prepare themselves through their CWA membership to be office-holders in," what McCurdy terms, "the coming theocracy."[29] One of the headline speakers was Elaine Donnelly, president of the Center for Military Readiness, an organization whose board includes Beverly LaHaye, Phyllis Schalafly, and Oliver North. In her speech, Donnelly "charged that the armed forces had become a perfect laboratory for President Clinton's social experimentation fueled by theories perpetuated by feminist activist retreads from the Carter administration" and that "especially dangerous were openly homosexual men and women in the armed forces." In a show of their power, the CWA organized its activists to jam Capitol Hill with 450,000 phone calls protesting Clinton's attempt to allow gay men and women to serve openly into the military.[30]

Sexual Politics

Just as LaHaye came to national prominence via the Moral Majority, his series of nonfiction books arguing that a secular humanist conspiracy had invaded America and displaced the biblical foundations of the country became popular in the evangelical community. The 1980 book *Battle for the Mind* laid the basis for the two following books, *The Battle for the Family* (1982) and *The Battle for the Public Schools* (1983). Tim LaHaye's nofiction books haven't made as much a splash on the mainstream as the Left Behind series, though they have long been prominent among fundamentalist readers.

Years before venturing into politics, both Beverly and Tim were more interested in sex and psychology than secular humanism. In 1966, Tim published *The Spirit Controlled Temperament*, in 1971, *Transformed Temperaments*, in 1977 *Understanding the Male Temperament*, and in 1984, *Why You Act the Way You Do*. Scattered in between these are the Christian sex and marriage manuals *How to Be Happy Though Married* in 1968, *The Act of Marriage: The Beauty of Sexual Love* written by Tim and Beverly and published in 1976, and Beverly's *The Restless Woman* in 1984. Beverly was also increasingly active, with her 1976 book *The Spirit Controlled Woman* (a spin-off of her husband's earlier book) and the 1977 *How to Develop Your Child's Temperament*. None of these titles were too terribly biblically literal or biblical at all. They are more of a new age–style hybrids of scripture, astrology, genetic theory, and handwriting analysis, also drawing on bastardizations of Freudian and Jungian psychological theories, more suited for the self-anointed self-help section of the bookstore than the theological or religious. In *Transformed Temperaments* there are references to personality types—Abraham, Moses, Peter, Paul—all of which are deciphered through what has been written about them. For people who claim the literal Bible as their source of inspiration, it is interesting how much of the secular they absorb and regurgitate in proselytizing.

More than most other Christian right commentators, Tim LaHaye has accentuated sexual and procreative aspects of marriage along with the male role as head of a biblically principled family unit. Karen Armstrong notes in her book on the history of fundamentalism, *The Battle for God*, that the LaHayes seem "deeply concerned about male impotence" and man's loss of certainty from the invasion of feminism. Men were becoming "feminized" or even "castrated" by the epidemic of feminist ideas.[31] The LaHayes hold women primarily responsible when their husbands stray from their marriage vows. Presumably, in this scenario, men who seek comfort outside the marriage bed have not had their sexual needs properly met by their wives. In this convoluted argument, their friend Anne Swaggart, wife of televangelist Jimmy Swaggart, whose prostitution scandal led to his fall from grace, is at fault for "his sins."

"The LaHayes emphasize that sexual energy is natural to men and caution wives not only to be aware of this energy, but also to give it every opportunity to be released," writes Detwiler.

"Thus relieved of sexual pressures regularly, husbands are free to devote their attention to matters of dominion and the proper exercise of authority over their family."

Yet, with all the focus on sex in his nonfiction books, LaHaye's treatment of sensuality is absent from the Left Behind novels, where extreme violence often takes the place of sexuality. The Left Behind novels are filled with orgasmic and cosmic violence perpetrated on helpless sinners and believers alike. When there isn't a focus on massive destruction, much of book *Tribulation Force* chronicles an ongoing romance between Buck and Chloe. The whole tryst becomes a propagation of LaHaye's ideas on family values and the roles of men and women in marriage.[32] Chloe finally ends up pregnant, though the reader never gets a sense that the couple had ever done anything more than kiss. For all the detailed and gory description of violence in the books, one has to wonder where sensuality fits into this worldview. The characters come off as unfeeling warriors concerned only in battling the Antichrist forces and bearing children who will possibly be sacrificed during End Times.[33]

A similar statement about marriage and family is made by focusing on the relationship between Hattie and Carpathia, but this time with its evil overtones instead of the banal exchanges between Chloe and Buck. It is likely no mistake that there is an absence of the sensual and sexual in these novels, as LaHaye argues, and this is one of his main basis for opposing sex-education in public schools—that couples can "learn all the basic ingredients [for sex] in two or three hours just prior to marriage" and that anything else leads to sex as "an obsession."[34]

Homosexuality

Tim LaHaye's 1978 book *The Unhappy Gays,* reissued in 1980 as *What Everyone Should Know About Homosexuality*, uses a mixture of biblical scripture, revulsion, and highly selective scientific data to back his claims about homosexuality. The book also uses associative assumptions about relationships between homosexuality and child molestation, and a causal connection between the immorality of homosexuality and the rending of the social fabric. Much of the scientific basis for these attacks can be attributed to psychologist Paul Cameron, an anti-gay campaigner and organizer who founded the Institute for the Scientific Investigation of

Sexuality and the Family Research Council, and who was influential in the National Association for Research and Therapy of Homosexuality. In 1983 he was expelled from the American Psychological Association after he claimed gays were ten to twenty times more likely to molest children, and that they were responsible for half of all sex murders.[35] In the late 1980s, during a Focus on the Family television program Cameron claimed that Thomas Jefferson had favored castration of gays and the drilling of a hole through the cartilage of the nose for lesbians.

Writing with his wife in their marriage manual *The Act of Marriage*, LaHaye argues that scientific advancements have made many of the Levitical prohibitions of the "Holiness Code" obsolete. It is these same Levitical codes that most Christian right activists reference in regards to prohibitions of homosexuality. As Reverend Michael S. Piazza notes, the irony is that "LaHaye draws heavily on the Levitical passages to explain his condemnation of homosexuality" as well as his ambiguity about whether the death penalty applied for these acts at the time has encouraged the leniency in our own, while explaining away the others in a biblically literal fashion. Piazza argues that it is hypocritical of LaHaye and other fundamentalists to dismiss what they deem unnecessary—such as codes prohibiting the eating of pork, shellfish, ritualized washing, not having sex with a woman while she is menstruating—while exalting other codes, like those forbidding male-male sexual acts to a status of literal dogma.[36]

At one point in the Left Behind books, Buck uses a character's homosexuality to blackmail her into keeping it secret from Carpathia that he thinks Nicolae is the Antichrist. Verna, his boss at the local offices of *Global Weekly* in Chicago, discovers that Buck believes in the Rapture and the conspiracy theories surrounding Carpathia, and hints that she doesn't like him pretending to be something he's not to the Antichrist. Buck counters that his private life and belief is his own business. Fair enough. But he has to push matters further, saying "if I knew you were a lesbian, I wouldn't feel it necessary to tell your superiors."[37] This type of characterization, transferred into the real world, follows some of the earlier activism LaHaye wanted to pursue regarding homosexual teachers in public schools—believing they should be outed and not allowed to teach American children. Here the character

Buck puts Verna's privacy about being a lesbian on the same level as his thinking his boss is "the Antichrist"—something which would probably affect that relationship with his superior.

A "homosexual-as-effeminate-artiste" character presents himself in the novel *Indwelling* by the name of Guy Blood, pronounced "Gee," which he makes certain they all know. When he isn't ranting nastily, Guy takes on the air of a flamboyant, pretentious, Frenchified, gay *artiste*—essentially the ultimate gay stereotype.[38] The authors seem to take delight in going on for pages and pages about how gay Guy acts, how "artistic" he seems to be, about his "genius" and his "muse," sort of a sad fundamentalist satire without much humor. Further on, Guy develops a sort of "Gay speak," a winking "hey, there mister," and "how you doin,' soldier?" language.

As has already been mentioned, perhaps the biggest case of blatant homophobia in the books is the characterization made in the first prequel book in the series *The Rising*, in which Carpathia is born from a conspiracy hatched by international bankers, in which he is fathered through by two homosexual men. These "evil seeds" set up the entire series and in essence, implying everything that comes from Carpathia after this is inherently evil.

Here is the passage from *The Rising* where Carpathia's mother finds that her former husband and his lover had been the sperm donors for this satanic experiment conceived by a shadowy group of "international bankers":

> Could these documents be forged? Had Viv hoped Marilena would one day discover them? Where they meant to torment her? Was it possible Sorin had been in this from the beginning? From before the beginning? And Baduna too? They were the sperm donors? Marilena could not make it compute. Sorin had attended a private school in Zurich, his prodigious mind earning him shoulder-rubbing privileges with the children of international wealth.[39]

Abortion

During the Rapture in the first novel, fetuses disappear from the wombs of unrepentant mothers and children under the "age of reason" are snatched to Heaven by Jesus, taken away in Pied

Piper fashion. Later, fetuses, as they are first described, are no longer called fetuses, but unborn children. [40] Hattie, the flight attendant who has become Carpathia's assistant, discusses how her sister just happens to work at a pregnancy clinic. Because the fetuses/children have all been Raptured, Hattie is worried her sister, a distant and undescribed person the reader never sees, will be out of work now that there are no more abortions. This passage conveys the message that abortionists are waiting with bloody scalpels to carve out fetuses for money, and that they need unwanted pregnancies so they can keep in business.

> Hattie seemed to be waiting for some signal of affirmation or acknowledgement that he was listening. Rayford grew impatient and remained silent.
> "Anyway," she said, "I won't keep you. But my sister told me they have zero business."
> "Well, that would make sense given the disappearance of unborn babies."
> "My sister didn't sound too happy about that."
> "Hattie, I imagine everyone's horrified by that. Parents are grieving all over the world."
> "But the women my sister and her people were counseling *wanted* abortions."
> Rayford groped for a pertinent response. "Yes, so maybe those women are grateful they didn't have to go through the abortion itself."
> "Maybe, but my sister and her bosses and the rest of the staff are out of work now until people start getting pregnant again."
> "I get it. It's a money thing."
> "They have to work. They have expenses and families."
> "And aside from abortion counseling and abortions, they have nothing to do?"
> "Nothing. Isn't that awful? I mean, whatever happened put my sister and a lot of people like her out of business, and nobody really knows whether anyone will be able to get pregnant again."[41]

Hattie gets into an abortion debate with the other characters of the Tribulation Force in the first Left Behind book, foreshadowing her own circumstances later in the series when the books revolve around whether or not Hattie, who has become

Carpathia's lover and is now pregnant, should have an abortion herself. Further debates surround Hattie possibly having the Antichrist's child out of wedlock. As it turns out, Carpathia is not only the Antichrist, but an awful husband and potential father too. He pressures her to have an abortion, even urges Rayford to convince her to have one, something that goes on behind the scenes through much of the third and fourth books. From *Soul Harvest*:

> "Do not be naïve, Captain Steele," Carpathia said. "All I want to know is that you will have the talk with Miss Durham."
>
> "The talk in which I tell her she can keep the ring, live in New Babylon, and then, what was it about the baby?"
>
> "I'm going to assume she's already made the right decision there, and you may assure here that I will cover all the expenses."
>
> "For the child throughout its life?"
>
> "That is not the decision I was referring to," Carpathia said.
>
> "Just so I'm clear then, you will pay for the murder of the child?"
>
> "Do not be maudlin, Rayford. It is a safe, simple procedure. Just pass along my message. She will understand."
>
> "Believe it or not, I don't know where she is. But if I do pass along your message, I can't guarantee she'll make the choice you want. What if she chooses to bear the child?"
>
> Carpathia shook his head. "I must end this relationship, but it will not go over well if there is a child."[42]

At another point Rayford, when mulling over Hattie's talk about abortion, decides: "She was not a believer. She would not be thinking about the good of anyone but herself." Furthermore, Rayford wonders if rape or incest victims are justified for seeking abortions, which is an abrupt turn from his wayward philosophy before the Rapture. Here, speaking to Hattie:

> "I'll even buy the argument that perhaps you regret the idea of having a child at all and would not be the best mother for it. I don't think you can shirk responsibility

for it the way a rape or incest victim might be justified in doing.

"But even in those cases, the solution isn't to kill the innocent party, is it? Something is wrong, really wrong, and so people defend the right to choose. What they choose, of course is not just the end of a pregnancy, not just an abortion, it's the death of a person. But which person? One of the people who made the mistake? One of the people who committed rape or incest? Or one of the people who got pregnant out of wedlock? No, the solution is always to kill the most innocent party of all."

Chloe offers Hattie comforting and contradictory messages about her possible abortion when she says things like "God will love you," regardless the decision Hattie makes and also that the decision is "a life-and-death, heaven-and-hell":

"Let me just tell you, Hattie, if it's love you're looking for, you came to the right place. Yes, there are things we believe. Things we think you should know. Things we think you should agree with. Decisions we think you should make. We have ideas about what you should do about your baby, and we have ideas about what you should do about your soul. But these are personal decisions only you can make. And while they are life-and-death, heaven-and-hell decisions, all we can offer is support, encouragement, advice if you ask for it, and love."[43]

Eventually Hattie ends up in a reproduction clinic (that happens to be in an old church) somewhere in Colorado, where the doctors are pushing her, at the Antichrist's insistence, to have an abortion. They also pursue cloning and "fetal tissue research" at the abortion-reproduction-church-clinic. Members of the Tribulation Force raid the clinic and escape with Hattie, shooting a guard to death in the attempt. All of this is surrounded by the language of martyrdom, of "dying for Christ" and "to die would be gain" in the pages after the successful raid. When confronted with the fact that they have just killed a guard at an abortion clinic and whether that means they should turn themselves over to the law, a new member of the group, Dr. Charles, asks, "If you shot an enemy in battle, would you turn yourself in?"[44] Hattie then begins a drawn out conversion process upon being accepted into the care of the group. For the intensity they give decisions like abortion, they brush aside other decisions where life is taken as an act of faith.

Pages later, the sadistic God the authors portray throughout the series rains blood from the sky, followed by a huge asteroid and tidal wave. Folloeing this, Carpathia blasts another asteroid out of the sky, but this one also happens to be the Revelation version of Wormwood that poisons most of the fresh water in the world. Little monster locust demons with three noses come to earth in *Apollyon* and "God uses them to torment" unbelievers, stinging and biting and generally causing a menace to anyone who isn't a premillennial fundamentalist by this time. Hattie, who still hasn't had a total conversion yet, goes through a torturous rehabilitation after being attacked by these things. Tsion Ben Judah, the former Jewish scholar and now premillennialist firebrand, says this is all part of God's love, that it is "all part of his master design to turn people to him so he can demonstrate his love."[45] Finally, after putting up with the Tribulation Force, one of many tortures of the Tribulation, Hattie converts in the book *The Mark*.

The authors, confronted with a Hattie about to give birth to Carpathia's evil spawn, have her give birth to a dead baby. About twenty pages later we are told that Carpathia had poisoned her, killing the baby-fetus.

When reading this, it is important to understand how biblical literalists justify their insistence on enacting laws, to reflect their values onto an entire populace. Legislating morality, they say, is essential in the battle toward building the perfect biblically based American society: there is no separation of church and state, and there is no separation between the lines which lead directly to the two from the home. "The condition of the state, like the condition of the church, is the condition of the home," writes LaHaye in *The Battle for the Family*.[46] The trinity of Church, State, and Family are absolutes and an abortion in one corner of the family affects moral fabric of the rest of the families of the larger trinity. For instance, a married or legally recognized homosexual union denigrates the insistence on the biblical designation of marriage as an act primarily for the purpose of raising children, one based solely on procreation. Sexual activity simply for enjoyment, marriage only for companionship, without attaining that primary act, should not be sanctioned in their eyes. This literalism would seemingly disqualify anyone who is sterile, past the age of bearing children, or those with no intentions of bringing up a child through their own intercourse or through adoption. On the other hand, this literalism would seemingly give sanction to a homosexual couple adopting and raising children. But in the end this is not that case. In the end, debate over abortion is not about the killing of babies or fetuses, the debate over homosexual union not about the raising of children—the debate is about who has the right to decide any of these choices: the individual, the state, or the church.

FROM THE WOMB TO THE TOMB

LaHaye has long been one of the leading figures of the fundamentalist attack on science. Much of the language now heard about creationism via "ccientific creationism" or "intelligent design" comes out of institutions LaHaye founded. In the first years of the George W. Bush Administration, over sixty prominent scientists from the Union of Concerned Scientists, twenty of them Nobel laureates, sent a letter to the White House accusing it of politicizing scientific research, twisting facts to support its own policies, and otherwise suppressing or distorting massive amounts of scientific data for its own agenda. These scientists claim that science issues from AIDS to stem cell research, from sex education to the environment were being manipulated to conform to the religious worldview of the voting base of the Republican Party.[1]

Creationism is a matter of faith, not science, based on the literal assumption that the world is exactly as old as the Bible saysit is, with little room for interpretation in regards to symbolism, allegory, or metaphor. Darwinism can be compatible with faith and Creationism only as long as biblical "truths" are taken as symbolic and not literal. This goes once again to the philosophical argument of literal versus allegorical interpretation of the Bible and the differences between fundamentalist worldviews and the worldviews of most Christian denominations.

The reason LaHaye and those like him continue to push scientific creationism at the same time they push prophecy is because their literal interpretations and assumptions do not hold up if one part of the Bible is taken as symbolic and open for a wide range of opinion, and another part is taken as a literal absolute. In the same manner, this is how the merry-go-round of conspiracy propaganda tied to prophecy functions. All the action of prophecy in the Left Behind novels occurs in the future, based upon sometimes broad and sometimes specific *symbolic* assumptions of the biblical past. Mixed into this are unfalsifiable rumors from conspiracy theories about institutions (such as the U.N.) in the current and recent past, as well as sometimes broad and sometimes specific *literal interpretation* of the prophetic works of the Bible, a work that has been translated and retranslated through the centuries. Thus it is a matter of faith, though a faith wrapped in the tangled web of metaphor, interpretation, symbolism, and allegory—interpretations that they so vehemently argue against.

From 1870 to 1925, this debate divided much of the evangelical community in the U.S., splitting it into modernists and fundamentalists: one side focusing on the social gospel of moral instruction and service, and the other, outright rejection of modernism in favor of strict literal absolutism. After the failure of Prohibition and the defeat of strict creationism after the Scopes trial in the early 1930s, fundamentalists retreated from the public scene and into increasingly isolated communities, increasingly gravitating toward the southern states. Helped along by the media mockery of fundamentalists during and after the Scopes trial, these communities nursed a strong sense of persecution. Much of this mindset gravitated toward the paranoid fantasies that all that was happening to them was part of a Communist plot led by Jews and anti-Christs. "The media subjected these fundamentalists to such ridicule that they slunk away," said Karen Armstrong. "But these fundamentalists were simply withdrawing in the time-honored way, leaving the mainstream denominations and founding their own churches, Bible colleges, broadcasting stations and publishing houses."[2]

From the 1930s to the 1970s, evangelical modernists and moderates largely controlled the Protestant denominations, often becoming tied to progressive social movements. The rise of the civil rights and counterculture movements toward the end of the sixties was set to change all that. For fundamentalists, these uprisings were seen as the last straw and signaled the whole nation was going further and further away from the myth of itself as the bride of New Jerusalem and closer toward the whore of the New Babylon. From the end of the 1970s on, fundamentalists eclipsed the modernist evangelicals through building an empire of media, education, and social organizations, by using the structures of modern society to deliver their literalist and absolutist message. With the clarity and organization of this machine, they have been able to remain remarkably "on message" through the last thirty years. One who deserves much of the credit for this is Tim LaHaye.

After building his Christian Heritage College near San Diego in 1970, Tim LaHaye founded the Institute for Creation Research in 1972 along with Henry Morris. An independent preacher from Virginia who had written the book *Genesis Flood* along with John Whitcomb in 1961, Morris came to LaHaye from mutual connections in the high level Christian right community through his writing and church building success after he left a separate Creation-Science Research Center in San Diego, headed by Kelly Segraves. *Genesis Flood*, which had been a sensation among the biblically literal community (two hundred thousand copies sold over twenty-five years) asserted that the earth was six thousand years old and that the six-day creation was to be taken literally as "created in six days." Drawing heavily on the writings of a self-taught geologist and Seventh Day Adventist named George McCready Price, Whitcomb and Morris had mixed creationism with science to account for the geological record, arguing that each of the geological time layers had been the result of the worldwide flood of Noah's time and God had put fossils there to test people's faith. This book helped create what is now known as scientific creationism, the type of creationism that many Christian activists argue should be included in the public school curriculum, not just in science, but in any subject where creationism could apply.

By teaming up with LaHaye, Morris finally had an academic institution to give credit to his theories and put a Dr. by his name, as well as funding from donors and tuition to expand on the teaching and dissemination of scientific creationism. In 1977, LaHaye and Morris set up a museum to display this mix of science, Genesis, the Flood and six thousand years of history to the believers The museum expanded from one room to nine rooms by the late 1980s. Much of the written material produced by the Institute for Creation Research (ICR) began to make its way into Jerry Falwell's Lynchburg Bible College as the basis for the biology curriculum during the latter half of the 1970s. When it came to the attention of the ACLU that graduates of the biology program at Falwell's University were teaching biology in Virginia public schools, the ACLU filed a complaint challenging their ability to teach biology with creationism as their basis of scientific thought.[3]

The tax-exempt ICR produces the prayer booklets *Acts and Facts* and *Days of Praise*. The contents are average prayer book issues—Pslams, Acts, and specific lines from various Gospels. Yet the main aim of the Institute for Creation Research remains promoting creationism, so in most pamphlets there are also advertisements for books such as these 1992 offerings: *Christian Education for the Real World*, *The Beginning of the World*, and a book for young creationists by Henry's son John Morris (now president of the ICR) and Ken Ham, *What Really Happened to the Dinosaurs?* Another Ken Ham book advertised by Master Books, called *The Lie: Evolution*, portrays a large serpent wrapping itself around the globe, an indication of Satan and the "big lie" of evolution. Master Books is a for-profit publishing arm of ICR, located in El Cajon, California. Ken Ham, chief executive of a group called Answers for Genesis, is currently helping build a one hundred thousand square-foot creationist institute complex near Cincinnati that includes a museum, classrooms, planetarium, and special-effects movie theater where viewers can get a glimpse of how Noah's flood created the earth.

The echo of persecution often reverberates through the letters written by John Morris that accompany the booklets—the language of the fight, the war, the enemy. By distributing their literature to churches, the ICR works to promote creationism, patriotism, and anti-secularism. There is only a small amount of Bible prophecy included in the literature, but there is a heavy dose of the embattled and the dire in many of the letters that accompany the booklets. "Wrong thought systems seem to be everywhere, affecting every arena," writes Dr. Henry M. Morris in a letter to members in 1997 in which he blames evolution, instead of the more obvious millennialism, as the "core belief" that drove the Heaven's Gate cult members to suicide. "This becomes blatantly obvious with the recent mass suicide here in San Diego County of 39 members of a New Age Cult. As expected, evolutionary theory was at the core of their belief . . . while camouflaged with pseudo-Christian lingo."[4]

Contributions to the ICR in 2002 totaled over $4.5 million with nearly the same amount of expenses—half of which went to salaries, over $2 million. John Morris, Henry, Gish, and treasurer Donald Rohrer paid themselves over $80,000 each for their duties at the institute. The two "research scientists" on staff included in the tax return were Russell Humphreys of New Mexico—who made nearly $70,000—and Andrew Snelling, a controversial geologist from Australia who stopped publishing in reputable scientific journals in 1992—he made around $100,000 (although, according to the *Princeton Review*, the average salary of a geologist, after ten or fifteen years in the field, is around $76,000).[5]

Assets for the ICR in 2002 were over $5.8 million of which nearly $1.5 million is invested in nontaxable stocks and bonds (ICR is a non-profit tax exempt private foundation under 501(c)(3)). Royalties off book sales from Master Books in 2002 were over $35,000, an amount likely to shoot up with the controversy over the book *Grand Canyon: A Different View*, that claims the Grand Canyon was formed in the biblical flood (and which has landed on the shelves of six bookstores within the National Park). *Grand Canyon: A Different View* was written by Tom Vail, a rafting guide in the canyon who converted to Protestant fundamentalism and then started a biblical canyon tour called Canyon Ministries with his wife Paula.[6] While not calling for the removal of the book from the stores, the presidents of seven scientific organizations did write to the park superintendent asking that it be "clearly separated from materials offering scientific information about Grand Canyon geology," causing a controversy between the scientific community and fundamentalists.

Total book sales for the ICR in 2002 were over $1.2 million.[7] In even deeper irony, deep in the 2002 income tax return for the creationist organization is a claim on $6,105 in royalties—on that good old fossil fuel created millions of years ago—oil.

Among the board of LaHaye's Christian Heritage College, a non-denominational four-year liberal arts college in El Cajon where the ICR is based, are Duane Gish and wife Lolly (the former being a co-founder of the ICR, and also members of the CNP and Pre-Trib Research Center). Pre-Trib Research Center member David Jeremiah serves as pastor at the college. In 2002, the school generated $7 million in revenue, and after expenses such as the over $3 million in salaries, could claim just over $3 million in assets.[9] Around $350,000 dollars was spent in hiring an outside marketing group to recruit students, while another $75,000 was spent for, oddly enough, flight classes.

Gish, a "creationist biochemist" and former member of the CNP along with Henry Morris, also founded the Creation Research Society (CRS), which exists as a separate entity today. This is the second arm of the scientific creationism machine. Based in Chino Valley, Arizona, as well as San Antonio, Texas, and claiming assets of over $1 million in 2002, the CRS is a smaller version of the ICR.[9] The main activities of this organization are publishing a quarterly journal and books on scientific creationism, giving lectures at churches and other religious organizations, and conducting research into scientific creationism—though only a paltry $26,000 went into research in 2002. Marketing scientific creationism was almost five times more costly to the "research" society.

From the CRS it's a quick fifteen minute drive over the Interstate 410 and the Interstate 31 Loop to the Covenant Foundation, a massive philanthropic institution with almost $40 million in assets at of the end of 2002, a year when it gave its second largest chunk of funding—over $1.6 million—to Michael Farris's Patrick Henry College. The largest gift, over $4 million, went to a similar institution—the Christian Academy of San Antonio. Around $12 million dollars total went to a wide variety of conservative social and political causes, nearly half located in Texas.[10]

One of the directors of the Covenant Foundation is Dr. James Leininger, a Texas physician and part owner of the San Antonio Spurs, who made much of his fortune off the sale of medical-bed manufacturer Kinetic Concepts Inc. and is one of the single largest donors to conservative political campaigns in

Texas. Molly Ivins has referred to him as the "Daddy Warbucks" of Texas social conservatism. A homeschooling parent himself, Leininger was a major advocate for voucher programs and has been influential in getting candidates elected to the powerful state school board in Texas. Besides these efforts, Leininger started the Texas Public Policy Foundation and the Texas Justice Foundation, which function as webs within webs for conservative causes from anti-abortion to low taxes, anti-homosexual rights legislation, and school voucher programs, as well as loan backers for candidates statewide. Leininger, yet another member of the CNP, also sits on the board of directors for Patrick Henry College, along with Janet Ashcroft, wife of the former Attorney General John Ashcroft, himself a former member of the CNP.[11]

Leininger was recently eclipsed as the leading Republican funder in Texas by Robert J. Perry, a Houston homebuilder who gave $100,000 to start the Swift Boat Veterans for Truth campaign, which aired the attack ad on John Kerry's war record midway through the 2004 presidential race.[12] Perry, himself a member of the CNP since 1982, gave over $3 million to Texas Republican candidates during the 2002 mid-term elections. A *Los Angeles Times* profile of Perry notes that he gave money to the last four Bush election campaigns and is closely tied with mutual friends of Bush, such as Karl Rove, who he's known since Rove's Texas days. The *LA Times* also notes that during 2002 Perry gave about $700,000 to the Texas GOP in its attempt to control the state house for the first time in 130 years. Of that largesse, $165,000 went to House Majority Leader Tom DeLay's Texans for a Republican Majority, a branch of DeLay's Americans for a Republican Majority. That takeover ultimately led to the GOP redrawing the congressional maps of Texas in attempt to "shore up Republican control of Congress," as well as helping push through further abortion restrictions and limits on medical malpractice cases in the state.[13]

Leninger's Texas Public Policy Foundation is especially important when it comes to the information schoolchildren across the country get in their textbooks. Between 1999 and 2001, the foundation received $200,000 in outside grants. With the support of large national conservative foundations, it undertook a review of social studies textbooks for students in grades six through twelve in the Texas school system, using carefully chosen conservative high school teachers and university professors; it later used the review to change social studies textbooks in the state.[14] As the second-largest purchaser of textbooks in the country, Texas-approved student books are often used by school systems in other states as publishers tailor their books to that market.

"One frightening thing the educators are advancing is 'global education' which is part of what Education 2000 is about," writes LaHaye, referring to President Clinton's Goals 2000 education reform program, in his August 199Pre-Trib Research Center publication, *Tim LaHaye's Perspective*. "After successfully ruining the best educational system in the world . . . they want to make their amoral socialistic form of 'education' global." In his book on the Christian right's efforts to redefine public schools, Fritiz Detwiler argues that because leaders like Beverly LaHaye, Robertson, Schlafly, and Dobson had been portraying the Clinton administration's education bill Goals 2000 as a big-government liberal conspiracy in order to promote a homosexual agenda, local activists familiar with this rhetoric who believe the conspiracy theories seek out these connections in their local schools.[15] It is something similar to what happened in the late 1970s in California, when Reagan didn't support LaHaye's public school anti-homosexual agenda for fear of witch hunts and paralyzing interference that paranoia has on children and their parents. For years, much of the fear the LaHayes have been spreading has prompted many parents within the evangelical community to separate themselves from public schools by pulling their children from them to be taught at home, with the utmost oversight, through homeschooling.

Homeschooling

During a discussion between Left Behind characters Bruce and Chloe about what ramifications bringing children into the world during the Tribulation would have, Bruce offers the tempting scenario of abandoning the educational system altogether. He states that Chloe "wouldn't even have to think about junior high school, let along high school or college. You would be raising that child, preparing him or her for the return of Christ in a few years."[16]

Much of the attitude about the alleged erosion of faith in the public school system is based on a "presuppositional" strategy, argues Detwiler, defining the presuppositional strategy of the

Christian right as proceeding "incrementally, first by gaining a hearing, then by defining the issues, and finally by reforming society to conform to Biblical principals." Put simply, first it must come to the table as a legitimate player, second, it must take control of the debate and undermine its opponent by adding conspiracies like "the homosexual agenda," and finally it attempts to control their own children's education, then onward into private and public schooling until the whole system of public education is destroyed and remade in these Christian's likeness. It isn't really this simple, but it is a good model for how these groups have worked their way into the debate to undermine the system.

"Christian Right leaders knew that, using presuppositional strategy, they had to convince the general public that the alarms they were sounding about public education were justified," Detwiler writes.[17] Ephemeral terms like "diversity" that are used often on the left get hammered by these folks and turned upside down. Instead of using terms like "inclusion" or "inclusiveness" which would bring in concepts and ideas from all groups, including biblical Christians as well as homosexuals, public schooling has been placed in an indefensible position due to the fact that an increasingly vocal outside grouping of people on the Christian right has undermined that term "diversity" to mean the "legitimization of homosexual values," while ignoring its functions in introducing the broad spectrum of American society. Instead of a middle ground, the attack on public schooling by the Christian right has created a condition where two equally ideological camps are sitting opposite each other with no room to maneuver.

Nearly 2 million American students—or one out of twenty-five—are now being taught at home by their parentsaccording to statistics given by the Home School Legal Defense Fund. In 1981, when Reagan came into office, it was illegal to teach students at home in most states. Just over twenty years later all states now allow homeschooling. Of those, twenty-eight require home-schooled students to take official evaluation tests and thirteen only stipulate that parents must inform the local officials that they've decided to teach their children at home. In Texas, parents don't have to do either. Upwards of $850 million in homeschooling products are sold per year. The Home School Legal Defense Association states that 76 percent of homeschooled kids between eighteen and twenty-four vote in elections, compared with an abysmal 29 percent in the same age group of those publicly schooled nationwide.[18]

In reality, there are many families that hold similar view on preparing their children for Jesus' return or theocratic America, whichever comes first. Around 42 percent of homeschooled children are from evangelical or mainline Protestant families, split half and half. Yet it is the growing power of the evangelical half that has been garnering the most attention for blending class credit and political activism—students getting credit for programs in government and civic involvement by working on conservative political campaigns. Critics have claimed Home School Legal Defense, which is headed by Michael Farris, a former attorney for CWA and founder of homeschooling college Patrick Henry College (motto "For Christ and Liberty"), is using its status as a promoter of all homeschooled children to become a feeder system for the fundamentalist political network.[19]

In the past few years the Home School Legal Defense Association launched a project called Generation Joshua, which gives high school credits in exchange for students joining voter drives and volunteering for local campaigns where conservative Christian candidates are in close races.[20] In the 2002 midterm elections, Ned Ryun—coordinator of Generation Joshua—sent teams of students to Missouri where they manned the phones for seven candidates in tight races, six of whom eventually won their elections. Ryun, son of sitting Congressman from Kansas, Jim Ryun, is a former presidential writer for George W. Bush.

In 2002, the Patrick Henry College's assets stood at $14.5 million quite a holding considering there were only 195 on-campus and sixty-eight distance learning students in 2002.[21] That same year out of one hundred interns at the White House, seven were from Patrick Henry College and about a dozen others were aides in the House and Senate. In mid-2002 Patrick Henry College was denied accreditation by the American Academy for Liberal Education (AALE) because it was teaching scientific creationism in biology classes, teaching creationism as a science and not as theology. Speaking to *Christianity Today*, Farris says students are taught evolution but "we just think it's bogus—bogus science, and bogus as a matter of faith."[22]

Besides president Michael Farris, among the current board of directors of Patrick Henry College are multimillionaire Texas fundraiser and CNP member, Dr. James R. Leninger; wife of former attorney general and CNP member John Ashcroft, Janet Ashcroft; Ken Raasch, a businessman who has made millions from marketing the works of artist Thomas Kinkade; Ramon Ardizzone, Chairman and CEO Emeritus of Glenayre Technologies, Inc., a developer and worldwide supplier of telecommunications equipment as well as chairman of the Bible Archaeology Search and Exploration Institute (his daughter Kristen was an executive director of Schalfly's Eagle Forum and a member of the CNP); Barbara Hodel, wife of former vice chairman of Texon Corporation and secretary of energy under Ronald Reagan; Donald Paul Hodel, who was also on the boards of Christian Coalition and Focus on the Family, as well as the CNP; and Paul De Pree, a senior leader at Dow Chemical Company.

Michael Farris's Home School Legal Defense Fund, a 501(c)(4) non-profit, shares the same facilities and some staff as Patrick Henry College, and functions as the lobbying arm for PHC and Farris's homeschooling interests. The Patrick Henry College Foundation is also on the premises—and besides granting to its own college, PHCF awarded nearly $30,000 to Eternal Perspective Ministries, the personal ministry of religion writer and anti-abortion activist Randy Alcorn based in Portland, Oregon.[23]

THE SEDUCTIVE APPEAL OF
THE IMMINENT RETURN

According to Heather Hendershot in *Shaking the World for Jesus*, there are three apparent goals of apocalyptic media—first, to entertain while also presenting the basics of their interpretation of Bible prophecy; second, to frighten people to convert before the "bleak future that awaits the unraptured"; and finally to covert those left behind if a Rapture occurs.[1]

It is the imminence or the immediacy of Christ's return that is so powerful in this set of beliefs, the idea that "at any moment" Jesus will blow his trumpet and send believers soaring into the air to meet him. Darby, the founder of the idea, had grown dissatisfied with the static church and knew from his studies of past movements that the hint of approaching "millennium" had always attracted many new converts. The trick of premillennialism is that its leaders often give a vague account of how imminent the return would be, at times insinuating that it is "close at hand" and other times saying "only the Lord knows the time and the date of his coming," in essence playing believers like an organ and often sharpening the rhetoric when it serves their political needs most fully.

LaHaye knows full well the effects of imminency, combined with conspiracy politics and mingled with a good dose of the Fear of God, has on winning converts to his brand of political religion, snapping people into his brand of holy living, and increasing the righteousness of the premillennialist line. These are God's Minutemen, ready at any moment. The more believers the ideology gains, the greater the power of its own reality. He also knows that the promised return of a physical king or messiah is much more tempting than the murky spiritual kingdom other Christian denominations preach to help guide people in their daily lives. Some premillennialists, including LaHaye, get around criticism of their use of imminent return theology with the vague "well, it could happen any moment . . . but it may not happen for a thousand years" line of reasoning. Of course they know what wins souls is the immediacy of the message, and this is displayed in all the premillennial literature including the Left Behind series. There are some within premillennialist circles who are aware of the dangers of the imminent return doctrine, saying it breeds speculation over whether this person or that person is the next Antichrist, or the desire to personalize biblical prophecy. Yet someone who has bought into the movement through mass culture means like the Left Behind series, would hardly know this unless they became a serious student of biblical prophecy. Not as culturally active or politically connected as LaHaye, Dr. Edward Hindson, who is dean of the Institute of Biblical Studies at Liberty University and a Pre-Trib Research Center member, warns against wild speculation about the "when, where, who or how" of prophecy, seemingly playing down the major draw of premillennialism—imminent Rapture.[2] As part of his case Hindson mentions the hysteria created by a prominent evangelical who saw the number 666 on automobile license plates in Israel which he took as a sign the "mark of the beast" had already come to the Holy Land. "The greatest danger of all in trying to interpret biblical prophecy is to assume that our speculations are true and preach them as facts," says Hindson.

One has to wonder how long and how taut that rubber band of imminent return can be stretched before it breaks into the mass despair of disappointment if the promised Rapture and imminent return don't come. The mass anxiety this generates in its believers is similar to the mass fear of nuclear annihilation during the cold war era. In fact, it is a comparison often courted and welcome in their writings. Except that instead of imminent doom of being nuked, there is the promise of imminent salvation by being Raptured. Only those left behind to face the torment of the Tribulation will be nuked—and often worse. There is a point, as many cult and millennial watchers know, when believers in the imminent return of Christ become impatient, disappointed that their visions have not conformed to reality, and are spurred to action. In the case of American premillennialists, much of that physical action can be seen in "prophecy pushing" such as helping fund diaspora Jews' return to Israel and funding settlements in the Occupied Territories. The urge to fulfill what they believe is the prophecy that the biblical "Land of Israel" must be the same Israel that takes shape today, as well as increased political activism to create the millennial utopia on the homefront, are all manifestations of this desire to action.

As with most messianic millennialist movements, the urge to action follows a sense of despair. When the message of prophecy hasn't been fulfilled, something must be done to help it along. In January 1999, fourteen members of Concerned Christians—a group based in Denver, Colorado—were deported from Israel because authorities suspected they were planning a disturbance leading up to the turn of the century. In Israel in the year leading up to 2000, psychiatrists saw a 50 to 60 percent increase of what they call Jerusalem Syndrome, in which pilgrims to the Holy City sometimes imagine they are figures from the Bible. Those diagnosed were predominantly Christians and Jews from the United States and Europe. One hotel in Jerusalem hoping to cash in on the millennial fever advertised to over two thousand Christian groups in the U.S. with the selling line of "How would you like to be staying at the Mount of Olives Hotel the day that Jesus returns?"[3]

Israeli authorities weren't the only ones on guard against possible violent acts around the millennium. In October 1999 the FBI issued a report called Project Medidddo, named after the prophesized location of the battle of Armageddon. The report warned of possible attacks by apocalyptic white supremacists and groups such as the apocalyptic-conspiracy movement Christian Identity wanting to ignite a race war, preemptive strikes by militia forces fearing a United Nations takeover of the U.S., suicides or other cultish behavior from those anticipating imminent return.[4] Among groups that made headlines through the final despairing act of suicide, the Heaven's Gate tragedy received the most attention in the United States. An even more violent end came when over one thousand followers of the Movement for the Restoration of the Ten Commandments were murdered in Uganda during the month of March 2000 after the cult leadership decided it was time to bring on the end themselves.[5]

"The real problem is that in the immediate period after disappointment," says Richard Landes, "the first decade of the next century—one of the tendencies of disappointed apocalyptic groups is to get nasty. They [will] look for scapegoats."

Landes outlines why apocalyptic beliefs have had such resiliency over time and why they have been so adaptable to the many narratives which incorporate them. He argues these beliefs play into the human yearning for justice to be meted out to the doers of evil and a search for a time when the good will no longer suffer from the injustice. This notion also incorporates the utopian dream of overcoming our human weakness and making the leap from our sinful nature into a higher state of being, a deliverance project incorporated into nearly every religion to varying degrees—be it Heaven, Enlightenment, Perfection, or Nirvana. Apocalyptic beliefs can be addictive in that they tend to heighten awareness and provide meaning in a world of random chaos. Everything from the news ticker across the bottom of the TV screen that relays the occurrence of yet another bombing in Israel, to the highly selective Bible passages read in apocalyptic literature, arouse, clarify, provide coherence, and delineate a clear path of action for the believer. In an apocalyptic community, the "sense of intimacy and purpose is far more potent than the wan ties that bind us in the messy grey world of civil society," says Landes. He also explains that millennial movements, when prophecy does fail to deliver, often reinterpret and move on, rather than totally abandon the ties that bind them.[6] Boston University professor of scripture and author of *Jesus of Nazareth, King of the Jews* Paula Fredricksen calls this improvisation "apocalyptic jazz."

> [Apocalyptic] expectations may be couched in sufficiently ambiguous language to cover a variety of human events," said Michael Barkun, professor of political science at Syracuse University on the PBS program Frontline's "Apocalypse!" series roundtable discussion. "Second, there may be a closed system of belief that resists disconfirmation. This is particularly the case

where conspiracy beliefs are involved, since conspiracy beliefs are nonfalsifiable. The ideas about a "New World Order" conspiracy that now circulate are of this type. That is, the theory itself asserts that seemingly contradictory information has been planted by the conspiracy and thus ought not to be believed.[7]

The vague quality of most events within the Left Behind books gives them many of the qualities outlined above, in particular the elasticity of happening today, tomorrow, or at any moment. In the first book of the series, Explaining why some Christians were Raptured and others were not, Reverend Barnes continues to foster the division between "true believers" and the rest of the mass of writhing humanity, that those Christians who had been left behind were never fully Christians. These divisions further separate people into good and evil camps.

The authors of *Strong Religion* offer an example of a certain "flexibility" some premillennialists have had that points more to the political agenda of "pushing prophecy" through their apocalyptic literature rather than a religious or spiritual one.

> The growing conviction of Jerry Falwell, Pat Robertson . . . and Tim LaHaye in the late seventies as to the possible emergence of a Moral Majority, likely to acquire hegemony in American politics and culture, made them introduce a "millennial window" into their premillennialism. They assumed that the arrival of the millennium depended upon their activism. Tribulation would precede Rapture, not follow it. In consequence, one could act immediately in order to better American society, otherwise devastation would be so comprehensive as to hit the saved as well, and anyhow, it might be so cataclysmic as to render the reconstruction extremely difficult. Only a daring bid for power, until then thought to be an un-Christian course of action, could save the day.[8]

Throughout the Left Behind novels, assumptions about the Rapture and second coming are leveraged by the characters in their interactions with one another, largely based on a condition of fear. After a massive earthquake in *Soul Harvest* wipes out millions of people, Rayford uses the fear of God when talking to his copilot Mac—who has yet to convert and is heavily weighing his own beliefs—telling him of how many preachers used to think that people couldn't become believers after the Rapture. He then nonchalantly reminds Mac that he hoped "there would be no aftershock or attack that might get you killed before you are assured of heaven."[9]

LaHaye and Jenkins frequently use reverse psychology when they have their post-Raptured, or left behind characters comment that the only people who believed in the Rapture before were religious nuts, cults, weirdos or radical fanatic fundamentalists, or simplify it down to disparaging comments like the Rapture is "pretty freaky stuff." Most often, these references occur when the characters are relaying their conversion stories and what their beliefs were before the Rapture. For readers who believe in the Rapture, reading these post-Rapture comments, lends a sense of righteousness to their belief. Passages like these also lend to the feeling that they are still embattled, since after all, they are just reading a fictional account of the future Rapture. The wavering between describing them as fanatics or religious nuts and describing them as "true Christians" also reinforces the belief that they are being persecuted, always manning the ramparts in defense of their belief.

On the very first page of the title novel, the reader is confronted with Rayford Steele's pre-Rapture antagonism to what the authors consider religion—which for them takes only the form of the narrow premillennialist line. Rayford finds himself "repelled" by his wife's "obsession with religion" (she is Raptured in the first book). But it isn't necessarily religion he is "repelled" by. What the authors go on to describe is his wife Irene's abandoning of their old church for a new, smaller premillennialist congregation, which takes up much of her time and creates a rift between these two due to her evangelistic zeal and Rayford's own static beliefs.[10] There is also some antagonism over their son Raymie, who accompanied Irene to the new church and became an integral part of that small group, "even when Rayford didn't go." Rayford remarks with shock that his son Raymie "even read his Bible and studied it"—and of course, Raymie is Raptured along with his mother. Only Rayford and his daughter, Chloe, who happens to be studying for what looks to be a promising future at Stanford University, are among the family members left behind to face the wrath. Chloe is later convinced by her fellows in the Tribulation Force, the group of premillennialist believers formed to battle the Antichrist, to abandon her studies at Stanford and instead study the prophetic books of the Bible at the church. This new church and Tribulation Force is formed by Pastor Bruce who started to build a bomb shelter from where they will be able to harass the Antichrist in Koreshian fashion.[11]

Before his conversion to the premillennialist belief system in the Left Behind series, the world-renowned journalist character Buck Williams insists on not being called a Christian. "Deist is as much as I'll cop to," the authors write him as saying, with all the Jeffersonian baggage of that claim. Buck then explains the familiar refrain of how he used to go to church when he was young, but the "the lack of any connection between his family's church attendance and their daily lives that made him quit going to church altogether the day it became his choice." A few pages later we find this is similar to one of the reasons the wife of Rayford Steele had left her church for her new premillennialist one where her pastor had "often spoken of the 'Rapture'"—she was disenchanted with the "lack of spirituality" in her old church. This came after Irene had begun listening with excitement to Christian radio and the biblically literal messages it exposed, something that actually made her disenchantment with her church stronger and gave Rayford the excuse not to attend altogether. Much of this is reflected in how Irene abandons what is described as the messy, chaotic, and liberal denomination to take on the cloak of a single-minded, literal system of belief—something that Rayford is uncomfortable with before he becomes a believer. He comments that he seems to always be on the top of her prayer list and confesses he feels "like a project," which in many ways has dehumanized him and driven a barrier between them. It is later revealed that Irene's preoccupation with the End Times events had made Rayford contemplate looking outside of marriage for another relationship, one that almost came from flirting with his flight attendant Hattie Durham.[12]

Another likely indication of how this sense of embattlement and the demarcation made between "true believers" and "others" has made premillennialists so insecure in their own beliefs is that they have to continuously wrap it in complicated theories of conspiracy and complex reconstructions from prophecy. For LaHaye, the world is divided into two camps—Christians and nonbelievers. Dividing this further, he would also argue that the dispensational premillenialism of the Rapture and the complex theological structure built around millenialists' literal interpretations of the Revelation is the only correct vision for Christianity, that all the other forms have been corrupted by modernist secular ideas. In all of these cases, and with the case of premillennialism today, there is a feeling of exclusiveness surrounding the belief—the us versus them, good versus evil, believer vesus nonbeliever aspects—which usually end up isolating and dividing people at the very least, and promote active persecution, destruction, or dehumanization of people at the very worst. Throughout the Left Behind series, the authors actively dehumanize an entire segment of humanity—the nonbeliever—simply because that unfortunate populace does not buy into the premillennialist beliefs. In fiction, this leads to violent depopulation through "acts of God" or through the forces of the evil Antichrist. As of now, thankfully, it remains in the realm of the sadistic slash-fic of apocalyptic Christian fictions. In the world of reality, the Japanese millennialist cult of Aum Shinrikyo turned to violent "catastrophic millennialism" against nonbelievers through its attacks on the Tokyo subway with sarin nerve gas. Timothy McVeigh, being taken in by conspiracy and apocalyptic fantasy and taking the further step to rise up and act out those fantasies in reality, is but another example.

Throughout the Left Behind series there is also a construction where personal criticism toward Trib Force members is mistaken for institutionalized persecution. The sense of being embattled for readers and believers in premillennialist prophecy is often reinforced by people like LaHaye, who see the power in it. This occurs to such a great degree that when their beliefs are questioned on a personal level, they think it is part of some larger conspiracy out to crush them, which is clearly one of LaHaye's intentions in using the secular conspiracy theories he does.

One example of this construction where personal criticism is taken for institutional persecution comes in the second book, *Tribulation Force*, when Rayford is reprimanded for proselytizing on the job to one of his cockpit mates. Here is the passage where he interacts with the other pilot, Nick:

"Is it going to offend you if I sit reading this for a while?" Rayford asked. [He'd just pulled out his wife's Bible.]

The younger man turned and pulled the left phone away from his own ear. "Say again?"

Rayford repeated himself, pointing to the Bible. It had belonged to the wife he hadn't seen for more than two weeks and probably would not see for another seven years.

"As long as you don't expect me to listen."

"I got you loud and clear, Nick. You understand I don't care what you think of me, don't you?"

"Sir?"

Rayford leaned close and spoke louder. "What you think of me would have been hugely important a few weeks ago," he said. "But—"

"Yeah, I know, OK? I got it, Steele, all right? You and lots of other people think the whole thing was Jesus. Not buying. Delude yourself, but leave me out of it."

Rayford raised his brows and shrugged. "You wouldn't respect me if I hadn't tried."

"Don't be too sure."

Obviously his fellow crewmate was uncomfortable with this kind of talk while he's taking a plane through its preflight check. Rayford confronts others about their beliefs many times throughout *Tribulation Force*. Through his connections Rayford manages to land a job flying a plane for the American president Fitzhugh, whom Reverend Barnes urges him to proselytize at one point. Bruce also begins to advise the other members of the Trib Force on what jobs they should be taking so they can be closer to power.[13] Through the reinforcing of the sense of embattlement and seclusion in the early Left Behind books, the paranoia that the group fosters for themselves is quite catching.

At the beginning of *Soul Harvest*, Rayford tries to figure out how to wiretap the plane he is now flying for Carpathia, who for the most part doesn't seem to be concerned that the people who think he is the Antichrist are flying his plane. It is obvious he is aware that the characters of the Tribulation Force believe him to be the Antichrist. During these scenes Rayford wonders if his co-pilot Mac is trying to entrap him for Carpathia. As "the believers" begin to meet other people, they usually have a great initial sense of distrust. Further on in the series, when believers get marks on their foreheads (which only other believers can see), distinguishing the good from the evil becomes much easier, the sense of paranoia is lessened, and instead jubilation replaces that old fear. At times the Tribulation Force starts to take on something of a Mafioso, "welcome to the family" air. When Mac does eventually convert, and the "mark of the believer" cross shows up on his forehead, Rayford tells him it "looks like what Catholics *used to* get on Ash Wednesday." At this point the Catholic Church had been easily swallowed up by Enigma Babylon in a matter of pages, so in the world of these novels, the Catholic Church is now past tense.[14]

Early in the second-to-last book, *Armageddon*, Rayford happens upon a woman who wants to accept the Lord by prayer, but had previously taken the "mark of the beast." The authors make it clear that she cannot come to Christ. It is too late.

> "Oh, God, oh, God and Jesus, help me!"
>
> "Ma'am," he said, reaching for her. She shrieked when he touched her, but he pulled at the sides of her head until he could see her hollow, unseeing, terrified eyes.
>
> "I knew before everybody disappeared," she said pitifully. "And then I knew for sure. With every plague and judgment, I shook my fist in God's face. He tried to reach me, but I had my own life. I wasn't going to be subservient to anybody.
>
> [. . .]
>
> Rayford knew the prophecy—that people would reject God enough times that God would harden their hearts and they wouldn't be able to choose him even if they wanted to.[15]

For the authors, if it is too late for this woman to become one of the believers, what is the rest of the Tribulation for if not simply revenge for rejecting Christ?

Rayford's paranoia manifests itself earlier when he wonders if his new believer wife Amanda, who had died in a plane crash during one of the massive earthquakes, was actually a spy for Carpathia.[16] Her mother's maiden name happens to be Fortunato, which is the name of Carpathia's chief henchman.

Another key feature of the Left Behind books is heavy quoting from the Bible along with the implication that these quotations are to be taken literally. Often characters say things like "Let me show you from the Bible exactly what has happened," as the former pastor of Bruce Barnes's church does when explaining the Rapture to the rest of the Tribulation Force through his post-Rapture video.

> "Let me show you from the Bible exactly what has happened. You won't need this proof by now, because you will have experienced the most shocking event of history. But as this tape was made beforehand and I am confident that I will be gone, ask yourself, how did he know? Here's how, from 1 Corinthians 15:51–57."
>
> The screen begins to scroll with the passage of Scripture. Rayford hit the pause button and ran to get Irene's Bible. It took him a while to find 1 Corinthians, and though it was slightly different in her translation, the meaning was the same.
>
> The pastor said, "Let me read to you what the great missionary evangelist, the apostle Paul, wrote to the Christians at the church in the city of Corinth:
>
> "Behold, I tell you a mystery: We shall not all sleep, but we shall all be changed—in a moment, in the twinkling of an eye, at the last trumpet. For the trumpet will sound, and the dead will be raised incorruptible, and we shall be changed. For this corruptible must put on incorruption, and this moral must put on immortality. So when this corruptible has put on incorruption, and this mortal has put on immortality, then shall be brought to pass the saying that is written: 'Death is swallowed up in victory. O Death, where is your sting? O Hades, where is your victory?' The sting of death is sin, and the strength of sin is law. But thanks be to God, who gives us victory through our Lord Jesus Christ."[17]

This picking and choosing from the Bible, and reading into it of all vestiges of proof of Rapture, is a preoccupation of premillennialists and one which leads them through a revolving door of repetition, a cyclical quoting of one another's quotes to back up their complex narrative of biblical prophecy that the lay person usually doesn't have time or energy to even desire to question or break down. Yet, in doing this elaborate dance, the pastor still always feels the need "translate" and "paraphrase" and "interpret" the "real meaning" to the group so that it will "be understood."

There are passages like this elaborate interpretation when the pastor on the tape goes on to tell the Tribulation Force that "Scripture indicates that there will be a great lie, announced with the help of the media and perpetrated by a self-styled world leader. Jesus himself prophesied about such a person." On the next page, the pastor explains that this "great deceiver," this Antichrist, may "emerge from Europe."

> "Let me warn you personally to beware of such as leader of humanity who may emerge from Europe. He will turn out to be a great deceiver who will step forward with signs and wonders that will be so impressive that many will believe he is of God. He will gain a great following among those who are left, and many will believe he is a miracle worker."[18]

Essentially this is an interpretation, mixed with the rightwing conspiracy narrative being delivered as literal biblical fact from the mouth of a fictional pastor used to instill fear, distrust, and undermine reasoning. There are also no references to where exactly this passage would be in the Bible. Further on, the pastor tells those who have watched the tape:

> "Bible prophecy is history written in advance. I urge you to find books on this subject or find people who may have been experts in this area but who for some reason did not receive Christ before they were left behind. Study so you'll know what is coming and you can be prepared."[19]

The pastor follows his teaching by telling the crew—"You don't need to understand all of this theologically. You can become a child of God by praying to him right now as I lead you." These new believers must give public declarations of faith, which is nothing new to most religious beliefs, but does aid in showing the influence peer groups have on those actions. The small group setting of the Tribulation Force functions much like an AA meeting. After this sermon the group officially forms the Tribulation Force, a vanguard and a microcosm of premillennial militancy, a shadowy group of underground cells consciously formed to attack the coming, but not yet arrived, global community run by the Antichrist figure of Nicolae Carpathia.

After telling believers that they don't have to understand theology, the authors turn the concept of "intellectual honesty" after Buck Williams has converted, writing that after the Rapture, "everyone in the world, at least those intellectually honest with themselves, had to admit there was a God after that night." After his conversion, Rayford himself battles with his own impulses about not wanting to offend his daughter by preaching to her, wondering if he's "liable to 'not offend' [his] own daughter right into hell." With renewed missionary zeal, Rayford makes up his mind that he must "direct people to the Bible," and especially "to the prophetic portions" as, for literal premillennialists. they were the most important. With what the authors have constructed around him it's no wonder that Rayford has the psychotic "confidence that things are happening exactly the way the Bible said . . ." The authors also get quite nervy toward the faith of others and sectarian at times, like in the instance where they have Chloe wondering "if God answers your prayers before?" . . . to which Buck finishes for her . . ."you're a born-again Christian?" No Catholics, or mainline Protestants need apply.[20]

Attempting to justify the literalism of the Revelation, the former rabbi and now premillennialist Tsion Ben Judah remarks that since he had always taken phrases like "Love your neighbor as yourself" and "do unto others as you would have done unto you" at their literal word, so why not do the same when "John the Revelator says he saw a pale horse"? Here the authors are simply elevating the words of Jesus to an equal place with the author of Revelation, never once acknowledging that this book almost wasn't included in the Bible, or any of the centuries long debate about the meaning in the book. There is no sense of proportion for the authors, their fixation on this one *Book of Revelation* is so total, so intertwined with the worldview they have constructed, that they do anything to attempt to prove its literal truth, including debasing the words accredited to Jesus, the God they say is a loving, redeeming God, while at the same time painting him as the vengeful, destructive God of Revelation.[21] In their fixation to prove that God is "not only love" the authors have swung so wildly in the opposite direction that they have created a God that is nearly pure hate.

At one point Tsion threatens a total dismissal of the Bible if the Revelation doesn't conform to future reality:

> "We are engaged in a great worldwide battle with Satan himself for the souls of men and women. Do not think I lightly advance to the front lines with this truth, not understanding the power of the evil one. But I have placed my faith and trust in God who sits high above the heavens, in the God who is above all other gods, and among whom there is none like him.
>
> "Scripture is clear that you can test both prophet and prophecy. I make no claim of being a prophet, but I believe the prophecies. If they are not true and don't come to pass, then I am a liar and the Bible is bogus, and we are all utterly without hope. But if the Bible is true, next on the agenda is the ceremonial desecration of the temple in Jerusalem by Antichrist himself, This is a prediction made by Daniel, Jesus, Paul and John."[22]

The authors also seem to raise Satan above God at points, for example when Rayford says "Little is our fault, anymore . . . Carpathia is in charge of everything now," showing a great lack of faith that God can actually do anything anymore. Further confusing the reader the authors have Tsion explain that "in Revelation 3:5, Jesus himself promises . . ."—in effect saying that Jesus was the author of the Revelation when before they were calling the author "John the Relevator.'"[23]

The terms "victory," "winning," and "losing" are often repeated throughout the books. It is a race to win souls, to defeat the Antichrist, to lose a loved one to the abyss of disbelief; all this comes across as a language tied more to American sports obsession than religious faith, a pseudo-faith more concerned with competition for converts and power than anything else.

"In a world where good people often suffer and the wicked prosper, the promise of an imminent moral accounting is often consoling," comments Michael Barkun. With all the inherent destructive qualities of apocalyptic belief, it can be extremely positive and proactive for those in the circle of this community. A sense of meaning, of belonging, a higher calling, a desire for greater good, for evolution (via the trigger finger of God, not some murky Darwinian theory) into a higher state of perfection—all of these could be considered healthy preoccupations.

They often lead to works of genius in art, science, literature, philosophy, and individual salvation. On a larger scale, one movement at the approach of the year 1000 in France harnessed their millennial energies into one of the first known peace movements in the world called the Peace of God. In one sense, this is condition is what Catherine Wessinger of Loyola University calls "progressive millennialism." Since the era of the "social Gospel" in the early twentieth century, Paul Boyer of the University of Wisconsin argues, this progressive millennialism has been sufficiently absorbed and secularized by the mainstream of American reform tradition that its biblically based elements cease to exist.

However, in other mass millennialist movements, one man's evolution or triumph is often another man's destruction or defeat. There was a heavy strain of messianic millennialist deliverance in Marxist Socialism, in German Nazism, and in Italian Fascism, for a few more recent examples of "catastrophic millennialism." What they all contain is a reliance on militant language and portraying everything outside their ideology as "evil" or so directly opposed to their worldview that they must be destroyed. In essence, this is what the purpose of the portrayal of a militant Jesus is about in the Left Behind books.

THE MILITANT JESUS

In his essay on the paranoid style of American politics, Hofstadter describes the "paranoid leader":

> He does not see social conflict as something to be mediated and compromised, in the manner of the working politician. Since what is at stake is always a conflict between absolute good and absolute evil, what is necessary is not compromise but the will to fight things out to the finish. Since the enemy is thought of as being totally evil and totally unappeasable, he must be totally eliminated—if not from the world, at least from the theatre of operations to which the paranoid directs his attention. This demand for total triumph leads to the formulation of hopelessly unrealistic goals, and since these goals are not even remotely attainable, failure constantly heightens the paranoid's sense of frustration. Even partial success leaves him with the same feeling of powerlessness with which he began, and this in turn only strengthens his awareness of the vast and terrifying quality of the enemy he opposes.

This, essentially, is a description of the militant Jesus that the authors paint in the Left Behind novels, as well as an apt description of the political mind of LaHaye.

Looking past all the violence, tribulation, and horror of the Left Behind novels, one can't help but wonder if there has ever been a series of bestselling books in which the main character doesn't show up until page 203 of the twelvth and final book of the series. The main character, the hero of the Left Behind novels, is Jesus Christ, the militant warrior messiah returning to conquer evil and bring a utopian paradise to the world. Upon His return tens of thousands of nonbelieving soldiers are struck dead. Here is LaHaye and Jenkins describing that final battle:

> Their innards and entrails gushed to the desert floor, and those around them turned to run, they too were slain, their blood pooling and rising in the unforgiving brightness of the glory of Christ.[1]

The Jesus the authors have created, with all his destruction and lust for power, often seems no better than the Satan he is fighting. "This vision of Christ, who eviscerates his human foes and drops them to the desert floor, is fast becoming the Savior for our times," writes Paul O'Donnell at Beliefnet in a review of *Glorious Appearing*.[2]

Hofstadter offers another thought: "Very often the fantasies of true believers reveal strong sadomasochistic outlets, vividly expressed, for example, in the delight of anti-Masons with the cruelty of Masonic punishments."

LaHaye truly accepts this version of a militant Jesus, the conquering knight on a white horse Jesus, the triumphant and warrior-like Jesus. "Unfortunately, we've gone through a time when liberalism has so twisted the real meaning of Scripture that we've manufactured a loving, wimpy Jesus that he wouldn't even do anything in judgment," LaHaye said in an interview with CBS's *60 Minutes* in early 2004. "And that's not the God of the Bible. That's not the way Jesus reads in Scripture." Jenkins echoes these sentiments in the CBS interview, saying, "That stuff is straight out of the Bible. The idea of him slaying the enemy with the sword, that comes from *his* mouth, which is The Word, and the fact that the enemies' eyes melt in their heads, their tongues disintegrate, their flesh drops off, I didn't make that up. That's out of prophecy." Here Jenkins and LaHaye willfully confuse the words of Jesus with the words written in the Revelation, mixing them the convoluted theology constructed through premillennialist teaching over the last 150 years.[3]

Reverend Barbara Rossing, who teaches at the Lutheran School of Theology in Chicago, attempts to debunk many of the Darbian premillennialist ideas about Revelation that LaHaye supports in a book called *The Rapture Exposed*. Her argument is that LaHaye and others are marketing a "false view" of this militant Jesus, pieced together from a variety of references in the Bible. She and most other mainline Christians insist on Jesus as a "non-violent lamb" who conquers through his dying for sin, not through slaughtering nonbelievers. "They make this an us vs. them kind of theology," she said. "If you're not with us, you're against us."[4]

In many ways Carpathia's utopian global society is a mirror of the utopian global society premillennialsts yearn for. The stark difference is the utopian society premillennialists urge is not of this world, not in human hands, but one which is promised after the destruction of that human world, to be later rebuilt and presided over by the militant and vanquishing God-King Jesus. Rayford Steele's daughter Chloe remarks early in the book *Armageddon* that they are "less than a year to real freedom"—a remark that essentially says freedom or hope in freedom is not of this world. Fortunately for her, she doesn't have to wait a year—she is captured and killed by the end of the book. She eventually does make a cameo appearance later when all the Tribulation saints return with the warrior Jesus in the final book.

Before she is executed via guillotine, Chloe combines the Americanist myth with the premillennialist narrative, directly equating her execution with Jesus's crucifixion, quoting Patrick Henry's famous regret about "one life to give"—but calling him a martyr instead of a patriot—followed immediately by Jesus's "they know not what they do."

> Chloe turned to the people and spoke softly. "A famous martyr once said he regretted he had but one life to give. That is how I feel today. On the cross, dying for the sins of the world, my own Savior, Jesus the Christ, prayed, 'Father, forgive them, for they do not know what they do.'"[5]

On the following page is a reference to the words of Jim Elliot, a missionary executed by a tribe in South America in

1956 for trying to convert them, a construction which attempts to bind patriotism and religious martyrdom together with Jesus dying on the cross.

The treatment of Chloe's death hints at a problem for premillennialists and prophecy believers in general—America doesn't appear in the Bible. To get around this they often say, as pastor Bruce mentions in *Tribulation Force*, echoing the real life words of LaHaye, that America will be sidelined and not a player in End Times events. Yet wherever possible LaHaye draws on Americanist myth in crafting their narrative, and combine it, as in Chloe's execution, with the premillenial narrative.[6] Other than these neopremillennialists and Orthodox Jews, the only group that doesn't fall for Carpathia's plan for world domination in the Left Behind books is the American militia movement; this group appears prominently in the novel *Tribulation Force*. Part of this militia rebellion is portrayed as resistance to Carpathia's aim to disarming the whole world, cleaning up nuclear weapons and attempting to impose peace. Here, Carpathia explains to Buck the purpose of disarmament:

> "Millions have vanished. People are scared. They are tired of war, tired of bloodshed, tired of chaos. They need to know that peace is within our grasp. The response to my plan to disarm the world has been met with almost unanimous favor."
>
> "Not by the American militia movement."
>
> "Bless them," Carpathia said, smiling. "If we accomplish what I have proposed, do you really think a bunch of zealots running around in the woods wearing fatigues and shooting off popguns will be a threat to the global community? Buck, I am merely responding to the heartfelt wishes of the decent citizens of the world. Of course there will still be bad apples, and I would never forbid the news media to give them fair coverage, but I do this with the purest of motives."[7]

Before the battle with Carpathia, militia groups had started hording weapons. Later, even the president of the United States lends his support in the militia sneak attack on Washington, D.C. and New York; groups of English patriots attack London.[8] By the end of that book the militia movement is for the most part destroyed, leaving behind a network of premillennialist militia forces—the Tribulation Force—to take its place.

Taking in these fictional accounts, it is not surprising that in real life the LaHayes have been associated with militia movements. In 1990 the Coalition on Revival brought together American Family Association leader Don Wildmon and the LaHayes and their CNP and CWA connections, along with gun advocate Larry Pratt (also of the CNP). Pratt, besides advocating the dismantling of the IRS, the Federal Reserve, and the public school system, has been actively involved with the creation of militias. His book *Armed People Victorious*, which appeared also in 1990, had been attacked in the media for his support of "death squads" in countries like the Philippines and Guatemala (death squads he had termed liberators). Pratt argued later in 1994 that semiautomatic rifles should be widely available to every American in order to prevent such government actions as the 1993 Waco tragedy of the Branch Davidians and Ruby Ridge standoff against the white-supremacist Weaver family in Montana in 1992. After the Ruby Ridge stand-off ended in tragedy, Pratt was one of 160 "concerned Christian men" who gathered at Estes Park, Colorado, for a meeting organized by Christian Identity pastor Pete Peters, a meeting which some analysts of the radical-right call the "birth of the modern American militia movement."[9]

Just a day after the Oklahoma City bombing in 1995, Pratt, Peters, and leading members of the Christian Identity movement Timothy McVeigh embraced, met along with 550 others at the International Coalition of Covenant Congregations Conference in Branson, Missouri. An attendee told the militia magazine *Freedom Writer* that he saw "not one shred of sympathy" for what had happened in Oklahoma City.[10] The Christian Identity conspiracy theology is similar to much of the conspiracy narratives borrowed by premillennialists—a New World Order led by the United Nations and "international bankers"—coded references to international Jewry—will take over the world, and religious freedom will be the first thing to go when they do. The federal government, its efforts to regulate arms, and just about any form of federalism, is seen as the device that these evil forces will work through to gain power. Keeping and bearing arms is central to Christian Identity ideology, as is a virulent anti-Semitism and white supremacy based on the belief that white Christians are descendants of the "Ten Lost Tribes" of Israel, whom they believe settled in Northern Europe. Another version of this called British-Israelism, played heavily in Anglican support of relocating Jews to Israel in the early twentieth century; identifies Great Britain as the home of the "Ten Lost Tribes" of Israel, essentially identifying Anglo Saxons as "God's Chosen People" instead of the historic Jews. Ideas similar to this were supported as far back as the Puritans, who claimed to be spiritually descended from the ancient Israelites.

While there are only approximately fifty thousand followers of the Christian Identity ideology in the United States, and these certainly aren't widely held views within most fundamentalist communities, the crossover as well as connections between the leadership of these groups does show how some of the ideas commingle. Specifically, the connections revolve around the right to bear arms, and interestingly enough, abortion—which both factions militantly oppose. The Christian Identity–inspired *Field Manual of the Free Militia*, which circulates through many militia groups, argues that the Bible is the literal and unerring word of God and expounds on the idea of a militant Christ, a Christ who authorizes Christians to bear, as well as take up, arms against foes to these ideas.[11]

The "desire for a militant, virile Christianity also explains Moral Majority's hostility to gun-control legislation," writes Armstrong. "This too was part of their campaign to revive upright, potent, and combative manhood."[12] In addition to his militia connections, Pratt was also the President of English First, a lobby group founded by H. L. Bill Richardson and based in Sacramento, California, and Falls Church, Virginia, that attempted to push legislation to declare English as the official national language. Currently Pratt is also director of the Institute for Christian Economics, based in Winslow, Arizona—the president is Rushdoony disciple Gary North, formerly of the CNP and a leading proponent of Reconstructionism. The Institute for Christian Economics is a free-market educational nonprofit that promotes "Christian economic ethics" as well as an unstated healthy dose of conspiracy theory, Dispensationalism and Reconstructionism.[13]

Reconstructionism is also often called "Dominionism." Its purpose is to remake the laws of the United States into Biblical law, much in the same way fundamentalists in Islamic countries try to impose Islamic law on their governments. The eventual aim is a government and nation governed by biblical principles.[14] The main difference between LaHaye and the Reconstructionists, however, is that Reconstructionists tend to believe in postmillennialism as opposed to premillennialism. But while they may differ on specifics of dispensationalism, their political aims remain largely the same.

Martyrs and Renegades

Hofstadter, in writing about the paranoid style, makes this comment about the prevalence of the renegade throughout far-right narratives:

> In the spiritual wrestling match between good and evil which is the paranoid's archetypal model of the world, the renegade is living proof that all the conversions are not made by the wrong side. He brings with him the promise of redemption and victory.

The idea of the new Christian believers, post-Rapture, as martyrs and renegades is an underlying feature of the Left Behind books. There are many instances in the series where the "believers" refer to themselves as martyrs in their acts of violence committed against the global community, such as the one already mentioned about Chloe before she is executed. These renegades are the lone holdouts against the evil of the global system. Besides displaying a militant mentality, the believers form groups of militia-like units to combat the growing influence of the Antichrist global system. When asked a question about images of martyrs in the Left Behind series compared to the Islamic terrorists who attacked the U.S. on 9/11, Jenkins poses a muddy hypothesis in a chat room conversation at CNN.com. "Readers who are really familiar with our stories realize that there can be no comparison between the believers in Left Behind and these clearly misguided zealots who were behind these attacks."[15]

In the final pages of the first book, we see the Tribulation Force beginning to prepare, as martyrs, for all the tribulations to come before them. They declare a willingness to become martyrs in their fight against Carpathia and the Antichrist system of global government, to establish themselves as Christian soldiers. This martyrdom idea is further explored through the use of biblical references toward the end of *Tribulation Force*, an idea the newly devoted unit duly discuss and debate. Rayford ruminates on writings sent to him by his pastor, Bruce:

> Between Bruce and Chloe, Rayford found his answers about the fifth and seventh seals. It was not pleasant news, but he hadn't expected any different. The fifth seal referred to the martyrdom of Tribulation saints. In a secured mail package, Bruce sent to Chloe—who forwarded it on to Rayford—his careful study and explanation of the passage from Revelation which referred to that fifth seal.
>
> John sees under the altar the souls of those who had been slain for the Word of God and for the testimony which they held. They ask God how long it will be until he avenges their deaths. He gives them white robes and tells them that first some of their fellow servants and their brethren will also be martyred. So the fifth Seal Judgment costs people their lives who have become believers since the Rapture. That could include any one or all of us. I say before God, that I would count it as a privilege to give my life for my Savior and my God. [16]

These martyrdom ideas are reinforced again near the end of *Nicolae* when Rayford gives a sermon to the Tribulation Force on the Revelation, again based on Bruce's notes (Bruce has since died under mysterious circumstances, which we later find to be poison, again by the hand of Carpathia), asking the crew, "Would you give your life for the sake of the Gospel?" After this come shouts of "I will! I will!" filling the church. Ultimately, the martyrdom angle takes its most succinct form when the Mark of the Beast is proclaimed official policy by Carpathia in the book *The Mark*. Those refusing to take the mark of Satan are subject to beheading by guillotine, at first as a method to persuade the reluctant and eventually as standard procedure for any believer caught without a mark.[17]

In essence this convert or die philosophy is also the expressed opinion of the books toward nonbelievers. The unconverted will die through militia force or through the final slaying from the militant Jesus. What much of this language is saying is that what they fear the most—global domination of a secular "Antichrist" seeking to convert Christians to its way of thinking or death—is exactly what the Tribulation Force members would like to impose on anyone who does not follow their belief. Throughout the books, those not taking the "mark of the believer" are in effect persuaded to become believers through God's violent Tribulations let loose on the earth, just as those who do not take the Mark of the Beast are slaughtered for their position. Later when the patience of both Carpathia and this militant God grows weary, believers and nonbelievers alike are subject to destruction as standard procedure.

Through most of *Nicolae*, Rayford has fantasies of assassinating Carpathia, an act he later carries out but bungles.[17] In the sixth book, *Assassins*, he pleads with God to appoint him to be the trigger man to kill the Antichrist. Other Tribulation Force members share these assassination fantasies as well, but it is Rayford who eventually gets the chance to practice tyrannicide as advocated by LaHaye in the name of this militant Christ. In the latter half of *Assassins*, Rayford is increasingly fixated on the lavishly described super-gun he has gotten hold of, becoming something of a Holy Travis Bickle.

> Rayford set the block on the ground and turned the gun over and over in his hand. Heavy as it was, it had excellent balance and settled easily into his palm. He worried it might be difficult to hold steady due to the weight.
>
> "That mechanism," Albie said, "is found in no other handgun. Only in high-powered rifles. It does not cock. It is semiautomatic. You have to pull the trigger anew for each shot, but it will fire off a round as quickly as you can release the trigger and trip it again. It is probably the loudest handgun ever made, and I recommend something in the ear nearest the weapon. For now, just plug your ear with your other hand."
>
> "I don't see a safety."
>
> "There is none. You simply aim and fire. The rationale behind this piece is that you do not separate the block and produce it unless you intend to shoot it. You do not shoot it unless you intend to destroy what you are shooting. If you shoot at that rock enough times, you will destroy it. If you shoot a person in a kill zone from within two hundred feet, you will kill him. If you hit him in the neutral zone from that same distance, your

ammunition will sever skin, flesh, fat, tendon, ligament, muscle, and bone and will pass through the body leaving two holes. Provided you are at least ten feet away, the soft hollow-point shell has time to spread out due to the heat of the firing explosion and the centrifugal force caused by the spinning. Rifling grooves etched inside the barrel induce the spin. The projectile then will be roughly an inch and a half in diameter."[18]

At a great gathering near the Wailing Wall, Carpathia kills the two prophet characters Eli and Moishe, but they resurrect Christ-like three days later and are taken to heaven in a cloud. The faux-pope, Peter the Second, is also killed and the new church, Enigma Babylon, abolished. After another great earthquake, Carpathia is assassinated—by whom the reader doesn't know until book seven, and at least 150 pages into it. Rayford has fired his gun, but Chaim Rosenzweig, the Jewish scientist who has since converted to the side of the believers, is the real assassin. Rosenzweig fakes a stroke, which gives him the opportunity to be alone for a long time, a time in which he trains to be the killer of Carpathia.[19]

Gershom Gorenberg in his book *End of Days*, an examination of how fundamentalists in Christianity, Judaism, and Islam are vying for control of the Temple Mount in Jerusalem, makes some striking comparisons from his reading of the assassination scenes from the Left Behind books to more recent history of zealotry justifying assassination. "There's one Jew whose psychology [LaHaye] can subliminally make sense of," remarks Gorenberg. "Yigal Amir, the religious extremist who gunned down Yitzhak Rabin for the 'sin' of making peace." In a discussion early in the book *Indwelling*, Chloe and Tsion go to great lengths to justify the assassination of Carpathia after the deed has been done, a time when they think Rayford may have been the trigger man.

"I know, Tsion. But you have been a man of the Scripture your whole life. This is new to Daddy. I can't imagine him actually standing there and doing it, but I'm sure he wanted to. If he did, it sure answers a lot of questions about where he's been and what he's been doing. Oh, Tsion! How will he get away? That they say he's at large makes me wonder if it's not just a lie, a smear campaign to make him and you and us look bad? Maybe he's a scapegoat."

"We can only hope."

She dropped into a chair. "What if he's guilty? What is he's a murderer? There's no exception to God's law if the victim is the Antichrist, is there?"

Tsion shook his head. "None that I know of."

"Then mustn't he turn himself in? Suffer the consequences?"

"Slow down, Chloe. We know too little."

"But if he is guilty."

"My answer may surprise you."

"Surprise me."

"Off the top of my head, I believe we are at war. In the heat of battle, killing the enemy has never been considered murder."[20]

After being assassinated, Carpathia is eventually resurrected in Frankenstein fashion, and begins to display even more characteristics usually attributed to Satan. During this episode he even uses the same language Jesus used at his resurrection. Carpathia also echoes George W. Bush's "Axis of Evil" speech when, after his resurrection, he says, "Only he who is not with me is against me," which is somewhat disconcerting, considering the book was published in 2000, a full two years before that State of the Union speech.[21]

Midway through *The Remnant*, another Tribulation Force member, George Sebastian, threatens to torture a nonbeliever. Here a Global Community soldier festering with God-given boils from one of the Judgments, pleads with Sebastian to be careful (at the same time he is asking to be killed) with him because of his ailment. The soldier gets the empathetic response of having a Directed Energy Weapon aimed at him. As it heats up, while Sebastian says, "This is what cooks your flesh, and there's plenty more juice in it." This comes moments after the character Mac has suggested their radio code should be Psalm 94:1—though he doesn't say the verse. It goes like this: "O God, to whom vengeance belongs, shine forth." In the final book, Mac shoots a Global Community trooper in the back, muttering Christian and secular platitudes to himself, bringing the act of murder down to a few simple clichés—live by the sword, die by the sword and all's fair in love and war.[30]

MUSLIMS, CATHOLICS, AND JEWS
—OH MY!

"Babylon was the capital of Satanic activity and Jerusalem the city of God,"[1] writes LaHaye in his Pre-Trib Research center bulletin. "It is interesting that many of the elite power brokers of today think that the world should be divided into ten regions each with its own king under the authority of a United Nations type of government to bring 'peace' to this war weary world." LaHaye gets this information largely from the world of conspiracy, although here it is stated as fact and taken as fact by less than astute followers of foreign policy.

One of the main themes in the first few books of Left Behind is the U.N. falling under the rule of the "peacemaker" Nicolae Carpathia, who later changes the name of the international body to the Global Community and appoints ten former U.N. ministers as kings of ten regions of the world. A good deal of the recent Biblical prophecy frenzy surrounds the historic city of Babylon, the whore to Jerusalem's bride, and Saddam Hussein's efforts to rebuild the city where it once stood in ancient times. Often this frenzy plays into the unqualified support believers in the End Times theories of the premillennialists have given to attacking Iraq in both Gulf Wars. In the books, the Antichrist figure of Nicolae Carpathia, as secretary general of the United Nations and later the "Global Community," moves the global institution to a newly built New Babylon in the middle of Iraq.

"Leaders have always invoked God's blessing on their wars, and, in this respect, the Bush administration is simply carrying on a familiar tradition," says Paul S. Boyer. "But when our born-again president describes the nation's foreign policy objective in theological terms as a global struggle against 'evildoers,' and when, in his recent State of the Union address, he casts Saddam Hussein as a demonic, quasi-supernatural figure who could unleash 'a day of horror like none we have ever known,' he is not only playing upon our still raw memories of 9/11. He is also invoking a powerful and ancient apocalyptic vocabulary that for millions of prophecy believers conveys a specific and thrilling message of an approaching end—not just of Saddam, but of human history as we know it."[2]

Muslims

One of the staunchest proponents of premillennialism and LaHaye's Left Behind books is the Pre-Trib Research Center steering committee member Thomas Ice, author of *The Truth Behind Left Behind*. Ice runs the Pre Trib Research Center, which functions as a centrifuge for exchanges in premillennialist ideas and a clearing-house for their works.

In February 2001, Ice lauded Joan Peters's *From Time Immemorial: The Origins of the Arab-Jewish Conflict Over Palestine,* which in most of the world has been blasted as a farcical ruse, but in the United States still remains a source of backup for Christian Zionist beliefs. So it makes sense that Ice would call upon this book and give it his highest recommendation, when writing that "Arabs popularly known as *Palestinians"* don't, in reality, exist. Much of the Peters book also makes this claim, but fails to notice that there are in fact people living in Israel and West Bank and Gaza Strip, as well as scattered throughout the world, who really do exist and are known to most of the world as Palestinians (or, if they live in Israel proper, Arab Israelis).[3]

Ice writes with the conspiratorial tendency to discount all media other than their own as untrustworthy sources of information. "I want to demythologize a number of popular notions about the land of Israel, so that prophecy-loving believers may not be taken in by what they hear and see in today's media. Perhaps the most maddening term that I hear today is related to the term *Palestinian*." In constructing his argument Ice draws upon the Peters book; plugs the "newly produced" *Tim LaHaye*

Study Bible, which insists on always using "Israel" and never the term "Palestine"; calls the Oslo Peace accords foolish (as they did later with the road map under the Bush administration), and claims that a twelve-year-old Arab boy videotaped being killed and dying in his father's arms during the Temple Mount Intifada was killed by Arabs as part of a propaganda coup to dupe the world media. Ice also discounts the Muslim legend of Mohammed's Night Visit to the Temple Mount in Jerusalem, one of the central tenets of the Islamic faith, as "Arab lying." To back this claim he points to his own book *Ready to Rebuild,* co-authored with Pre-Trib member Randall Price.

In the fervor to push prophecy into reality, one of the pre-millennialists' avowed hopes is that the Jews will rebuild the temple on the Temple Mount, which they think will lead to Jesus' Second Coming. They are backing that with words and money. To get there, they have to first wrest control over the Temple Mount from Muslims. A group called the Temple Mount Foundation, which comprises members of LaHaye's Pre-Trib Research Center including Randall Price, has set its sights on this battle. Some of the best ways for them to get by the fact that Muslims are in control of that piece of land is to deny their existence or dehumanize them. "As believers in God and His Word, we should not be surprised that Satan and the world system is anti-Israel," Ice writes. "We should not be surprised that in spite of the justice of Israel's cause, the international media echoes Satan's voice instead of God's." Prior to this strategy of simply denying Palestinian existence, some apocalyptic narratives anticipated a much more bloody outcome. Hal Lindsey's 1996 novel *Blood Moon* foresees the genocide of the entire Arab world, through a preemptive nuclear attack by Israel, fearful after uncovering a plot to nuke Israel and all the sacred Muslim holy sites within it.[4]

David Cook, an expert on Islamic apocalyptic literature, argues that Christian millennialism is one of the roots for current Islamic millennial fundamentalism. This argument points specifically to works like Lindsey's book The Late Great Planet Earth, which pitted Islam against Christianity in a struggle of good versus evil. Islamic apocalyptic literature, Cook says, had been dormant for centuries until the perceived threat from Christian fundamentalist apocalyptic narratives became so prevalent. This has even led to Muslim writers mining the same prophetic books like Daniel, Ezekiel, and Revelation to craft their own versions, with themselves as the persecuted and ultimately triumphant. "In my view the reason why Muslim writers have used this Biblical [Christian] material is because of the fixation upon Israel and the Jews," Cook wrote.

> Biblical material gives them judgment, negative comments about the Jews' behavior (ascribed often to God), and read through a Christian interpretation, an end to the situation.
> After major setbacks or problems in the Arab world these books appear. For example, Safar al-Hawali's (a well-known Saudi radical) book The Day of Wrath (appearing after the beginning of the 2000 intifada) was a best seller and very influential. Books predicting the end of the United States or of Israel are often cited in even mainstream press.[5]

LaHaye and Falwell are on a similar wavelength to Ice on Muslims as well, discounting the mainstream faith of one billion, most of which doesn't follow the fundamentalist line of the Wahhabists or Al Qaeda, as most mainstream Christians don't follow the same time of premillennialist doctrine LaHaye does. "We should not be deceived by the well publicized belief in *Allah* as though the Muslim and Arab world truly believe in God," he writes. Like much of the language in the Left Behind novels, he blames religious tolerance and its murky postmodernism for the Western attitude toward the Muslim faith, and in absolutist terms proclaims there is only one true religion, Christianity.

Considering how central a role Israel and the Middle East play in the Left Behind novels, Arabs and Palestinians are hardly mentioned at all. This follows the strategy Ice has of ignoring them. When they are mentioned it is usually as terrorists: It is Muslims who attack the two prophets Eli and Moishe at the Wailing Wall. Their culture and history is predominantly brushed aside without much as a hint to its existence.[6] There are minor references to how some fundamentalist Muslims are holding out against the new world religion Enigma Babylon, but this occurs in the space of one paragraph. Furthermore there is little acknowledgement of the Islamic faith or what its tenets are at all. Despite the significance of the Temple Mount to Muslims, they appear to have simply have abandoned it to Jewish control in the books; one of Buck's journalist friends says, "Nothing's going to stand in the way of the Jews rebuilding their temple because no one but the Jews care." A reporter does later ask Carpathia what will happen to the Dome of the Rock, the Islamic Holy site on the Temple Mount—as it turns out, the Muslims have agreed to move the entire thing to New Babylon in Iraq, quite a task really, and one that puts them right in the Biblical womb of the whore.[7] Other charged statements put Iraq in the center of evil, referring to the Euphrates as symbolic of where Israel's enemies live and where the final sins of man will culminate, backing both neoconservative, premillennialist Christian, and hard-right Israeli agenda.[8] Eventually the Euphrates dries up so the forces of the Antichrist "in the East" can invade the Holy Land.

When the reader finally sees the appearance of a Muslim character, the man has converted from Islam and become "a believer," and taken the unlikely name Abdullah Smith. Buck, ever the culturally sensitive globetrotting journalist, just happens to wonder what this fellow did before he turned his life over to Christ—"Maybe he'd been a terrorist."[9] Abdullah relays a story in *Assassins* about how he became a Christian late in the game, after he had divorced his wife because she had become Christian a few years before he had come to the faith. "Imagine your wife taking up a religion from some mysterious, faraway country," he says.[10] Today, six percent of Jordan's population is Christian, which is not much, but it does belie the notion of Christianity as the "mysterious" religion of a "faraway country"—in fact next door is the birthplace of all monotheistic religions. The authors seem to be referring more to their Americanist brand of premillennial Protestantism as this "religion of a faraway country." By their disregard for all other denominations of Christianity, they seem to reflect only that extremist brand.

There are many reasons why the hope of a coming Final Battle did not die off as fast as other millennial flukes had after the year 2000. Dire news kept feeding the fire, largely due to the attacks on September 11, the continued conflict in the Holy Land, and the war in Iraq. Anticipation about the coming of an Antichrist, the return of Jesus or his Rapture of the believing church, the kindling being piled for the battle of Armageddon, wars, rumors of wars, and continued natural disasters throughout the world have all stoked the feeling of impending apocalypse among those keeping track. As millennialist movements grow off their narratives, so the ideology grows. Islamic apocalyptic narratives have been perpetuated by the resurgence of Christian apocalyptic narrative. Leading the way has long been the dominant Christian concept of a millennial reign, based on the older versions of a messiah promised to the Jews, and now fueling fundamentalist Islamic narratives as well. Consider this: if an Islamic fundamentalist author used the exact same story line as Left Behind and inserted Islamic characters instead of Christians, portraying a triumphant and avenging Mohammed returning to take back the Holy Land and slay all the nonbelievers and infidels in order to install a utopian era of Islamic rule, outrage would ensue across the United States. At the heart of it, this is what the Left Behind books describe: a triumphant and avenging Jesus returning to eradicate all nonbelievers and establish the millennial reign of Christianity over the entire world. At the center of this mass removal are those who premillennialists most often say they supports, Israeli Jews.

Anti-Semitism

A prominent aspect of dispensational premillennialism is its deeply rooted Christian anti-Semitism. Though most believers adamantly deny any presence of anti-Semitism in their ideology, it cannot be ignored that those who cry most loudly about loving Israel approach Jews only as players in a grand drama. It is a drama outlined in their prophecy, that eventually, they believe and ultimately pray for, will lead to the destruction of the Jews. At least the ones who don't convert to their form of Christianity—a group they repeatedly reference as being 144,000 converts. This displacement theology aims to pave the way for their Messiah to return to the Holy Land and reign over a millennium of Christian peace. This evident in the entire series of Left Behind novels.

The founding of Israel in 1948 and the taking of Jerusalem's Old City in the 1967 Six-Day War figure prominently in the chain of events for premillennialists, actions seen as starting the countdown clock toward Armageddon. But in order to get there, they believe the entire biblical Holy Land of greater Israel within God's grant to Abraham must be established, which according to Genesis 15:18 is everything from "the river of Egypt" (the Nile) to the Euphrates in Iraq. These are what commentators call Christian Zionists and their unwavering support of settlements in the West Bank and Gaza Strip has tied them inextricably to the most far-right elements and messianic movements within Israel. This linkage is central to why two-state solution is not acceptable to either the far-right in Israel or the far-right Christian community in the United States. An ever hopeful LaHaye, commenting on the length of the Israel-Arab dispute—"We think it will go on. Unfortunately, the hatred between Arabs and Jews is so intense and of such longstanding that is seems clear the Holy Land will be in a state of turmoil right up until Christ comes."

In that same interview with *Insight on the News*, a conservative news magazine owned by Rev. Sun Myung Moon's News World Communications, Jenkins says the two were "stunned at a *Time* magazine cover article speculating that evangelicals support Israel in the ongoing conflict because they think it has to be in Jewish control for Christ to return. I've been an evangelical all my life and I never heard that. In my mind, such statements reflect an attempt to make us look anti-Semitic. In effect it says, Christians will support Israel only because they have to, because they want Christ to return," he said.[11]

Jenkins's statement is true if one listens to mainline evangelical theologians, but the Left Behind books do not come from a mainstream evangelical position. In July 2002 nearly sixty mainline evangelical theologians wrote to President Bush to urge him to adopt an even-handed policy toward Israel and the Palestinians, support a two-state solution, and recognize the "degrading Israeli settlement movement" was involved in the "theft of Palestinian land." Yet, in all of LaHaye's narratives, it is Christian Zionism ideology that gets the most attention. Bishop Munib Younan of the Evangelical Lutheran Church wrote from his office in Jerusalem that "Christian Zionism is the enemy of Peace in the Middle East." Others have called the premillennialist version "heresy" and a "menace" to the region.[12]

Many followers of premillennialist Christian Zionism are spurred on to open their pocketbooks to fund settlers in the Occupied Territories in an effort to fulfill the prophetic vision of a Greater Israel, to rebuild the Third Temple, and to support mutually exploitive rightwing Israeli political parties at whatever cost. For example, between 2000 and 2001, Israeli rabbi Yechiel Eckstein raised around $15 million for his Jerusalem Friendship Fund from premillennialist Christian groups. His Jerusalem Prayer Team membership roster includes people like Jerry Falwell and John Ashcroft, who follow LaHaye's line of belief.[16] In the late 1990s, John Hagee's Cornerstone Church in San Antonio, Texas, gave a $1 million donation to Eckstein's organization to help settle Jews from the former Soviet Union in the disputed territories of Jerusalem and the West Bank. In the Denver suburb of Arvada, Colorado, members of the Faith Bible Chapel raise $100,000 a year on fruit basket sales to support the West Bank settlement of Ariel. Another group, American Christians for Jewish Immigration to Israel, raised $20 million in 2002 to settle Jews in the Occupied Territories.[13] In this battle over the Holy Land, hope has been debased into meaning that redemption will only come from destruction, a destruction brought by the fulfillment of prophecy.

Thus, in 2002, when President Bush began calling for Israel to curtail its military operations in the Jenin refugee camp, premillennialist Christian Zionists bombarded the White House with over one hundred thousand emails, a tactic long used by groups like the Lahaye's Concerned Women for America. After that outburst, Bush was quite reticent about any criticism of Israeli military actions against the Palestinians during that period. When the "road map to peace" began to be pushed by the Bush administration, House majority leader Tom DeLay flew to Israel and told Likud representatives in the Knesset not to worry about the plan, that it would never get the support of the Christian community.[13] LaHaye, Falwell, Robertson, and a number of other prominent members of the religious right issued an internet petition through their Religious Freedom Coalition called "The Bible is My Road Map" in order to rally support against the agreement.

So, if premillennialists support Israel, how can they be anti-Semitic? "I've often characterized the leaders of the religious right, for example, as being simultaneously pro-Israel and anti-Semitic," writes Randall Balmer at Slate.com.

> They favor Israel because they believe that the State of
> Israel will be a crucial player in the unfolding of the
> apocalyptic prophecies that LaHaye and Jenkins write
> about, and so people like Jerry Falwell and Pat
> Robertson are always advocating a pro-Israel foreign
> policy. At the same time, the only good Jew for most
> fundamentalists is a converted Jew. They refuse to rec-
> ognize Judaism on its own terms. Jews who have not
> converted, who have not recognized Jesus as messiah,
> are "incomplete Jews."[20]

There are also a number of problems with the way Israelis
and Jews are depicted in the Left Behind novels, especially Israeli
scientist Chaim Rosenzweig and later Tsion Ben-Judah, the
rabbi who converts to a premillennialist version of Christianity.
At times it is difficult to discern whether the authors are being
naïve in these depictions or transferring subconscious versions of
their own prejudices about Jews and Israelis. For example,
Rosenzweig creates a formula that makes Israel's deserts bloom
but does not allow any other nation in the world have access to
this. The authors, whether intentionally or unintentionally, leave
his reasoning for this ambiguity—whether it is greed behind his
hording of this secret or is it his nationalistic and racial pride the
reader never really finds out. The reader is treated however to
the caricature of "Jew-speak" and debating manner from a car-
toonish Rosenzweig and later Ben-Judah, with boisterous excla-
mation punctuated sentences and a halting style of ending sentences with a question mark.[15]

Gershom Gorenberg, an American-Israeli religion journalist who wrote the book *The End of Days: Fundamentalism and the
Struggle for the Temple Mount* talks of the jarring experience he
had reading the Left Behind books, which describe a Galilee
which didn't exist anymore and tour boats "plying" the river
Jordan—jarring for him because while he was reading *The Rise
of the Antichrist* he happened to be sitting right in the town of
Galilee, jarring because the current Jordan River is little more
than "a narrow trickle not fit for navigating." "I'm reading a
book set largely in the country where I live—but not really,
because the authors' Israel is a landscape for the imagination, and
the characters called 'Jews' might as well be named hobbits and
warlocks," he writes. It is the land of imagination and Christian

myth, so far removed from the reality of Israelis and modern-day Jews. Yet, in myth there is often power, and as he warns, the apocalyptic vision portrayed by LaHaye "misdirects the relationship between real-life Jews and born-again Christians, and in the worst case could bend the future of the Middle East."[16]

Through Tsion, the authors of the Left Behind novels also attempt to link Israel and the United States in this circular logic of American myths and Israel's place in prophecy, using the terms "sacred duty," "calling," "history," and "country," they describe how both nations, Israel and the United States, are connected in their Manifest Destiny. It is at this point in *The Mark* that Tsion is trying to convince Rosenzweig that he should become a "new Moses," delivering the new Christianized Jews into the millennial kingdom of Christ. The Trib Force members later create a robe that will make him look more Moses-like for his return to Jerusalem.[17]

"God has given us in the Bible an accurate history of the world, much of it written in advance," says Tsion Ben-Judah in *The Remnant*. "It is the only truly accurate history ever written."[18] In *Armageddon*, one finds that after the Babylonish physical world is destroyed, Jerusalem will be the Messiah's world capital, the premillennialists' fetishized bride. Of course the rest of the world seems pretty useless now that God has destroyed it—a nuked world, ravaged by countless earthquakes, rivers and seas full of blood sounds much more hellish than heavenly. Would He really want it after selfishly ripping it apart in order to "persuade" people to believe in Him? Who would? The authors get by this simply through the way they get by anything—making a miracle happen. A final earthquake swallows up the hundreds of thousands of bloodied bodies rotting like raisins in the sun, sanitizing the destruction, erasing the residue of war.

One of the deepest antipathies toward Jews through the ages derives from their denial of Jesus Christ as the Messiah, or from the Islamic end, Muhammad as the true prophet springing from the line of Abraham, thereby making Jews the central players in the fantastical prophetic drama of each group, much to Jewish dismay.[19] After the Rapture occurs in the first Left Behind book, the authors allude to a meeting in Manhattan called by a Jewish Nationalist conference that is behind a "new world order government." The New World Order government is looking to rebuild the Jewish Temple in Jerusalem and reaching out to interfaith groups in order to get support for their plan. On the next page, the authors easily turn to talk of "international monetarists" and the United Nations. Much of this is similar to the disturbing *Protocols of the Elders of Zion*—propaganda used by anti-Semitic groups in the Christian and Muslim world to construct an elaborate conspiracy around a Jewish plot to take over the world.

At one point, Buck Williams happens to comment that "the Israelis hate Jesus," which kind of pops out of his mouth without all that much consideration over what that "hate" actually is, as well as insinuating that all Israelis are Jews (believing or otherwise). This is uttered in the context of the book to be something nearly as cliché as "the Lord works in mysterious ways." It's a very odd thing for an Ivy League graduate and an international journalist of his stature to say. When that type of remark comes out of a cardboard character like Williams, and then on the next page the authors remark about secret meetings and "international bankers," it tends to take on the larger context of reinforcing anti-Semitic generalizations.[20] Following this are the same old notions of one world conspiracy theories and shadowy references to "the power behind the power," which built upon the veiled *Protocols of Zion*–type references, charges these messages with a distinct anti-Semitic quality. Buck, in *Soul Harvest*, when talking to Tsion lets loose another bit of nativist bigotry: "You're a recognizable guy, even in Israel where everybody your age looks like you."

Drawing further on old-time conspiracy, the authors bring in the names of Joe Kennedy and the Rockefellers as reminiscent of the "power behind the power," which is embodied by the international banker character Jonathan Stonagal (who has the backing of "an international brotherhood of financial wizards"). These are names long intertwined with paranoid theories about Catholic and Jewish power cabals.

> "It still smells major to me," Buck said. "Rozenzweig was high on this guy, and he's an astute observer. Now Carpathia's coming to speak at the U.N. What next?"
> "You forget he was coming to the U.N. before he became president of Romania."
> "That's another puzzle. He was a nobody."

"He's a new name in disarmament. He gets his sea-
son in the sun, his fifteen minutes of fame. Trust me,
you're not going to hear of him again.
"Stonagal had to be behind the U.N. gig, too," Buck
said. "You know Diamond John is a personal friend of
our ambassador."
"Stonagal is a personal friend of every elected official from the president to the mayors of most medium-
sized cities, Buck. So what? He knows how to play the
game. He reminds me of old Joe Kennedy or one of the
Rockefellers, all right? What's your point?"
"Just that Carpathia is speaking at the U.N. on
Stonagal's influence."[21]

Both men have previously been rumored to be associated
with the Antichrist in their own times. Joe's son John F. Kennedy
for his 666 votes at the 1956 Democratic Convention and his
being shot in the head (a reference to Revelation 13:1–3 where
one of the seven heads of "the beast" seemed "to have received a
death blow"), and David Rockefeller, co-founder of the Trilateral
Commission in the 1970s (a group which prophecy watchers suspected as a shadowy organization bent on world domination).[22] A
page after mentioning these names, between references to
Orthodox Jews wanting to rebuild the temple and international
monetarists setting up one world currency, Buck complains to his
boss that he's "being overrun by Jews."

"You are short on sleep, aren't you, Buck? This is why
I'm still your boss. Don't you get it? Yes, I want coordi-
nation and I want a well-written piece. But think about
it. This gives you automatic entrée to all these digni-
taries. We're talking Jewish Nationalist leaders interested in one world government—"
"Unlikely and hardly compelling."
"Orthodox Jews from all over the world looking at
rebuilding the temple, or some such—"
"I'm being overrun by Jews."
"—international monetarists setting the stage for
one world currency—"[23]

Returning to the premillennialist fascination with the conversion of Jews to Christianity, the figure of Rabbi Tsion Ben-
Judah appears in the book *Tribulation Force* to proclaim this good
news to Jews over worldwide television. After three years of

study he has found that the Messiah predicted by the Scriptures is in fact Jesus, that the Rapture has occurred, and that the legitimate study of Bible prophecy could only lead to Jesus as the Messiah. The bumbling Jewish scientist Rosenzweig is referred to as a "pawn in an end of the world chess game" by the Tribulation Force, although they later befriend him to fight against Carpathia. In the meantime, Orthodox Jews left and right throw off thousands of years of religious culture to become converts to Christianity, mirroring groups today like Jews for Jesus, an outreach group meant to convert Jews to Christianty. Buck, in describing Ben-Judah, says, "He's Orthodox" then qualifies it with "but he knows the New Testament, at least intellectually."[24] From studying the character of Tsion Ben-Judah though, it doesn't seem he knows much of the New Testament other than the Revelation and a few well placed quotes from the Gospels. Everything else is brushed aside. Later Rosenzweig says that the "religious zealots" in Israel "hate a person who believes that Jesus is Messiah." Cleverly the authors have a secular Jew saying this instead of one of the Tribulation Force.[25] Toward the end of the series, Rosenzweig wonders how he had ever been so blind to the faith that now buttresses him, claiming "I was too intellectual," thereby equating intellect with a lack of faith.

In *Nicolae*, the Third Temple in Jerusalem has been rebuilt, "illuminated magnificently and [looking] like a three-dimensional picture show."[26] This image is striking because in the real world, Christian Zionists—such as those who run the Temple Mount Foundation—have been creating models to show off what they believe the end result should look like.

At this point, Carpathia has also made a pact of peace with Israel to protect it from its enemies, providing years of peace Israel has never seen. Peace for Israel, through the Antichrist, means, in evangelical eschatology, eventual destruction and the resturn of Christ. At the beginning of book five, *Apollyon*, tens of thousands of Jews have converted to Christianity (Israel is described, rat-like, as "crawling with" them) and "tens of thousands of clandestine house churches" have sprung up to form communes and a separatist underground economic system fueled by Tsion's sermons and Buck's *The Truth* magazine via the Internet. How they reach millions of people across the world by using only English is also a miracle. Tsion, instead of "speaking in tongues" begins to type in tongues. Finally, in *Glorious Appearing*, the premillennialist fantasy of a mass conversion of Jews takes place.[27]

While premillennialist Christian Zionists often embrace Israelis with moral and monetary support, behind their backs they hold sharp knives. In many ways, this belief system is similar to Islamic fundamentalism preached by Saudi Wahabbists and political-Islam radicals who have hijacked that faith with their absolutist vision. For these premillennialist "believers," the barriers between religion and political activism have eroded somewhere between their destructive beliefs for the future and their psychotic readings of the past into a hijacking within the U.S. Among the prophetic fantasies of the Left Behind novels, none are as prominent than the characters Eli and Moishe, who appear at the Wailing Wall in Jerusalem preaching in archaic faux-Biblese and attempt to convert Jews to Christianity. These take on sinister tones considering some of the real and present political issues surrounding the Wailing Wall, and the Temple Mount and Jerusalem in particular. In part, this is due to the dispute about who has dominion over the Temple Mount, which rages between orthodox Muslims and Jews. In this instance—the authors allude to how "the Orthodox Jews are in an uproar" over the appearance of these two prophets.[28] The old Revelation number 144,000 pops up again as the number of Jews to be converted, to premillennialists post-Rapture, in order to push prophecy and bring about the Second Coming, and along with it the Millennial Reign of Christ. A problem with this is that there are laws against overt proselytizing by Christians of Jews in Israel. An Israeli 1977 anti-proselytizing law prohibits people from giving or receiving material benefits from conversion, though reports about enforcement of these laws are few.[29]

As all this is happening in the books, Bruce Barnes goes through flip charts and sermons of his former pastor to explain just what is to lie in store for the Tribulation Force—seven years of extremely violent depopulation of the earth through a variety of terrible judgments, which the premillennialists lift from Revelation and set in the current era. Describing the bleak future that awaits, Barnes seems nonchalant about the whole ordeal, about the millions upon millions killed in the earthquakes and floods; by meteorites and man eating locusts; and those armies of ghost horsemen who slaughter a third of the world's population. The authors often use the word "clear"—as in "to make clear" and "becoming clear" and "Scripture was clear" and "it was clear that the new world order was the enemy of God"—through these passages to reinforce the already apparent message they have constructed out of the Revelation. Barnes reassures the Tribulation Force about where their allegiance lies, referring to the two prophets at the Wailing Wall: "We're on their side. We have to do our parts"—though like much of the novel, he remains vague about what that allegiance really means.[30]

Not appreciating that the Wailing Wall has been taken over by the two prophets, a couple of Orthodox Jews, described in the books as zealots "wearing long, hooded robes and [being] bearded," attack the prophets with an Uzi and a long knife but die mysteriously before reaching their target. Carpathia, embarrassed by the media attention on the two witnesses at the Wailing Wall (though he owns all the media), reenacts what seems to be the Jesus-Barabas-Pilate scene from the Bible by asking the crowd that has gathered around the Temple Mount what they want to do with the two. Toward the beginning of book five, he orders them to be shot on sight.[31]

In *Glorious Appearing*, the character of Chaim Rosenzweig, a former secular Jew and now "believing Jew"—a new convert from Judaism to Christianity—reinforces the power of the premillennialist line about the "at any time" imminent return toward the closing of the Tribulation: "God has his own economy of time. Do I believe Messiah will return today? Yes. Will it trouble me if he does not return until tomorrow? No. My faith will not be shaken. But I expect him soon."[32]

As Jews and Christians are now one and the same through the miraculous changing of names to "believing Jews," Carpathia's orders of pogroms and death to any Jew in the world essentially creates a mixed message. It is never fully explained in the series of books how or why Carpathia has become an anti-Semite, it is simply understood that this is the case. There is a segment here where Carpathia's forces are rounding up Jews and Chinese Muslims in Zhengzhou, China. The Christians, who had come to convert the Jews and Muslims before they were massacred, tell them reassuringly: "Resist the temptation to choose the guillotine without choosing Christ the Messiah."[33]

Despite the explicit disavowal of anti-Semitism, LaHaye has made odd comments about Jews in the past, saying to journalist Jeffrey Goldberg in an article at Slate.com that "some of the greatest evil in the history of the world was concocted by the Jewish mind," and that "Sigmund Freud, Marx, these were Jewish minds infected with atheism." Goldberg, unsure of what LaHaye was getting at, asked him to tell more about the Jewish mind. "The Jewish brain also the capacity for great good," said LaHaye. "God gave the Jews great intelligence. He didn't give them great size or physical power—you don't see too many Jews in the NFL—but he gave them great minds."[34]

Eugenicist and CNP member Ernest Van Den Haag has also written about "the Jewish mind" in such terms—his book *The Jewish Mystique* has been used by white supremacist publications like *The Christian Vanguard* for years. In the June 1972 issue of that magazine, an excerpt of Van Den Haag's book is prominently displayed below the title "Are Jews Smarter Than Other People?" In the 1970s the *Christian Vanguard* regularly published articles defending the *Protocols of Zion*; calling Jews "the Christ Haters," as well as claiming they were not "the real Jews" at all and that Jesus was never a Jew; frequently painting John F. Kennedy and Martin Luther King Jr. as Communist agents; claiming 75 percent of the LSD in the United States was shipped from Israel; and insisting that the social unrest of the "Negro power" was inspired by Jewish agents of Communist conspiracy.[35]

Anti-Catholic

Early in the series the authors refer to Carpathia (readers already have a clear idea that he is supposed to be the Antichrist), as having the popularity of Lech Walesa and Mikhail Gorbachev one a Catholic socialist and the other an atheistic Russian Communist who many premillennialists once thought could be the Antichrist because of the birthmark on his head, a supposed "Mark of the Beast." (These references are probably lost on the average reader, but for prophecy and conspiracy buffs, they certainly hit their mark. One example is the 1988 book *Gorbachev! Has the Real Antichrist Come?* by Robert Faid.)

Toward the end of Chapter nineteen in the first book, Buck wonders if Carpathia could be another Lincoln, Roosevelt, "or the embodiment of Camelot that Kennedy appeared to some."[36]

To most this statement looks insignificant. But considering the history of Protestant fundamentalist support of racism and segregation in the South, the large architecture of far-right conspiracy built around Roosevelt and his New Deal, and the anti-Catholicism aimed at Kennedy by the predecessors of the authors, the statement takes on a more sinister air, especially considering two of these men were assassinated. Similar to the muted anti-Semitism noted above, the anti-Catholicism functions below the surface of most of these novels, a backdrop of assumptions, stereotypes, and sometimes outright bold bigotry.

The advent of the printing press in the 1450s and the first mass produced scriptures written in local languages—not simply the Latin of the Roman Catholic Church—led to widespread individual interpretations of the Bible. The Protestant Reformation in the sixteenth century and its insistence on decentralized power over the Word of God and orthodoxy facilitated the development of millennialism as well as its cyclical rise and fall. The decentralization of the Word of God into the common languages of the people opened the field to wide interpretation of the Bible, one of those being millennial interpretation. By applying biblical prophecies to events in their own ages, many Protestants had discovered how useful and galvanizing the ideas of an imminent return were to spreading their brand of Christianity.

Interfaith denomination outreach and their ecumenical ways have long been a bane to hardcore fundamentalists, who feel they erode their literal teachings and corner on belief. They have long been intertwined into the conspiracy narratives constructed by premillennialists who felt liberal denominations were infested with communists and secular humanists, using ecumenical impulses to undermine the truth about God and salvation. The Left Behind novels use this narrative as one of the central themes in the push for a "one world religion."[37]

This leads to one of the premillennialists and LaHaye's major arguments with the Roman Catholic Church. From AD 325, when the early Church started to abandon the idea of Christ returning any time soon, until Martin Luther's Reformation, LaHaye believes the Catholic Church had been "corrupted" by St. Augustine's adoption of Greek philosophy and interpretation of literature—and thus the Bible as allegorical and metaphorical.

One of the reasons St. Augustine opposed the literal reading of Revelation was because it heralded the imminent return of Christ and thereby inspired religious fanaticism. This amillennialism, or abandonment of the immediacy of Christ's return, according to LaHaye, led to the Dark Ages when Church hierarchy took over and left the common man out in the mud to shake his head in wonder at all that Latin gibberish. Thankfully, LaHaye says, closet evangelicals and heretics from the early Church kept the idea of Rapture alive and didn't fall for the Church in Rome, the domination of the Pope, the pagan idolatry and Greek humanism.[38]

In *Tribulation Force* the reader learns that the new Pope, who took over the Catholic Church a few months before the events in the books happen, had been among those Raptured. It is also discovered that he apparently had embraced the "heresy of Martin Luther," converting to a form of premillennialist Protestantism. A minority of Catholics appear to have been Raptured as well, although most were left behind. The future Pope and eventual leader of a worldwide ecumenical church, Cardinal Peter Matthews of Cincinnati, explains this by saying that those "opposed to Orthodox teaching of the Mother Church were winnowed out from among us." The reader learns all this as Buck is interviewing Cardinal Matthews for a story he is writing on the "disappearances" for *Global Weekly*. In that interview, Buck uses his newfound premillennialist fundamentalism to query Matthews about the "faith" versus "good works" argument, quoting a single passage from Ephesians (2:8–9) to dismiss the Catholic position on "good works"—something reiterated throughout the series—and assert that Christians are not saved through good works but grace and faith.[39]

But there is an important paradox represented in the anti–good works argument—what happened to all these people who thought they were performing good works and died before the Rapture? Did they go to heaven or not? One character, Floyd, hints why the authors use the fundamentalist sectarian line about good works when talking about his own conversion. He's talking about how his wife had used to say good works wouldn't get him into heaven, and that if Jesus returned *before* he died to Rapture "his Church," he'd be left behind. In this line of reasoning, anyone who didn't believe in the born again style of

Christianity was doomed to hell or doomed to Tribulation until they convert to the fundamentalist line.[40]

Buck then writes the story about Matthews and editorializes it through his new premillennialist lens. A favorite scene is where the authors have Cardinal Matthews—it is already taken for-granted he'll become the next Pope—offering Buck champagne during a flight, sometime around six in the morning.

Pages later, when the Catholic Church with Matthews at the head starts down the road of one world religion, these small pre-occupations take on much larger significance. Whenever the mainline Christian argument surfaces that the Revelation is to be taking symbolically and metaphorically, it is always from the mouth of the Catholic representative Matthews, who by this point is already saddled with the evil shroud of one-worldism through his Enigma Babylon Church—a religion which is no longer Catholic but a pseudo New-Age manifestation of the liberal aspects of all religions.[41]

When Cardinal Peter Matthews becomes the new pope, and later the head of Enigma Babylon he claims the title Pontifex Maximus Peter Matthews Supreme Pontiff of Enigma Babylon One World Faith. This starts the treadmill for what looks like an endless inside premillennialist joke as various people serving under Carpathia assume spectacular titles and insist on everyone using those titles: potentate, minister, supreme commander, etc. A lot of this starts to snowball after Carpathia apparently raises one of his assistants, Leon Fortunato, from the dead and starts entertaining thoughts that he could possibly be the Messiah. After that the fixation on how characters like Carpathia and Fortunato have to be addressed goes on and on with a somewhat silly, though populist, anti-Catholic, and anti-elitist, purpose. The Pontifex Maximus Peter Matthews Supreme Pontif insists on being called "Peter the Second" and eventually shrouds himself in absurd garments, overly absurd even for the Pope-bashing overtones of the series.[42]

Other Kinds of Racism

In Left Behind, other faiths are also simplified into either an after-school-special quality of just a few words of jargon. Hindu belief, for example, is just a matter of good karma or bad karma. Here Carpathia, talking to Buck, says: "By committing suicide and killing Todd-Cothran in the process, my old friend Jonathan Stonagal took care of the problems we both had. That is good karma, if I understand my Eastern friends."[43]

With the introduction of Hannah Palemoon, the reader also gets a token Native American character, who in describing the stereotypes people often perceive about Native Americans, is fundamentally stereotyped herself by the authors. Beyond these descriptions, only a cardboard character exists. Chapter thirteen of *The Mark* Palemoon describes her conversion to another character, as well as misconceptions about Native Americans. "Now it's Indian this, Indian that. Indian tribes. Cowboys and Indians. Indian nation. Indian reservation. The Indian problem. American Indians—that's my favorite. And of course, anyone who hadn't visited the reservation assumed we lived in tepees," says Palemoon. A page later she remarks, showing pictures of where she lived: "The pictures are from the tourist sites. They want to see old Native American culture; we're happy to show it. Dress in the old garb, dance the old dances, sell 'em anything they want made of colorful beads." In bringing in these token characters the authors attempt to be inclusive, but really just reinforce the caricatures of these minorities.

The only real acknowledgement of Asians up until late in the series is a brief mentioning of Chinese food.[44] One of the main reasons for the Asain absence is because at the time John was writing the Revelation, China and Asia were so distant they could have been on the moon. The media eventually gets a couple of stock stereotypical Chinese characters with names like Ming Toy and Chang Wong, the woman-girl, a cold hearted prison guard, the man-boy an over-achieving technology genius. They too eventually come under the sway of the Tribulation Force and become more real to a greater degree than other characters not endowed with the premillennialist belief system.

Another aspect that deserves serious consideration is the treatment of race within the Left Behind series and in the Christian right as a whole. While attempting to achieve race reconciliation over the last decade through faith—and groups such as the Christian Coalition have active in promoting themselves as colorblind—structural racism and discrimination has been largely overlooked.

"In order to enlist the loyalty of people of color," writes Andrea Smith, a Cherokee and co-founder of Women of Color Against Violence,

> the Christian Right transfers the label of "oppressed" from people of color to the Christian right itself. Ralph Reed is particularly adept at appropriating oppression language, with such chapter titles as "To the Back of the Bus: The Marginalization of Religion" in his After the Revolution. He argues, "Evangelical whites are the new marginalized community, those likely to be reviled for our political activism." This appropriation neutralizes the definition of "oppression" to mean being forced to live in a society where not everyone agrees with you. The Christian right cannot make any convincing argument that evangelicals are victimized by hate crimes, are forced to live near toxic waste dumps and uranium mines, or are systematically denied occupational and educational opportunities."[63]

CONCLUSION

Around the age of ten, about 1984, I often had the feeling of dread that nuclear apocalypse would strike at any moment. My town, I'd found out, was among the top ten cities to be struck first by the Soviets because of an U.S. Army armory located there on an island in the middle of the Mississippi River—the Rock Island Arsenal. I vaguely knew that high precision firing mechanisms were made there, along with tank turrets and other parts important to the American military machine. For this reason, among others, I developed an acute sense of doom about this eventual catastrophic occurrence. For me this meant a fascination and interest in military matters far beyond G.I. Joe and into the realm of survivalism and even studying how to survive a nuclear winter. For hours I would draw intricate pictures of underground bunkers, much like the tunnels used by the Vietcong in Vietnam, but also with rooms for schools, hospitals, barracks, parking for tanks, silos for missiles—something I shudder at thinking about now. I would browse through books about the military and weaponry for long hours when I should have been outside enjoying the fresh air (which could have been my last!). On long trips with my parents I would sometimes find myself staring out the window and wondering where a mushroom cloud would appear. I often wonder why I was burdened with a sensitivity toward this apocalypse when others of my age around me didn't seem, or at least didn't let on, to harboring the same fears and fascinations. I later brushed this off as cold war paranoia manifested in my growing little mind, and as puberty hit, largely forgot about most of these private terrors. Still, the melancholy of these thoughts touched me deeply, and I believe it is still with me today. From my reading of the Left Behind series these psychic cold war fears are similar to those formed by concepts such as the Rapture and the theology contained in these books. This "mind siege" as LaHaye calls it, is perhaps better described as "psychic terrorism"—especially when marketed toward children.

But then, while reading the adult version of Left Behind series, I sometimes couldn't help but wonder if Jerry B. Jenkins was perhaps one of the most brilliant satirical writers alive. If someone were to write a satire of the beliefs of dispensational premillennialism, they would be hard pressed to render it better than the current series.

The Left Behind books, much like Roland Emmerich's 1996 alien apocalypse movie *Independence Day*, if viewed as satire, are much more entertaining. However, Emmerich's 2004 environmental apocalypse movie *The Day After Tomorrow* was less tongue-in-cheek, though so equally absurd in its dire predictions that NASA scientists denied requests to consult on the film. In many ways, far-left visions of apocalypse are as politically expedient as their rightwing brethren. In this case, however, environmental catastrophe is physically more pertinent than premillennial apocalypse, though the use of such efforts in bringing attention to global warming and environmental degradation cheapens the science and does much to spread the seeds of hopelessness, fear, and anger in the same way premillennial apocalyptic visions cheapen religious belief and lead to fear and despair. No, neither of these examples are satire. They are much more serious than that.

A similarly named movie in the 1980s called *The Day After* painted a vision of apocalyptic nuclear holocaust after a cold war exchange between the U.S.S.R. and the U.S.; it was a film often blasted by rightwing critics for being a propaganda tool for leftwing pacifists. According to Victor Goodpasture, former president of the rightwing group Young Americans for Freedom in Lawrence, Kansas (the town fictionally obliterated by a mushroom cloud in the first scenes of the film), *The Day After* was merely another "left-wing political maneuver that failed."[1] Yet

from the rightwing came movies like *Red Dawn*, which predicted a surprise Soviet invasion (without the use of nuclear
weapons) directly into the heart of America, the small town of
Carbondale, Colorado. What I remember is that *The Day After*
probably gave me more nightmares and contributed to a feeling
of nihilistic hopelessness during my childhood than any other
film I'd seen. On the opposite end *Red Dawn* had the affect of
increasing and early interest in paranoid survivalism, commando
tactics, and other means to battle the Communist foe.

Looking back, I wish someone would have made me watch
Dr. Strangelove much sooner than I did come to it. Far from being
amusing, belief in imminent Rapture can have a profound psychological affect on those who adhere to their doctrines, especially children. From reading the Left Behind series, watching the
movies, and researching the premillennialists, after seeing the
influence the ideology had on my landlord David, I can't help but
wonder what the psychological impact vision of the world has on
children exposed to it.

One way to judge a cultural movement is by the art it produces. So far all one sees from this one are paranoia-based mass-
market thriller novels and soulless Christian rock music. This
may be because art is not as large a concern to them as is using
"the Word" as an instrument of evangelism. It is also so prominent largely because major publishers, Christian and secular,
tend to rely on marketing gadgets and celebrity names instead of
looking intrinsic artistic worth. Such is the case with "brand
LaHaye" and his co-writer Jerry Jenkins. Turning LaHaye loose
to write his own work of fiction based on his interpretation of the
Revelation would likely have been a disaster. Instead, by water-
ing it down with Jenkins's writing, Tyndale House was able to
present a slightly more tolerant face to LaHaye's usual divisive
rhetoric. In 1993, journalist Edward Plowman, a longtime writer
for Christian publications, derided Christian publishing as "grist
for ghosts, grinding away for people long on reputation but short
on time, self-discipline, or writing ability."[2] Mainly this criticism
has to do with the type of writing, which relies on ghostwriters,
and in its hunt for biblical literalism and political expediency, has
ignored powerful works of allegorical and mystical Christian
spirituality. Writers like C. S. Lewis and J.R.R. Tolkien come to
mind in this area, writers with deep Christian beliefs who used

those beliefs to create great works of fiction in the past century. The major difference was that these were created with artistic intentions; the purpose of the Left Behind books is not art, or even entertainment, but seems to be simply proselytizing and propagandaCompared to these great works, the Left Behind series is a hollow, hateful, and spiritually corrupt attempt at mass-marketing conspiracy and fear—and in this they succeed very well.

There is other contemporary art, a sort of paranoid neo-Americana surrounding the Rapture, besides novels and music. Bumper stickers proclaiming "In case of Rapture, this car will be driverless" are now countered by the humor of other bumper stickers asking "In case of Rapture, can I have your car?" In houses of some Rapture believers in the Bible Belt there are paintings showing scenes of disappearance or post-Rapture horror felt by those left behind, looking to the sky to find where their loved ones have gone.

Roman Catholic and mainline Protestant interest in Revelation has traditionally been expressed through high art, comments Bob Hodgson of the Institute for Biblical Scholarship at the American Bible College. Stained glass windows, paintings, allegorical and mystical poetry have all been depicted with Catholic renderings of the Revelation. Historical critical methods of literary interpretation, not systematic theology, have defined the Apocalypse in Catholicism for centuries. "It's a complicated process," says William Pottier, a theologian at Mount St. Mary's University in Emmitsburg, Maryland. "Opposed to looking at it as a kind of code you need to crack, which is how prophecy people read it."[3]

It is perhaps unfortunate that Revelation is the last and final book of the Bible. The complex scaffolding Left Behind builds around a singular interpretation of this badly placed book, wrapped with paranoia and fear more appropriate for an issue of the cold war–era "Red Menace" rag *Christian Crusade* than the present day, isn't an innocuous phenomenon. Those believing in the premillennialist interpretation of the Revelation have, for one striking example, parted with large sums of money for such ventures as adopting settlements in the Israeli-controlled but disputed West Bank, thinking they are helping fulfill prophecy, when in reality they are helping to scuttle any hope of peace and a two-state system for Palestinians and Israelis. Those looking toward a warm and fuzzily destructive apocalypse, while harboring naïve views of a mythical American exceptionalism free from moral corruption, tends to choke out any sense of the present reality in regards to the actual people they may be affecting in places like Israel. Because of a warped reading of history, combined with a yearning for the realization of apocalyptic "imminent future events," there is a great disconnect from any reality unless it conforms with a delusional worldview constructed on a complex framework of interpretation of prophetic biblical passages. Interpretation is a key word here.

LaHaye and other writers of premillennialist fiction and nonfiction would like readers to believe their writings are simply based on what is literally written in biblical prophecy, that current events mirror scriptures written millennia ago, that the current Israel and Iraq confrontations can be read like a news ticker slowly scrolling across the pages of the Bible. Meanwhile, these philosophies can lead believers to ignore pressing social and moral issues closer to home such as poverty, environmental degradation, racial inequality, or inadequate public education due largely to an absence of hope in the earthly reality of life and a grand hope for mass eternal salvation in death. It is also this type of disconnect which could lead more militant believers to act when history fails to match the insular pinball world of prophecy literature interpretations, pulpit jeremiads, and the promises made by premillennialist spokesmen in evangelical radio and television empire.

Like many prominent conservatives over the last thirty years, LaHaye has been on the forefront of promoting theories that the ACLU, the NEA, and the "thousands of other liberal organizations are out to destroy the Biblical principles this country was founded on and replace them with freedom from responsibility." Essentially, support for any of the above named organizations, retaining the separation of church and state, or religious liberty in general and freedom from proselytization makes you LaHaye's enemy and an enemy of his view of America, an idyllic land of biblical principles he believes once existed and should be returned to that heavenly state.

The aim is theocracy, not democracy, and one that blindly ignores the natural cultural evolution over the last century. Of course socialist and Marxist ideas have been introduced into the American culture, as they have all over the world, there is no denial of that. The delusional belief LaHaye has, and others on the far-right over the past half-century have had, is that this injection of ideas was part of a mysterious communist and social-ist conspiracy. They do not take into account that these are part of the natural exchange, transformation, construction, and deconstruction that comes from the free dissemination of ideas, an exchange that a democracy embraces through free speech and the free market of ideas. Nor do they take into account the vast demographic changes that have occurred in America since their "land of Biblical principles" was founded—namely the emanci-pation of African-American slaves and the influx of immigrants of all religious persuasions from all corners of the globe. The fan-tasy world of that mind harkens back more to the "untainted" Puritan America rather than the current Constitutional one. To these believers the evolution of the United States over the last 230 years is of little significance. The Puritan America they would like to return to was never a very democratic community either, and much of that system in early America was thankfully mar-ginalized by leaders like Jefferson, Madison, and Franklin in developing the Constitution. Democracy and evolution have never been very palatable to LaHaye. Pulpit politicking, a vast infrastructure of inbred and corrupting nontaxable foundations hiding behind their religious designation, charities and churches, a bullying evangelism, and the gullibility of Americans willing to give up their hard earned money in the faith that it will make them better in the eyes of God, has gotten them where they are over the last thirty years.

Among Christian commentators like LaHaye and Falwell, the utopian fantasy of a time when all was well—the Garden of Eden, the newfound United States, or the 1950s—has always been something of a goal for the embattled, a paradise to strive for, a heaven to take by force. Writing in 1998, LaHaye harkens back "to the good old days of 40 or 50 years ago" when divorce, crime, and single-parent family rates were low.[4] Yet a Barna Research report from September 2004 found that born-again Christians are just as likely to get divorced as non-Christians, 35 percent respectively. Protestants also had a higher divorce rate of 39 percent, actually above the national average, than Catholics, who had a rate of 25 percent.[5] According to the Bureau of Justice Statistics, the rates of the two most critical crimes—violent crime and property crime—had already gone into a steady decline by the time LaHaye made these statements. By 2003, violent crime had reached its lowest level in twenty years of data surveyed, with around 20 out of 1,000 people being victims of violent crime in that year, compared to peaks in the early 1980s and early 1990s when those rates were nearly 50 per 1,000. Property crime has seen an even greater decrease since a high in the early seventies at over 500 incidences per 1,000 households, to a figure that is now under 200 per 1,000 households. In 1972, the U.S. prison population was approximately 330,000—today it is over 2 million. That golden era forty or fifty years ago? The prison population in 1964 was higher than it was in 1972. It was in the late 1970s when the use of incarceration took a dramatic upturn, hitting the million mark in the early 1990s, and the 2 million mark in 2003. Between the early 1990s and today crime rates have continued to drop as incarceration rates climb. Much of this is due to prosecuting drug offenses harshly. In 1980, around forty thousand people were in American prisons on drug related offenses—now it is close to half a million, or a quarter of all inmates.[6]

That the idyllic era that LaHaye talks about was also a time before feminism and women's rights began to bring women out of the home and into the public sphere, and before the civil rights movement released African Americans from their apartheid and began to repair the damage the sins of slavery, shows the naivety of his hopes for a return to an "unspoiled past." Yet it is also because of these monumental changes in American society that people like LaHaye have wallowed in a sense of embattlement, feeling that their world has been turned upside down and that the only hope to return to such a state of perfection is to turn back the tide. It is strikingly clear that things have changed. That it is all part of a grand conspiracy is where LaHaye goes overboard into the murky sea of paranoia instead of realizing that these changes have come about because large groups of people had become empowered and more free.

What LaHaye fails to recognize is that American has transformed tremendously since those Puritans first landed on New Jerusalem's shores, that American is no longer only a WASP Christian nation cutting itself off from the world. It is one that now has all faiths and all races of all nations within—where one can be religious or nonreligious, where one is free to choose how to think and what to think. If there really was the vast secular humanist conspiracy LaHaye likes to pulpit pound about, does he think the mainstream "secular" publishing industry currently so happy to propagate his books would be interested in undermining their own perfect society?

There are also those like LaHaye who believe that to be worthy of the blessing of God one must evangelize and display an aggressive and often exhibitionistic religious attitude toward what they term "non-believers." As if they know what is in our hearts. This grand assumption reeks of intimidation through mass participation. It's almost a *Turn On, Tune In, and Beam Me Up, Jesus* holdover from the aggressive liberalism of the late 1960s counterculture, a counterculture that, when it coughed its dying gasps of nihilism, left many wondering what messianic community they could join next. Quite a few washed upon the shore and turned the energy of their floundering new-age philosophy into a neotraditional religiosity, but this time with its fair share of neon, media empires, foundational grassroots organizing, political clout, and Disney-style superchurches.

Like many on the extreme ends of the left and the right, LaHaye is obsessed with what he perceives as the rapid dissolution of American society due to globalization. While those in the anti-globalization wing of the left would say that amoral corporate domination of multinational companies, the free market, and free trade agreements are crushing the American Dream, those on the paranoid fringe of the anti-global right rail against a imaginary socialistic global government controlled by the United Nations which infiltrates every aspect of their lives, "global bankers" plotting their global dominance, a global monetary system, and an anti-Christian world crashing down the gates.

In seriousness, much of the reaction against globalization on the religious-conservative side points directly to their fears of modernity clashing with their cultivated traditional values. The dilemma arises when fear takes over reality. When those fears are packed into a worldview that encompasses, perpetuates, and in fact embraces the idea that the rapid changes over the last century toward global connection are a sign of the Last Days and that all the advance societies have made toward interconnectivity in

the world—communication, security treaties, travel, health—
lead straight to the Antichrist, the only hope is the one LaHaye
and Co. are selling—disengagement, despair, and separation. It is
an assumption within the point of view of the community
LaHaye represents that everyone and everything not buying into
that community is part of the evil outside force that must either
be destroyed, converted, or disengaged from.

There is a cause and effect to the rhetoric, though it often
difficult to gauge how much is actual reality, and how much the
rhetoric influences the reality. We must ask, what are their priorities? For the writers of this the premillennialist creed, the
danger of pornography outweighs the danger of poverty; the
absence of their religion in public schools outweighs the access
to education and literacy through public schools; the rights of
the unborn triumph over the rights of the living. In essence
there has been no grand conspiracy at all on the right, just a
massive amount of grassroots organization, the handyman of
constructed paranoia and conspiracy theories, the construction
of a media and publishing empire to spread them, a healthy
dose of self-righteousness, and the abduction of the religious
culture in America for political purposes.

Former President George H. W. Bush, while serving as
President Reagan's vice president, spoke at the National
Religious Broadcasters Convention in 1987, at a time when the
politically active Christian right had begun to build a separate
media empire of its own largely though the help of the LaHayes.
Bush had words of warning for them, and for the people:
"Initially you sought freedom. In the process you gained power,
and with power, a small minority now want control. There are
those who would seek to impose their will and dictate their interpretation of morality on the rest of society . . . there are those who
would forget the need for tolerance." Hope? Tolerance?
Cooperation? Dialogue? No, say the Left Behind books—the
future holds only violence, destruction, division, and doom.

APPENDIX: SYNOPSES OF THE BOOKS

Synopsis of the twelve books in the Left Behind series. Also included here are descriptions of the main characters of the novels discussed in this study.

Book One – LEFT BEHIND: A NOVEL OF EARTH'S LAST DAYS (1995)

The first book begins thus:

> Rayford Steele's mind was on a woman he had never touched. With his fully loaded 747 on autopilot above the Atlantic en route to a 6 a.m. landing at Heathrow, Rayford had pushed from his mind thoughts of his family.

Not a very dramatic opening, but it does set the scene for what is to immediately follow, as well as for the rest of the book. Rayford Steele, a pilot and average family man, has his eye on one of the flight attendants, Hattie Durham, when the event which sets up the entire series of novels occurs.

The Rapture.

In a "twinkling of an eye" many of the people on the flight vanish out of their clothes leaving the rest of the passengers scrambling for some clue as to where they have gone. So it begins. Millions of people have supposedly disappeared off the face of the earth, including all children and fetuses. The Pope, whom the authors describe as having come into a more premillennial line of theology, has also been taken to Heaven with a shout. Left behind are the unbelievers, including Hattie, Rayford, and the rest of the characters who will be shortly introduced. In the immediate aftermath of the Rapture, mass orgasmic violence and destruction ensues due to pilotless planes, driverless cars, and all manner of drastic possibilities which would occur if millions of people vanished in an instant. Many people commit suicide during this phase of the book, as well as throughout the series when the mounting destruction causes many to opt out of eventual global obliteration. The first signs of the vanquishing God of the Old Testament and Revelation described in the novels develop here, as opposed to the loving God of the Gospels.

Rayford Steele's preoccupation with Hattie is a major significance throughout the books, first to show how his "unclean thoughts" about her have signaled infidelity to his wife, a wife who has become a believer and devoted herself to her local church. Steele's wife and son are among those Raptured (his twenty-year-old daughter Chloe is also left behind), so through much of the first novel Steele is battling with the guilt of being left behind as well as how his mental infidelity (he never physically engaged in any sexual conduct with Hattie) has perhaps cost him a spot alongside his wife during the Rapture.

Backtracking slightly, on page 10 we join the famous international journalist for Global News Network, senior writer for Global Weekly, Ivy League grad, and a self-proclaimed Deist, Buck Williams in Israel, where he is working on a story about the miracle in the desert. Jewish scientist Chaim Rosenzweig has created a formula that makes the dry earth bloom and makes Israel rich through agricultural output. The secret formula is solely for Israel alone, though if sold to the rest of the world could end hunger. From what we can garner, this prompts an attack from Russia (significant in much of popular premillennialist prophecy debate over the past few decades has been an attack on Israel "from the North" which they have taken to mean Russia), but another miracle occurs—Israel is unharmed by the bombs and the Russian planes are blown out of the sky by God's protection.

Back to the Rapture. Buck Williams just happens to be on the same plane with Hattie Durham and Rayford Steele when the event occurs. When they finally land in Chicago they find that everything is in chaos—homes have burned down, transportation is nearly impossible, communications are disrupted. Many people speculate that aliens have taken people, others that some new weapon (from what enemy?) has zapped them, or that an unnatural natural phenomenon has whisked them away.

Stepping in to fill the void and help direct the world back to some semblance of order is the United Nations. Here we meet the Antichrist, or the eventual Antichrist, Nicolae Carpathia, a civil servant from Romania who becomes president of that country under mysterious circumstances, then gives an address at the U.N. wherein he says the name of every country in the world, something that obviously seems to qualify him to be secretary general. We later hear that when George H. W. Bush gave his New World Order speech, it resonated deep within Carpathia's young heart. Through all this the authors make feints and hints to conspiracy narratives through mentioning "one world government" and Jewish Nationalists, rebuilding the temple in Jerusalem, one world currency, interfaith dialogue, allusions to an Antichrist coming from Europe, great lies, one world religious orders, and other similar conspiracies to rule the world under one mantra. Underlying all this are suggestions of "power behind the power" a world of international bankers (often used in early rightwing conspiracy theories to signify Jews)—such as a man named Jonathan Stonagal and another named Joshua Todd-Cothran, who one of Buck's sources thinks are behind a plan to institute one world currency, a plan which eventually comes true. Of course all the conspiracies do come true, and very easily so it seems.

Eventually Rayford finds his way back to his home in the Chicago suburbs where he finds that his wife Irene and son Raymie have also disappeared, though his daughter Chloe, a student at Stanford University, has not. She also makes it home and they go to the old church where Irene was a member. There they find Bruce Barnes, the pastor, has also been left behind. Barnes brings the two under his wing and shows them the post-Rapture video the prior pastor had left in case the circumstances called for its viewing. Much of the middle part of the first book wavers between describing Rayford and Chloe interacting with Barnes and showing Buck the reporter as he begins to uncover the massive conspiracy with has created a one world government which Carpathia at the helm. Carpathia, a low level civil servant a few months before, even addresses the World Council of Churches and a conference on eschatology. In one of the greatest career leaps of the novels after Carpathia himself, Hattie Durham, the former flight attendant, meets Carpathia and swiftly becomes his personal secretary.

Toward page 300 of the first book the prophets Eli and Moishe appear at the Wailing Wall and begin trying to convert Jews to Christianity, or the premillennial version at least. Around this time Barnes outlines Revelation and the Tribulation for the Steeles while the plotline following Buck through his own discoveries about Carpathia and conspiracies also develops in parallel. The new global community rapidly develops through the latter part of the book, with even Botswana joining the European Common Market (though this really doesn't seem to matter much anymore as everything is rapidly moving toward a one-world currency). Carpathia proposes moving the U.N. to Iraq and rebuilding Babylon, another strong highway sign for prophecy buffs. Buck himself, that skeptical, cynical journalist (as he is described by the authors) begins to believe in "the Rapture thing" and becomes involved with the Steeles and Barnes as part of the early formations of what Barnes goes on to call the Tribulation Force. Buck is finally converted toward the end of the first book, describing himself now as "intellectually honest" and wondering what kind of "despicable subhuman creature" he was before he became a believer. By the end of the book, Carpathia has assumed global hegemony and is pushing for one world religion, one world language, one world government and currency, and finally rebuilding the temple in Jerusalem. The Tribulation Force begins to discuss martyrdom and the members are portrayed as Christian soldiers by the authors; here the group begins to become more solid and militant as the members reinforce one anothers beliefs. While not yet taking the on the same significance as a militia, the Tribulation Force only a book away from this eventuality.

Book Two – TRIBULATION FORCE: THE CONTINUING DRAMA OF THOSE LEFT BEHIND (1996)

Rayford begins to go deeper and deeper into Revelation in the second book of the series: only this one book could hold his interest now. The Tribulation Force becomes more insular and Rayford himself reinforces his new beliefs in a division of believers between good and evil. After trying to convert his co-pilot, he is reprimanded for proselytizing on the job, something he takes for persecution. Rayford also continuously berates his "'old self," at one point (28) bemoaning that he had been a skeptical cynic, a neglectful father, a lustful husband with a roving eye. Bruce Barnes, the pastor of New Hope and the head of the Tribulation Force, wonders, like most prophecy buffs, why America plays no role in Revelation, and like LaHaye in his nonfiction writings, believes that the U.S.A. will be sidelined in the final days. Chloe, contemplating going back to Stanford, is encouraged by Barnes to "go to college" here at the church. After this he starts to discuss his plans for building a bomb shelter below the church where they can hide out from "the Tribulations" as well as Carpathia's henchmen. The early part of this book details much of what Barnes says is in store for the world, the Four Horsemen of the Apocalypse, the seven judgments, further ratcheting up the fear factor and further alienating the Tribulation Force from the world outside. "The millenniums-old account reads as fresh as tomorrow's newspapers," he says. (67)

Also early in this book, the Jewish scientist Rosenzweig comes under the spell of Carpathia. A demonic aura is beginning to be given off by Carpathia, which, of course, is only

detectable by the believers. The reader is also introduced to
Rabbi Tsion Ben-Judah in this book. Tsion, a prominent Jewish
theologian, has recently completed a three-year study about
who the Messiah is or isn't, and will soon declare to his fellow
countrymen that it happened to be Jesus Christ, that they
missed it and that they now all should become good Christians.
Not exactly in those words, but in effect.

On page 127 we find that "the American militia movement" is the only group who has not fallen for Carpathia's plans
for world domination, which is significant because after "the
American militia movement" is destroyed later in the book, the
Tribulation Force becomes the de facto "American militia
movement" against the forces of the Antichrist. Carpathia
begins to also gobble up the media of the world, including the
entities where Buck works. Further toward the end of the book,
the militia movement begins to horde weapons and the
American president seems to lend his support to them in their
fight against the eroding of U.S. sovereignty. Following this is a
pact of worldwide disarmament, where the nations of the world
turn over most of their weapons to the U.N. (by now the Global
Community), after which the U.S. president begins to plot
along with the militia to oppose Carpathia. In the final pages,
the militia (along with militia from the U.K. and Egypt) attack
D.C.; in retaliation, London, Chicago and New York are
attacked by Carpathia.

Buck and Chloe become romantically involved through
this book as well, something which takes up a great deal of
space, and otherwise lightens much of the heavy violence and
destruction of the books. Barnes urges Rayford to proselytize to
the president of the United States (he's been chosen to fly the
president's plane and later becomes Carpathia's pilot), though
he hasn't had much luck with his other co-workers so far. He
also begins advising members of the Tribulation Force on jobs
they should take so as to be closer to power. Pastor Bruce himself goes around the globe to spread his message and is felled by
a mysterious illness, which the reader later finds was a poisoning ordered by Carpathia.

Toward the middle of the book, Buck interviews the soon-to-be Pope, the American Peter Matthews, who is drinking champagne at six in the morning. Around this time the Catholic Church is at the forefront of establishing a one world religion and the temple in Jerusalem is being rebuilt, a feat accomplished by moving the Muslim Dome of the Rock to the New Babylon in Iraq. Throughout the book the prophets Eli and Moishe are preaching at the Wailing Wall and increasingly drawing the ire of Orthodox Jews, Muslims, and Carpathia. Buck meets with the otherworldly prophets in attempt to interview them.

Book Three – NICOLAE: THE RISE OF THE ANTICHRIST (1997)

"It was the worst of times; it was the worst of times."
—Nicolae, p. 1

Washington, D.C, New York, and parts of Chicago lay in ruins at the opening of the third book, which chronicles the rise of the Antichrist, the villain Carpathia, aided by massive conspiracy, the promoter of peace, the head of the United Nations, former-ly a low-level civil servant in Romania. The Red Horse of the Apocalypse has ridden through the lands, so say the authors, as this first war testifies. The American militia forces have, for the most part, been defeated—stepping in to take their place is the Tribulation Force of believers, who begin to form bands to take action against the rule of Carpathia. Talk of assassination of this "global deceiver" begins to make its way into the books, which largely, are very repetitive in tone, though as they proceed they grow much heavier in carnage and violence. Global currency has been issued, and heavy global taxes are levied by the Global Community; one world religion, formed under the auspices of the Roman Catholic Church, has been instituted. Carpathia even proposes to integrate social services worldwide so as to equal the playing field for the Third World countries; abortion, euthanasia, and worldwide healthcare run rampant. All major media outlets are now owned by the Global Community.

Democracy is suspended for global socialism as signified by Carpathia and his Global Community (formerly the United Nations) bureaucrats. The secret formula developed by Chaim Rosenzweig to turn Israel into an agricultural paradise has been turned over to the Global Community, thus making desert into farmland worldwide (which in theory would probably collapse world trade in agriculture and give local communities autonomy over their food sources, though this is not mentioned). A plan hatched by Carpathia provides this secret formula to all countries that destroy 90 percent of their weaponry and turn the last 10 percent over to the Global Community. All the while, the two prophets at the Wailing Wall issue their reports of doom to come. The temple in Jerusalem has been rebuilt. Jewish "evangelists" begin to convert from Judaism to premillennial dispensational theology—the significant 144,000 being gathered to the flock. Buck continuously jokes that their new Tribulation Force could also be considered "International Harvesters." The battles between militia and the Global Community forces rage on, World War III (or is it IV?). Bruce Barnes, the first leader of the Tribulation Force, has died from a Carpathia poisoning but leaves behind massive notes on Revelation for the Tribulation Force to interpret and disseminate to bring other possible believers into the flock, martyrs "willing to die for the sake of the Gospel" (though there isn't much talk of the Gospels here; instead the fixation is mainly on the Revelation). Pontifex Maximus Peter Matthews, Supreme Pontiff of Enigma Babylon One World Faith assumes leadership of an ecumenical world church. Only Orthodox Jews, some fundamentalist Muslims, and the Tribulation Force "believers" have not joined the worldwide church. Matthews, and hearing it from him we are meant to believe the following statement to be evil or on the wrong side, in response to literal interpretation of the Book of Revelation by the believers, calls it: "wonderful, archaic, beautiful literature, to be taken symbolically, figuratively, metaphorically." Toward the end of the third book, ambassadors from the Ten Regions of the Global Community vote to fund abortions for women in underprivileged countries. (It seems this secret formula meant to give people control of their local agriculture has been forgotten, as well as the global health care instituted by the Global Community—would there still be underprivileged countries? Passages like this point to the logic of propaganda in tapping into present political and social hot spots and not a logic central to the books themselves.) Global Community Morale Monitors roam the earth. To end this book, a new Tribulation sent from on high ravishes the earth—a massive, worldwide earthquake destroys much of what the Global Community has built thus far.

Hattie Durham, who had become Carpathia's assistant, now becomes his lover and pregnant with the spawn of the Antichrist. Through much of this book, going into the next, debate over whether Hattie should have an abortion takes center stage while millions of other unfortunate souls around the globe are killed through the various Tribulations sent down from God above. Are both of these acts murder? "She was not a believer. She would not be thinking of the good of anyone besides herself." (295) Also throughout the book the members of the Tribulation Force debate with Hattie and attempt to sway her from deciding to abort the Antichrist's child, quite a dilemma if there ever was one.

Book Four – SOUL HARVEST: THE WORLD TAKES SIDES (1998)

At the start of the fourth book, the great earthquake has shaken the earth to its foundations; the seventh seal has been broken. Extreme violence, more of it at least, continues. People commit suicide all around and others plea to be put out of their misery. Many, many people have died as a result of this earthquake, including Rayford Steele's new wife Amanda, a person painted vaguely through the last couple of books, intentionally so it seems—it becomes known that she was perhaps one of Carpathia's spies. Odd that Carpathia would nuke entire cities but simply poison a pastor of a church (Bruce Barnes) and come up with a scheme to have a spy marry his pilot (Carpathia seems well aware that the Tribulation Force members think he is the Antichrist). I mention this, not to simply state how absurd the books are, but more to point to the intentional, or unintentional (it's difficult to discern the authors' intent here) creation of paranoia about believers and nonbelievers, as well the political manifestations which are loaded into anyone who is not a believer. It is in this book that Carpathia also begins to develop special powers—he raises his right-hand man Leon Fortunato from the dead after the earthquake and begins to think he, himself, is the Messiah. On the other end of the extreme, the Tribulation Force begins to resemble something more like a cult or a militia group than a group of Christians concerned about theological questions surrounding Revelation. Revelation has become real and they have become the front line forces of the Lord. At one point early in this book, Rayford seems more concerned with converting a fellow named Mac McCullum (who later is converted) than he is about how his daughter Chloe (Chloe becomes pregnant as well in this book) and son-in-law Buck have survived the earthquake or not. Rayford insinuates that becoming a believer like himself is the true path to heaven, and even threatens Mac with damnation, it seems: "I hope there is no aftershock or attack that might get you killed before you are assured of heaven." (135) After Mac does convert, both of them begin to see crosses on each other's foreheads, the Mark of the Believer, which only believers can see.

Much of *Soul Harvest* concerns various characters finally realizing there had been a Rapture and that Carpathia is the Antichrist, so a number of conversion stories begin to develop, including those of a number of Jews, mainly through the urging of Rabbi Tsion Ben-Judah. Rayford, who is still close to Carpathia as his personal pilot (and spying on him by listening to his conversations over a microphone in the passenger cabin of the plane), is urged by the Antichrist to speak to Hattie about having an abortion, something Rayford certainly will not do—he turns to intensive Bible study to fight off these thoughts.

Daughter Chloe has been nearly killed in the earthquake and Hattie is in a reproductive clinic (which used to be a church but is now involved in cloning and fetal tissue research) in Littleton, Colorado, adding to much of these notions of embattlement as well as using the memories the name Littleton happens to foster. Rayford and Company attack the reproduction clinic to rescue Hattie from the abortion and in the process shoot one of the guards, which Rayford harbors some guilt about but which Tsion brushes off by saying: "If you shot an enemy solider during battle would you turn yourself in?" (363) As in many cases throughout the books, martyrdom and a militant dying for Christ is accentuated along with phrases like "to die would be gain" (attributed to St. Paul, but used to justify such actions as Rayford has just taken, not the other possibility that he may have meant passing into heaven).

Toward the middle of the book, Tsion explains that the earthquake and the mass destruction, offered by the authors in delightful detail, have ushered in the second twenty-one months of the Tribulation (to last a total of seven years). Tsion also details the atrocious calamities that this (sadistic? loving?) God is about to visit on the remaining people of the earth. "How can a thinking person see all that is happening and not fear about what is to come?" wonders Ben-Judah. (246) Among these Tribulations are significant tax increases imposed by the Global Community, which, after the earthquakes have damaged nearly every form of transportation in the world, isn't so far fetched. Once again, the logic of the propaganda (painting tax increases as evil) supercedes; there is no account taken into the actual logic of the books. Tsion later, through his internet sermons and Buck's *The Truth*, rails against everything from Satan and one world government to the "moral relativism" of the Global Community, as well as "vile and lascivious images" on television, which seems to have developed into showing real violence, actual torture, sorcery, black magic, fortune telling, and all manner of witchery for entertainment. "My challenge to you is to choose up sides. Join a team. If one side is right, the other is wrong," writes Tsion in one of these sermons, coming off more as a Vince Lombardi or General Patton than the serious theologian he is supposed to be. All of this, of course, is meant for the reader to *take into the present*—the books are shaded mirrors of current reality. At the end of the book, those Tribulations Tsion foretold surely come to pass—fire and brimstone rain down on the earth, blood streams down from the sky, one asteroid his the earth and creates a tidal wave, another asteroid heading toward earth is blown out of the atmosphere by a nuclear warhead but this still causes "Wormwood" to poison all the fresh water on earth. All becomes chaos and destruction, punishment for God's children who failed to be taken in the Rapture.

Book Five – APOLLYON: THE DESTROYER IS RELEASED (1999)

One place that hasn't been touched by all these Tribulations so far is Israel. Jews are converting to the new form of Christianity en masse. Tens of thousands of underground "house churches" have sprung up around the world, essentially small Tribulation Forces militia devoted to the premillennialist idea of God. Eli and Moishe are still there at the Wailing Wall defying the orders of Carpathia to leave. After all these new destructions, Tsion once again launches into his Internet sermons with militant ferocity: "Lead, follow, or get out of the way."(39) He addresses the crowds in Jerusalem and gives a Bible lesson to the thousands. He had "explained the truths which had so recently become clear to these initiates, that man is born in sin and that nothing he can do for himself can reconcile him to God. Only by believing and trusting in the work Christ did for him on the cross can he be born again spiritually into eternal life." After this, Peter II (formerly Peter Matthews, then Pope, then head of Enigma Babylon) and Leon Fortunato give a wildly new age sermon to the crowds. Later they are among the plotters to detonate a bomb to blow up the prophets and blame it on terrorists.

It's found out that Hattie has been poisoned by Carpathia and she gives birth to a dead baby, so all the abortion debate was for naught and the authors get an easy out from having the Antichrist's kid running around. All the while, Carpathia is still intent on building his global village, though it's a wonder there are many people left to inhabit it after millions of people have been destroyed through the first tribulations. The authors have him reiterate the themes of one currency, one government, one language, one religion—and also have him debunk the idea of a Rapture (in essence, putting any critical thought on the subject in the mouth of the Antichrist). He orders that Eli and Moishe should be shot on sight as Jerusalem and falls into debauchery (strip clubs, tattoo parlors, XXX shows, prostitutes—"Not the Israel [I] remembered" thinks Buck; though this oldest profession is pretty commonplace in Israel today, especially in Tel Aviv). Orthodox Jews once again use the Temple for sacrifices.

Large sections of this novel are taken up by Tsion's sermons, either to the crowds or via the Internet. "They will say ours is not a message of ecumenism and tolerance that they promote, and I say they are right. There is right and wrong, there are absolute truths, and some things cannot and should not ever be tolerated." (189) The next judgment is detailed midway through the book by Tsion, and he also begins typing in tongues (or using new translating software). Severe cold covers the earth, shooting stars strike the earth and blacken out the sun, and later little mechanical locust-like metallic monsters with three noses start attacking nonbelievers. These little beasts sting unbelievers and afterward they suffer terribly for weeks, to which Tsion brushes off: "I beg of you not to look upon God as mean or capricious when we see the intense suffering of the bite victims. This is all part of his master design to turn people to him so he can demonstrate his love." (330)

Book Six – ASSASSINS: ASSIGNMENT: JERUSALEM, TARGET: ANTICHRIST (1999)

At the start of book six, Rayford Steele pleads with god to anoint him to be Carpathia's killer. We also find out that the believers have created a vast underground economy and only trade with one another. Both Mac McCullum and a character David Hassid fantasize about murdering Carpathia, and though Rayford is the most fervent about doing the deed, it is eventually Chaim Rosenzweig who takes the task upon himself.

Tsion continues his literalist prophecy: "For centuries scholars believed prophetic literature was figurative, open to endless interpretation. That could have not been what God intended. Why would he make it so difficult? I believe that when Scripture says the writer saw something in the vision, it is symbolic of something else. But when the writer simply says that certain things happen, I take those literally. So far I have been proven right." (90)

So much right that the next Tribulation is an invasion of 200 million horsemen which slays one-third of the population on earth with their swords and the poison the horses breathe, sparing only believers (unbelievers cannot see the horsemen). The Global Community blames this on a chemical attack by "religious dissidents." After this, Carpathia seems to say what many Christians also say about the heavenly kingdom of the millennial reign of Christ: "The day will come when we live as one world, one faith, one family of man. We shall live in a utopia of peace and harmony with no more war, no more bloodshed, no more death." (147)

A passage in which Tsion addresses believers comes to the paradoxical conclusion that the Tribulation is both necessary and unnecessary. If God is omniscient as they portray here, wouldn't he already know who will turn to him and who will not, and in this sense would it be needless that he torment and torture those he's trying to persuade? "God is still trying to persuade mankind to come to him, yes, but this destruction of other remaining unbelievers may have another purpose. In this preparation for the final battle between good and evil, God may be winnowing from the evil forces the incorrigible when he, in his omniscience, knows would have never turned to him regardless." (174)

Chaim himself, as yet still an unbeliever and tormented by the Tribulations, rebukes God for this cruelty. He does soon convert however, through the urging of Buck. Though Chaim is also planning his attempt to assassinate Carpathia, the reader is presented mainly with the thoughts of Rayford as the authors give great detail to a special gun he has now obtained, making him come off as a Holy assassin. After Carpathia shoots the two prophets, Peter the II is killed and one-world faith is to now take shape as Carpathianism. Three days after they are killed, the prophets resurrect and they are raised into the clouds. The book ends with Carpathia being shot, but it isn't revealed who the killer is until later in the next book.

Book Seven – THE INDWELLING: THE BEAST TAKES POSSESSION (2000)

By the seventh book, Hattie, who had attempted to go back to her family, has been found and interred in a high-security women's prison in Brussels, Belgium. One character named Leah, a part of the Tribulation Force, goes to Brussels to try to get her released and meets a prison guard named Ming Toy from China, a closet believer whose brother Chang Wong, also a believer, eventually becomes the computer guru for the Tribulation Force. The new Church of Carpathianism has supplanted the Enigma Babylon Church, formerly with the Roman Catholic Church at the head. Carpathia is "dead" but will soon rise at the Beast, the fully realized Antichrist.

Later the reader discovers that Chaim had faked a stroke so he could be close to Carpathia and had been training with a small sword in order to know how to kill him. This all occurs as Rayford is on the run from the Global Community forces who think he has killed Carpathia. Throughout these passages, Carpathia is lauded as a savior, compared to the Messiah, and even called the Son of God by the followers of Carpathianism. Statues are built in his image. Following this is Carpathia's funeral. Michael the Archangel appears at one point to Tsion, as well as a vision of Lucifer, who turns into a serpent and then a dragon, which Michael slays with a sword. Another dream brings the angel Gabriel and Michael again. Chaim, who had had yet to become a "full believer," now appears with the mark on his forhead.

At the end of the book, Carpathia rises from the dead, like a Frankenstein-Christ; his words mirror the words of Jesus upon his own resurrection: "He who is not with me is against me."

Book Eight – THE MARK: THE BEAST RULES THE WORLD (2000)

Once Carpathia has risen, Carpathianism (which seems to have developed into a mixture of Satanism and vestiges of Roman Catholicism) takes on an even greater role with Leon Fortunato as the high priest. He is proclaimed spiritual leader of Carpathianism at the Sistine Chapel in Rome. A huge statue of Carpathia is erected in New Babylon. Carpathia, holding the Bible, says sportingly: "This is the playbook for those who oppose me." (80) This being necessarily so, it becomes law that all those reluctant to take the Mark of Loyalty to Carpathia (the Mark of the Beast) will either be forced to or guillotined. The mark of loyalty consists of a biochip embedded under the skin, as well as a symbol which describes what region of the ten regions of the world the person is from, is located on either the forehead or the right hand. At first those not getting the mark of loyalty would simply not be able to buy or sell within the Global Community system and citizens are urged to report those not taking the mark. This new symbol of loyalty is first instituted at jails and prisons. Later executions for not taking the mark begin.

Hattie, now safely with the Tribulation Force again, converts to their Christianity and the mark of the believer appears on her forehead. She had finally "joined the team." "In many ways she was the same forthright woman she had been before, nearly as obnoxious as a new believer as she had been as a holdout. But of course, everyone was happy she was finally on the team." (308) Tsion, getting bolder now, calls out Carpathia as the Antichrist through his Internet sermon. "Woe to those who believe that God is only love," states Tsion. "We are engaged in a worldwide battle with Satan himself for the souls of men and women." (148) Later, Tsion leans toward a total dismissal of the Bible if it's literalism doesn't hold up: "If [the prophecies] are not true, and don't come to pass, then I am a liar and the Bible is bogus, and we are all utterly without hope." So, to fulfill prophecy, the authors write it into fiction. Here we find out that Carpathia wants to ride a pig into Jerusalem, which should be sacrificed at the Temple in Jerusalem in order to fulfill prophecy. Now in the middle of the eighth book, the Tribulation Force encourages Chaim to be a New Moses in Israel to lead the "believing Jews" and the Christians (aren't they both Christians now?). His task is to lead the "believing Jews" to Petra in a manner similar to Moses leading the Exodus. The last holdouts to Carpathia's plans are messianic Jews, Orthodox Jews, and the premillennial Christians.

Book Nine – DESECRATION: ANTICHRIST TAKES THE THRONE (2001)

"Desecration" may be too timid a word for what the authors have the former peacemaker come Antichrist, the Beast, Nicolae Carpathia do to Jerusalem and the Temple. Essentially he plays the figure of Jesus riding in on a mule, instead using the doubly (triply if we include Muslims who have by now been totally forgotten) offensive massive pig as his steed. Carpathia plans to imitate the Passion once the pig has been ridden and the slaughter been made. The vision-susceptible Tribulation Force members keep seeing angels, including Hattie who sees the Archangel Michael and after this meeting decides to confront Carpathia herself. Hattie, never a character with any definition for herself other than as a symbol for first, a wanton woman who gets pregnant out of wedlock (with the Anticrhist, no less!) and contemplates an abortion, and later as a devoutly changed believer, is easily dispatched from the rest of the series as she confronts Carpathia and is burned by Fortunato (who now has fireball powers). After this, Chole envies Hattie's martyrdom and will soon find her wish granted. Up next on the prophetic calendar is the destruction of the Temple and the Temple Mount, central to the books, and central to the three monotheistic religions that claim Jerusalem as a holy city. The rebuilt Temple, "a sparkling replica of Solomon's original" must be destroyed in the biblical timeline constructed by premillennialists before the Messiah can finally come.

Following on the heels of the other torments and Tribulations are a plague of boils which, once again, appear on anyone who has taken the Mark of Loyalty to Carpathia. Chaim, who in his new Moses role insists on being called Micah, intends to lead the "believing Jews" to Petra in Jordan. Carpathia continues to mock both Jews and Christians in the Temple, sacrificing the pig he rode in on in the Holy of Holies and washing his hands in the blood. Chaim, now Micah, meets Carpathia at the Israeli Kenesset to persuade Carpathia to let the Jews go to Petra while preaching in much the same language that Tsion (a "believing

Jew" and once formerly a rabbi) has used throughout the books, that Jesus is the Messiah. Another Tribulation comes, turning all the water in the world to blood. Michael the Archangel appears again throughout the book, to Rayford, as well as to the "exodus" of believers from Jerusalem to Petra. Carpathia sends his troops after them, and with similar Moses imagery, they are swallowed up by an earthquake instead of the parting of waves. Like manna from Heaven, a great flock of quails appears for the believers at Petra, which they roast over open fires. By the end of the book, Carpathia has also become quite antagonistic toward Jews and orders a Holocaust and extermination of Jews worldwide, though no explanation of this is given—the reader must take the fact that he is evil, the beast, the Lucifer as evidence enough that he hates Jews. The book ends with Carpathia ordering that Petra be nuked . . . to find out what comes next, the reader must rush out to buy . . .

Book Ten - THE REMNANT: ON THE BRINK OF ARMAGEDDON (2002)

Miracle of miracles! Petra has been nuked, but the believers remain unharmed. Seas have turned to blood, making trade difficult for both believer and unbeliever alike. After all these losses, Buck Williams, of the team destined to win, remarks: "I can't imagine how Carpathia deals with this. You can spin it, you can't gloss it over. Thousands are dying every day, and think of the crews marooned. They'll eventually all die." The Jews seem to have no friends anymore—Carpathia is trying to kill them all and the believers are trying to convert them. To attune to Revelation, the authors have Carpathia start up training schools for false messiahs. Much of this novel is action packed, full of guns and violence, battles, militias. One believer, George Sebastian, tortures a Global Community peacekeeper with a high-energy gun, saying: "Oh God, to whom vengeance belongs, shine forth." (199)

The guillotining of believers and those others who refuse to take the Mark of Loyalty to Carpathia continues unabated. Tsion, in his continued Internet sermons about the "Glorious Appearing" to come, explains, "God has given us an accurate history of the world, much of it written in advance. It is the only truly accurate history ever written." (228) He also explains that five more judgments remain and the Tribulation Force relocated to underground bunkers in the San Diego area. Toward the end of this book, Tsion and Fortunato duel and debate, with Tsion using Michael the Archangel as his magic (he turns all the fresh water to blood) and Fortunato using his own magic tricks. Finally total darkness descends on the earth, causing blindness as well as an unexplained itching which in nonbelievers.

Book Eleven – ARMAGEDDON: THE COSMIC BATTLE OF THE AGES (2003)

The second to last book opens with militia holdouts, not believers, being executed in Los Angeles. Back in New Babylon, where Rayford currently is, a strange segment occurs that seems to question the pointlessness of the whole Tribulation and paints God as a sadistic avenger with no mercy left (and there is still about a year left in the seven-year tribulation)—a woman tells him that she wants to accept the Lord by prayer, to become a believer, but she has already taken the mark of loyalty to Carpathia, so for her it is too late. "He couldn't make it compute with the God he knew, the loving and merciful one who seemed to look for ways to welcome everyone into heaven, not keep them out." (18) For nonbelievers and those not loyal to Carpathia, the fate is the same. Jews are taken to concentration camps on Carpathia's orders. If they would have gotten the mark they would have eventually have been killed by God. Their only hope is in conversion. Chloe now is hoping for the "real freedom," which is less than a year away, but she is captured by Global Community forces, given a truth serum which makes her talk about the truth of God, and thereby reveals much of the black and white theology the authors hold, which essentially paints Jews (who must make a choice) who do not convert as choosing Satan: "How someone could see all that had gone on during the last six years and not realize that the only options were God or Satan—or worse, could know the options yet choose Satan—she could not fathom." (232) Across the global television system (the blindness and darkness seem to be gone now), the executions of believers become the most popular program, lasting hours and showing slow-motion replays of "the most gruesome deaths.'"(243) However, it's not certain how many people remain to actually view these programs after the population had been cut from, first the Rapture, then by thirds in any number of the Tribulations, and finally by the various pogroms and attacks by Global Community forces around the globe. At one point the angel Caleb appears and smears the camera shot so Chloe's execution cannot be seen around the world. Chloe co-opts the language of Patrick Henry as well as missionary Jim Elliot (killed in Ecuador in 1956 by a tribe who didn't want to be converted) before she is executed, blending an Americanist religious patriotism with martyrdom. Following this is a massive triumphalist (the readers all know who will eventually triumph) sermon on the prophecies that have been fulfilled as well as those to come. Tsion mentions that "a third of the remaining Jews will turn to the Messiah before the end." (306) By the end of the book he is preaching to the remaining Jews in Jerusalem in a last attempt to convert them. It will be much more beautiful and efficient without them it seems, but why would they want to run off to the desert if this is what awaits them?

> "Do you know what will happen here, right here in Jerusalem? It will be the only city in the world spared the devastating destruction of the greatest earthquake known to man. The Bible says, 'Now the great city'— that's Jerusalem—'was divided into three parts and the cities of the nations fell.'
>
> "That, my brothers, is good news. Jerusalem will be made more beautiful, more efficient. It will be prepared for its role as the new capital in Messiah's thousand-year kingdom." (336)

Finally Carpathia identifies himself as Lucifer, seemingly also with Hitler ("My forces and I almost had them exterminated not so many years ago . . ." (297)), and eventually calls his troops to rally on the Plains of Megiddo where the Battle of Armageddon is to take place. Tsion goes on to reveal the last bits of Revelation and three beasts come to Carpathia's side. During the Battle of Armageddon, the language of the book takes on an even greater triumphalism as the blood of the Antichrist's armies "flows as high as a horse's bridle." (312) Carpathia has decided, in order to conform to scripture it seems, to attack the Christians with soldiers on horseback. At the end of the book, Tsion is killed in battle. Buck and Rayford are also mortally wounded and waiting, now, for Jesus to return.

Book Twelve – THE GLORIOUS APPEARING: THE END OF DAYS (2004)

Before Jesus does arrive however, Mac shoots a Global Community trooper in the back then mutters those clichés— "Live by the sword," and "All is fair in love and war." Carpathia himself isn't faring much better on the moral scale at this point, he even uses the "Cradle of Jesus" as a septic tank. He institutes a call to kill everyone without the Mark of Loyalty on sight. Early in the book, the fantasy of Tsion comes true—a mass conversion of Jews takes place, millions (a third of those left?) come to Christ.

Lucifer appears out of Carpathia's body at one point, makes a grand speech, then goes back into Carpathia. After this a meteor shower of asteroids strike the earth. Rayford has survived enough to grunt at what he sees happening all around. "All Rayford could do was grunt. Sometimes scripture had that effect on him. There was nothing more to say. At least not by him." (136) After this, his mortal wounds heal as the cross of Christ appears in the sky.

Finally, on page 203 of the final book in the series, Jesus arrives. Tens of thousands of the Global Community soldiers are instantly struck dead. "Their innards and entrails gushed to the desert floor, and as those around them turned to run, they too were slain, their blood pooling and rising in the unforgiving brightness of the glory of Christ." (226) You are either with Jesus or against him, it seems: "Every spirit that confesses that I came in the flesh is of God, and every spirit that does not confess that I came in the flesh is not of God. And this is the spirit of the Antichrist."

Before all calamity is over though, a worldwide earthquake swallows the hundreds of thousands of bodies which lie at the foot of the Lord. No residue of these final battles remain. The three beasts who had come to Carpathia's side kneel before Jesus and repent. Jesus promptly puts them to death. Next come the just deserts for Leon Fortunato, who is sentenced to eternal damnation in the Lake of Fire. Nicolae (Satan has been released from his body now) comes next and is also sentenced to the Lake of Fire. After this, Michael wrestles with a dragon, which is Lucifer. Before sentencing Satan to Hell, Jesus gets in a good jab on evolution vs. creationism: "For all your lies abut having evolved, you are a created being." (318) Jesus also seems to accuse him of trying to establish a "Babylonish" (or Catholic) religion: "It was you who attempted to establish a universal, idolatrous religion in Babel, then the largest city in the world, to keep mankind from worshiping the one true God." (320) Michael then binds Satan in chains and drops him into a bottomless pit. The rest of the novel is taken up by complicated passages on millennialism, premillennialism, postmillennialism, etc., and eventually all those Raptured or who have died during the Tribulation as believers return to their loved ones on earth.

So begins the Millennial Reign.

ENDNOTES

Citations from the Left Behind series are given by title only. All were written by Tim LaHaye and Larry B. Jenkins, and published by Tyndale House. For date of publication, please see appendix A.

Introduction
1. Thirteen as of July, 2005.
2. There were twelve original novels and three prequel novels, one of which has been released as of July 2005.
3. "The Rise of the Righteous Empire," *CBS News*. February 8, 2004, http://www.cbsnews.com/stories/2004/02/05/60minutes/main598218.shtml.
4. Barna Research Group, *Church Demographics*, http://www.barna.org/FlexPage.aspx?Page=Topic&TopicID=11.
5. *Assassins*, 147.
6. Teresa Malcolm, "Fearful Faith in End Times Novels," *National Catholic Reporter,* June 15, 2001.
7. *Tribulation Force*, 72.

A House Divided
1. The Biblical "Land of Israel"—based on when Israel was at its greatest expansion—stretches from the Sinai in what is now Egypt all the way to the Euphrates in present-day Iraq.
2. (My emphasis.) Mark Hithcock and Thomas Ice, *The Truth Behind Left Behind,* (Sisters, Ore: Multnomah, 2004.), 179-180.
3. Anti-Defamation League letter to Wal-Mart, September 21, 2004, http://www.adl.org/misc/wal-mart-protocols-ltr.asp.
4. Though these aren't mutually exclusive, at least on the white supremacist side. Most white supremacist groups are strictly Christian and adamantly so (though some do reject Christianity as well), and even

more specifically they are Protestant adherents, especially where this mixes with the Christian Identity movement.

5. I went to parochial school from kindergarten through high school and besides daily religion classes attended church weekly.

6. "Different Groups Follow Harry Potter, Left Behind and Jabez," Barna ResearchGroup, October 22, 2001.

7. The United Nations has changed its name to the Global Community and moved to New Babylon in Iraq.

8. *Assassins*, 34–35. It is also worth noting that the massive earthquake she is talking about had been sent by God, though this bit of irony, God slaying her family in order for her to come to believe in Him, does not seem to register.

9. *Assassins*, 37–38.

10. Amy Frykholm, *Rapture Culture: Left behind in Evangelical America* (New York: Oxford Univ. Press, 2004), 30.

11. FamilyChristian.com, www.familychristian.com/books/ jenkins.lahaye.asp.

12. "Left Behind: Interview with LaHaye and Jenkins," *Food For the Hungry*, www.parable.com/fh/spotlight.asp?sid=25&ct=interview.

13. "Tyndale House Kicks Off Highly Anticipated Left Behind #7 With San Diego Event," PR Newswire, April 10, 2000.

14. Abbas, interview.

15. Dee Ann Grand, "Tim LaHaye Keeps Readers Everywhere Enraptured with Tales of Those Left Behind," *Book Page*, April 2001, www.bookpage.com/0104bp/tim_lahaye.html.

16. "Three by LaHaye for Kensington," *Publisher's Weekly*, December 20, 2004.

17. Jeremy Lott, "Surviving Soul Survivor," *Christianity Today*, by Jeremy Lott, October 30, 2002.

18. Nancy Shepherdson, "Writing for Godot," *Los Angeles Times*, April 25, 2004.

19. Baker, John F., "Three by LaHaye for Kensington," *Publisher's Weekly*, December 20, 2004 hhtp://publishersweekly,com/ index.asp?layout=articleprint&articleid=CA488835

20. "Left Behind Series Sells 50 Millionth Copy," PR Newswire, January 15, 2002.

21. "Worldwide Phenomenon Left Behind Extends Reach With Airborne Entertainment," Business Wire, October 14, 2003.

22. "Apocalypse!" *Frontline*, PBS. www.pbs.org/wgbh/pages/frontline/shows/apocalypse

23. "The Greatest Story Ever Told" 60 Minutes II CBS, April 14, 2004, 1; Nielsen Bookscan.

24. "Religious Beliefs Remain Constant But Subgroups Are Quite Different," Barna Research Group, March 19, 2004.

25. Teresa Malcolm, "Fearful Faith in End Times Novels." *National Catholic Reporter*, June 15, 2001.

26. *Left Behind*, 48.

27. "Judge Dismisses All Claims Brought by Tim LaHaye Against Cloud Ten," PR Newswire, March 27, 2003.

28. "End of the World Panics," Ontario Consultants for Religious Tolerance, August 14, 2004, http://www.religioustolerance.org/end_wrl3.htm.

29. Hendershot, *Shaking the World For Jesus*, 196.

30. *Left Behind*, 209.

Wars and Rumors of Wars

1. "Left Behind Author Jerry Jenkins on God and September 11," CNN.com, October 3, 2001. www.cnn.com/2001/COMMUNI-TY/10/03/jenkins/index.html.

2. Tom Bissell, "A Comet's Tale: On the Science of the Apocalypse," *Harper's Magazine*, February 2003, 33-47.

3. Karen Armstrong, *The Battle for God*, (New York: Ballantine Books, 2001), 138.

4. "The Left Behind Books," discussion between Randall Balmer and Michael Maudlin, executive director of editorial operations for *Christianity Today*, June 22nd, 2002, http://slate.com/id/2000179/entry/1005559/.

5. "Apocalpyse," entry in New Advent Catholic Encyclopedia Online, 2003, http://www.newadvent.org/cathen/01594b.htm.

6. *Soul Harvest*, 411.

7. *The Mark*, 147–148.

8. *Tribulation Force*, 62.

9. *Tribulation Force*, 63–67

10. *Tribulation Force*, 72, 74.

11. "Apocalpyse," entry in New Advent Catholic Encyclopedia, 2003. http://www.newadvent.org/cathen/01594b.htm.

12. Tom Bissell, "A Comet's Tale: On the Science of the Apocalypse," *Harper's Magazine*, Feb, 2003.

13. "Apocalypse!" *Frontline*, PBS.

14. Carl E. Olson. "Are We Living in the Last Days?" *The Catholic Faith*
    5, No. 6 (November/December 2001), 46–47.
15. Cathleen Falsani, "Bishops Warn Catholics About Left Behind
    Books," *Chicago Sun Times*, June 6, 2003.
16. John Dart, "Beam Me Up Theology," *Christian Century*, September
    25, 2002.
17. "Religious Beliefs Remain Constant But Subgroups Are Quite
    Different," Barna Research Group, March 19, 2004.
18. Kenneth Woodward, "The Way the World Ends," *Newsweek*,
    November 1, 1999.
19. "Some Believers Waiting for Apocalypse—But Not on New Year's,
    Experts Say," CNN.com, December 25, 1999, www.cnn.com/SPE-
    CIALS/1999/at2000/stories/religion/.

Polyester Revolutionaries

Epigraph. Richard Hofstadter, "The Paranoid Style of American
          Politics," *Harper's Magazine*, November 1964, 77–86.
1. Nancy Shepherdson. "Writing for Godot," *Los Angeles Times*, April 25,
   2004.
2. Tim LaHaye, *Battle for the Mind*, (Old Tappan, NJ: Revell, 1980), 179.
3. Richard Hofstadter, "The Paranoid Style of American Politics,"
   Harper's Magazine, November 1964, 77–86)
4. Martin Surham, *The Christian Right, The Far Right and the Boundaries*
   of American Conservatism, (Manchester University Press: 2001), 108–109.
5. U.S. Religious Breakdown, CIA World Factbook,
   http://www.cia.gov/cia/publications/factbook/geos/us.html#People.
6. "Religious Beliefs Remain Constant."
7. "Election 84" Special Edition, *Christian Inquirer*, University of Iowa
   Social Documents Collection)
8. "The Greatest Story Ever Told," *60 Minutes II*, CBS, April 14, 2004.
9. Tim LaHaye and David Noebel, *Mind Siege: the Battle for Truth in the*
   New Millennium, (Nashville: World Publications, 2000), 271.
10. Robert Dreyfuss, "Reverend Doomsday," Rolling Stone, January 28,
    2004.
11. Hank Kurz Jr., "Falwell Plans for Evangelical Revolution," *Associated*
    Press, November 9, 2004,
    http://story.news.yahoo.com/news?tmpl=story&cid=519&e=6&u=/ap/f
    alwell_new_coalition.
12. Nancy Shepherdson, "Writing for Godot."

13. Jane Lampman, "The End of the World," *Christian Science Monitor*, February 18, 2004.

14. Tona J. Hangen, *Redeeming the Dial: Radio, Religion and Popular Culture in America*, (Chapel Hill, NC: University of North Carolina Press), 2000, from the introduction.

15. "Reverend Doomsday," Rolling Stone.

16. Tim LaHaye, *Rapture Under Attack*, (Eugene, Ore: Harvest House), 2005.

17. Shepherdon. "Writing for Godot."

18. Durham, "The Christian Right."

19. Cited in *Ilbido*, 59.

20. *Battle for God*, pp. 274. Armstrong.

21. "Reverend Doomsday," *Rolling Stone*.

22. Sara Diamond, Facing the Wrath (Monroe, ME: Common Courage, 1999), 60.

23. John Micklethwait and Adrian Wooldridge, *The Right Nation: Conservative Power in America* (New York: Penguin Press, 2004)., 83–84.

24. Armstrong, Battle for God, 310.

25. David Snowball, Continuity and Change in the Rhetoric of the Moral Majority (New York: Praefer, 1991), 77.

26. Rob Boton "If Best-Selling End-Times Author Tim LaHaye Has His Way, Church-State Separation Will Be Left Behind," February 2002, http://www.au.org/site/News2?page=NewsArticle&id=5601&abbr=cs.

27. Fritz Detwiler, *Standing on the Premises of God: The Christian right's Fight to Redefine America's Public Schools* (New york: New York University Press, 1999), 137. Also, Sara Diamond, *Spiritual Warfare*, 106.

28. Nancy Shepherdson, *Writing for Godot*.

29. Nina Easton, *Gang of Five : Leaders at the Center of the Conservative Crusade* (New York : Simon and Schuster, 2000). 215.

30. Sara Diamond, *Spiritual Warfare*, 66.

31. "Reverend Doomsday," *Rolling Stone*.

32. Linda Kintz abd Julia Lesage, "Clarity, Mothers, and Mass-Mediated Soul," *Media, Culture, and the Religious Right*. (Minneapolis: University of Minnesota Press, 1998), 116.

33. Sara Diamond, *Spiritual Warfare*, 70.

34. *Christian Inquirer*, October 1983, Social Documents Collection, (University of Iowa Libraries Special Collections), 6.

35. Sara Diamond, *Spiritual Warfare*, 43.

36. Terry Gross, interview with..., "Fresh Air," with Terry Gross, WHYY, March 12, 2004.

37. Rob Boton, "If Tim LaHaye Has His Way," February 2002, http://www.au.org/site/News2?page=NewsArticle&id=5601&abbr=cs
_.

38. LaHaye's response to this was that there had been no objection to these particular books, but an broader objection to reading books which 'advocate lying, endorse disobedience to parents, and ridicule their faith and other principles that subscribe to historic, traditional American values,' which, in absolutist language would mark Huck Finn, and thus Twain's book, as heretical—Huck often lies, sometimes nobly in defense of his friend Jim; Huck wouldn't be around very long if he didn't disobey and lie to his alcoholic father; and certainly blind faith and assumptions about historic, traditional American values are among the main ideas pilloried in Twain's satire of America.

39. "Reverend Doomsday," *Rolling Stone*.

God's Own Media

1. FamilyChristian.com interview at www.familychristian.com/books/jenkins.lahaye.asp

2. *Left Behind*, 394.

3. *Left Behind*, 101, 357

4. *Left Behind*, 394–395.

5. *Left Behind*, pp. 426; *Nicolae*, 108.

6. *Tribulation Force*, 338.

7. There is a definite and recognizable decision to attempt to define the term "Christian" in this movement as "real believers" meaning only conservative Christians, but in doing so they co-opt the entire term "Christian," which they use in a very effective way: when questioned they can claim "anti-Christian" bias when there is any criticism of the movement.

8. "Tim LaHaye's Perspective," Pre-Trib Research Center newsletter March 2000.

9. Elizabeth Bernstein, "All the candidates' clergy," *The Wall Street Journal,* August 13, 2004.

10. Micklethwait & Woolridge, *The Right Nation*, 84.

11. Jane Lampman, "The End of the World."

12. "Christian Mass Media Reach More Adults With the Christian Message Than Do Churches," July 2, 2002. Barna Research Group.

13. "Reading at Risk," June 2004, National Endowment for the Arts, http://www.nea.gov/pub/ReadingAtRisk.pdf.

14. Weyrich's Free Congress Foundation, funded by the Coors family, and on which Jeffery Coors sits as a board member, was set up to oppose the American Bar Association and actively work to promote conservative judges for state, local, and federal judicial positions. Robert Bork, a favorite often lauded in old CWA bulletins, was heavily promoted by the FCF. This is the group that formed from Weyrich and Coors' Committee for the Survival of a Free Congress founded in 1974 and which worked to erode support for unions and argued against nuclear weapons treaties with the U.S.S.R such as the SALT II agreement. The other Coors-Weyrich creation was the massive Heritage Foundation, which was started in 1973 with a $250,000 start-up fund provided by Joseph Coors. Between the years 1995 and 2002, the Coors foundation, Castle Rock, gave nearly $2 million to the Heritage Foundation and a little over $1 million to the FCF.

15. Chip Berlet, "Who is Mediating the Storm?" Media, Culture, and the Religious Right, 265-67.

16. Michael Shermer, *Scientific American*, September 2002; Keven Sack, "Apocalyptic Theology Revitalized," *New York Times*, Novemeber 23, 2001; "'Left Behind' Author Jerry Jenkins on God and September 11," October 3, 2001, CNN.com.

17. Brendan I. Koerner, *Onward Christian Moguls*, American Prospect, January 1, 2002.

18. "Trinity Broadcasting Network's Coffers are Overflowing with Cash," Ministry Watch, March 12, 2004.

19. In the mid 80s, Norman Geisler of LaHaye's Pre-Trib Research Center writes on the "Biblical View of Government" in one of the Rutherford Institute publications: "Secularism will crush Christianity." Much of the same language of persecution, embattled against the forces of the ACLU, and other "secular" institutions like Planned Parenthood, which they see as an "abortion industry," can be found in the Rutherford Institute literature; Armstrongm *Battle for God*, 172.

A Battle for the Mind

1. LaHaye, *Battle for the Mind*, 26.

2. Susan Friend Harding, *The Book of Jerry Falwell: Fundamentalist Language and Politics* (Princeton, N.J.: Princeton University Press, 2000), 242.

3. LaHaye, *Battle for the Mind*, 218–219.

4. "Election 84," *Christian Inquirer*.

5. Detwiler, *Standing on the Premises*, 191.

6. Lampman, "The End of the World."

7 Jeremy Lott, "Jesus Sells: What the Christian culture industry tells us about secular society," *Reason*, February 2003.

8. Aaron Rench, interview with Larry Jenkins, http://www.credenda.org/issues/15–3counterpoint.php Counterpoint, Vol 15. Issue 3.

9. Kenneth Woodward, "The Way the World Ends," *Newsweek*, November 1, 1999.

10 Two-thirds of these End Times believers think Jesus will return, and nine out of ten evangelicals who hold End Times beliefs assert the same. A total of 77 percent of born-again Christians think the Christian messiah will return. Of these End Times believers, 40 percent felt the apocalypse was likely or very likely to come in their lifetimes. And those who believe the End Times would come in their lifetime were a pretty confident lot about their chances of getting to heaven, around 61 percent. Overall, 87 percent of Evangelical Christians thought they would go to heaven, higher than born again Christians (77 percent), Catholics (53 percent) and non-Christians (surprisingly, 43 percent). Half the respondents to the poll thought that the Middle East would play heavily into the End Times events. PR Newswire, October 16, 2001.

11. This is actually from 1 John 4:3, John writing, not Jesus speaking. It is also worth noting that the word "antichrist" appears only in the Gospels of John and seems to point not to a single individual in the future but a "position" opposite that of Christ.

12. *Glorious Appearing*, 248.

Antichrists Among Us

1. http://www.pbs.org/wgbh/pages/frontline/shows/apocalypse/antichrist/quiz.html

2. KennethWoodward, "The Way the World Ends."

3. "Review of Armageddon," *Affairs*, September/October 2003.

4. *Left Behind*, 71, 243, 245, 255.

5. *Left Behind*, 352; *Nicolae*, 125; *The Mark*, 80; *Apollyon*, 105–107; *Nicolae*, pp. 132; *Apollyon*, pp. 102.
6. *Nicolae*, 300; *Left Behind* 414; *Indwelling*, 284; *Glorious Appearing*, pp. 45; *Desecration*, 36.
7. *Left Behind*, pg. 14. Here is the passage from Ezekiel, as interpreted by the Scofield Reference Bible, in which premillennialists get their idea of Russian and European attack:

> That the primary reference is to the northern (European) powers, headed up by Russia, all agree. The whole passage should be read in connection with Zechariah 12:1–4; 14:1–9; Matthew 24:14–30; Revelation 14:14–20; 19:17–21, "gog" is the prince, "Magog," his land. The reference to Meshech and Tubal (Moscow and Tobolsk) is a clear mark of identification. Russia and the northern powers have been the latest persecutors of dispersed Israel, and it is congruous both with divine justice and with the covenants (e.g. "Genesis 15:18" See "Deuteronomy 30:3" that destruction should fall at the climax of the last mad attempt to exterminate the remnant of Israel in Jerusalem. The whole prophecy belongs to the yet future "day of Jehovah"; Isaiah 2:10–22; Revelation 19:11–21 and to the battle of Armageddon Revelation 16:14 See "Revelation 19:19" but includes also the final revolt of the nations at the close of the kingdom-age. Revelation 20:7–9.")

8. http://www.raptureready.com/rap2.html
9. "European Union in Prophecy," Rapture Ready, www.raptureready.com/rr-eu.html.
10. http://www.christiandestiny.org/
11. Gayle White, "Countdown to the End Times," *Atlanta Journal Constitution*, May 17, 2003.
12. "Tim LaHaye's Perspective," September 1999. Pre-Trib Research Center.

Early Propaganda

1. Julian Foster, "None Dare Call It Reason," (1964), University of Iowa, Social Documents Collection.
2. *The Birch Log*, JBS publications, University of Iowa, Social Documents Collection; John F. McManus, *The Insiders*, Belmont, Mass.: John Birch Society, 1983; http://www.jbs.org/
3. http://www.dixienet.org/—League of the South homepage
4. John R. Ice biography, *Sword of the Lord*, http://www.swordofthelord.com/biographies/johnrrice.htm; Dr. Robert

L. Moyer, *The Sword of the Lord*, Social Documents Collection, Microfilm S-40; Ilbido., September 16, 1960.

5. *Alarming Cry* 5,1, University of Iowa Social Documents Collection; This was published out of Englewood, Colorado that year (Oshkosh, Nebraska, later in the 60s, and in Los Angeles and Pasadena before this)—many of these publications tended to move around a lot and only issue P.O. box numbers as addresses.

6. *Christian Intelligence Digest*, University of Iowa, Social Documents Collection.

7. *Flag of Truth*, August 1964, University of Iowa, Social Documents Collection, PR F20 microfilm, 10.

8. Ibid.

9. *Humbard Christian Report*, September 8, 1974, University of Iowa, Social Documents Collection, advertisement bottom left page 6.

10. *Christian Crusade*, Letter by Billy James Hargis, July 31, 1970, University of Iowa, Social Documents Collection, H-14OK microfilm.

11. http://www.guardian.co.uk/religion/Story/0,2763,1370739,00.html

12. "A Candid View of the Corrupt Liberal Establishment," Christian Crusade, 1967, University of Iowa, Social Documents Collection, H-14OK, microfilm, 13.

13. *Left Behind*, 358.

14. David A. Noebel, "Two Faces of the IRS," *Christian Crusade*, December 1966, University of Iowa, Social Documents Collection, H-H microfilm, reel 61.

15. *American Opinion*, University of Iowa, Social Documents Collection.

16. Chip Berlet and Margaret Quigley, "Theocracy & White Supremacy," in *Eye's Right! Challenging the Right Wing Backlash*, eds. Chip Berlet, (Boston: South End Press, 1995).

17. *Christian Crusade*, University of Iowa, Social Documents Collection, reel 61 H-10 microfilm.

18. R.J. Rushdoony, *The Religion of Revolution*, University of Iowa, Social Documents Collection.

19. *Applied Christianity*, University of Iowa, Social Documents Collection; "Invitation to a Stoning" *Reason*, Walter Olsen, November 1998, http://reason.com/9811/col.olson.shtml.

20. Berlet and Lyons, *Right-Wing Populism in America*, 212.

21. Jerry Jenkins with Bob Smietana, "Interview about the Left Behind Series," *The Covenant Companion*, July 2002.

22. Hanna Rosin, "Apocalypse Doomsayers Change their Story," *Washington Post*, January 1, 2000; Robert Sheaffer, *Skeptical Inquirer*,

May 2000, "Apocalypse Lost"; Gary North, "History of Economics Through Purtian New England," PhD diss., University of Iowa, Social Documents Collection; Gary North, "Writing Conspiracy History: Lists are Not Enough, http://www.cephasministry.com/nwo_cnp_gary_north.html.

23. *McAlvany Intelligence Advisor and African Intelligence Digest*, University of Iowa, Social Documents Collection.

24. Conservative Caucus file, University of Iowa, Social Documents Collection; http://www.armageddonbooks.com/20tidal.html; Larry Abraham, *Call It Conspiracy*, (Seattle, WA: Double A Publications, 1985).

25. "Bush Will Receive Petition Citing Perjury in Fraud Case," *Washington Times*, April 13, 2004.

26. Alan Pendergast, "Party Crasher," *Westword*, January 16, 1997.

27. "Tim LaHaye's Perspective," *Pre-Trib Research Center Newsletter*, August 1999,

28. *Washington Times* interview, "Election 84," Christian Inquirer; "Tim LaHaye's Perspective," Pre-Trib Research Center, September 1999.

29. Rosin, "Apocalypse Doomsayers Change Their Story"; "The Prophetic Significance of Sept. 11, 2001," Pre-Trib Research Center website; Tim LaHaye, *Unhappy Gays: What Everyone Should Know About Homosexuality*, Tyndale House, 1978.

30. "The Case for Imminent Rapture of the Church," Pre-Trib Research Center, February 2001.

31. Gerald A. Laure, "The Bible and the Prophets of Doom," *Skeptical Inquirer*, January-February 1999.

32. Teresa Wantanabe, "Millennium Madness," *Los Angeles Times*, March 31, 1999.

33. Rosin, "Apocalypse Doomsayers Change their Story"; Wantanbe, "Millennium Madness."

34. "The Prophetic Significance of Sept. 11, 2001," Pre-Trib website.

35. (www.schoolofprophecy.com/struggle_world_domination.html)

The Octopus
1. "The Greatest Story Ever Told," *60 Minutes II*.

2. Detwiler, *Standing on the Premises*, 190.

3. National Committee of Responsive Philanthropy, *Axis of Ideology: Conservative Foundations and Public Policy*, March 2004, 9.

4. University of Iowa Special Collections, Social Documents Collection.

5. Once known as Richard Nixon's "hatchet man," Colson pleaded no contest to obstruction of justice charges in the Watergate scandal and around the same time found Jesus. Upon release from prison in 1976, Colson founded Prison Fellowship, a group which attempts to reform prisoners through evangelism and is now funded partly through Bush's faith-based initiative programs. Some activists have argued that prisoners are being forced into fundamentalist Christianity through coercive faith-based treatment and preferential treatment for those who go through these programs over those who opt out but are not offered alternatives.

6. Arthur S. DeMoss Foundation, *The Rebirth of America*. University of Iowa Special Collections, Social Documents Collection.

7. National Committe of Responsive Philanthropy, *Axis of Ideology*, 10, 13, 21, 12, 37, 10, 16, 18, 16.

8. James Edwards, "Newfound Respect," *American Enterprise*, January-February 2003. "Axis of Ideology," 26–27.

9. CNN http://www.cnn.com/2004/ALLPOLITICS/11/07/specter.judiciary

10. Summit Ministries box, University of Iowa Special Collections, Social Documents Collection.

11. "Reverend Doomsday," *Rolling Stone*.

12. Ibid.

13. Since its founding, the CNP's membership list has included many of the heavy hitters of the hard line conservative and religious right—along with those already mentioned, members have included Howard Phillips; Gary Bauer (Family Research Council); Edwin Meese (former attorney general under Reagan); John Whitehead (Rutherford Institute); Michael Farris (Home School Legal Defense Association); D. James Kennedy (Coral Ridge Presbyterian Church); Beverly LaHaye; Pat Robertson; Ralph Reed (formerly of the Christian Coalition and in the 2004 presidential race, Bush's organizer in the Southeast); Bill Bright (Campus Crusade for Christ); Alan Keyes; Donald Wildmon (American Family Association); Henry Morris (of LaHaye's Institute for Creation Research); Louis "Woody" Jenkins (former Republican congressman from Louisiana); former Senator Jesse Helms; Jeffrey Coors, Holland Coors, Carin Coors, and Darden Coors of the Colorado Adolph Coors Co. family; Morton C. Blackwell (International Policy Forum); Reed E. Larson (National Right to Work Committee); Rich DeVos Sr. (cofounder of Amway); Oliver North (USMC Ret., of Freedom Alliance and former Iran-Contra

Affair celeb), George Grant; Paul Weyrich (Free Congress Foundation); Larry Pratt (Gun Owners of America); and Paul S. Godwin (Washington Times Corp.) Besides the organizations represented by these people, there are also the Eagle Forum, Chalcedon, Traditional Values Coalition, the American Center for Law and Justice, Wallbuilders (David Barton), Plymouth Rock Foundation (Rus Walton), Regent University's Robertson School of Law and Government, the Heritage Foundation, the American Enterprise Institute, and the Institute for Educational Affairs. Donald P. Hodel, former executive director of the Christian Coalition sits as the current president of the CNP.

14. IRS Form 990 #72–0921017.
15. Jeremy Leaming and Rob Boston, "CNP, Religious Right and Bush," San Francisco Indymedia, http://sf.indymedia.org/news/2004/10/1704827.php.
16. "Reverend Doomsday," *Rolling Stone*.
17. Joe Conason and Gene Lyons, "Circle of Deceit," *Arkansas Times*, May 5, 2000.
18. "Reverend Doomsday," *Rolling Stone*.

Concerned Women for America
1. Durham, *Christian Right*, 37.
2. Diamond, *Spiritual Warfare*, 108.
3. Form 990 ID #95–380834.
4. Kintz, "Clarity," 132.
5. *Christian Inquirer*, August 1983.
6. Diamond, *Spiritual Warfare*, 107.
7. Durham, *Christian Right*, 35, 37.
8. Diamond, *Spiritual Warfare*, 105.
9. *Concerned Women for America Newsletter* Vol 7. No 10, October 1985.
10. Sara Diamond, *Facing the Wrath: Confronting the Right in Dangerous Times* (Monroe, Me. : Common Courage Press, 1996), 14, 107.
11. Durham, *Christian Right*, 121; Diamond, *Spiritual Warfare*, 109; *CWA* newsletter, February 1987, 12.
12. Kintz.
13. Diamond, *Spiritual Warfare*, 84.
14. Ibid., 83.
15. Kintz, "Clarity," 129.

16. Kris Jacobs, "Kitchen Table Lobbyists," *Interchange Report*, Winter/Spring 1985.
17. "The Untold Story of Christian Genocide in Nicaragua," *CWA Bulletin*, November 1986, 11.
18. Diamond, *Spiritual Warfare*, 110.
19. "Colonel Oliver North, National Hero," *CWA Newsletter* 9, February 2, 1987.
20. Dr. D. James Kennedy, "Surviving the Nuclear Age," and John Kwapisz, "SDI: Protecting the Future of America's Families," *CWA Bulletin,* October, 1985.
21. Ian Bremmer is President of Eurasia Group, Senior Fellow at the World Policy Institute, and a columnist for the *Financial Times*. "Evaluating Ballistic Missile Defense," *In The National Interest* 3, Issue 24, June 16, 2004, http://www.inthenationalinterest.com/Articles/Vol3Issue24/Vol3Issue23Bremmer.html.
22. World Policy Institute http://www.nuclearfiles.org/hinonproliferationtreaty/2000npt_pr-wpf.html)
23. DOE Press Release, http://usgovinfo.about.com/gi/dynamic/offsite.htm?site=http://www.doe.gov/news/releases00/aprpr/pr00106.htm.
24. http://www.whitehouse.gov/omb/budget/fy2005/energy.html.
25. Jennifer Block, "Christian Soldiers on the March," *Nation*, February 2003, www.thenation.com/doc.mhtml?i=20030203&s=block.
26. Just two weeks after the re-election of George W. Bush to the White House, the FDA slapped new warning labels on abortion pill RU-486, also known as mifepristone, after it had been found that 3 women had died from taking the pill since 2000—3 out of nearly 360,000 women. CWA, which has campaigned against RU-486 and has petitioned the FDA to withdraw the drug, stepped up the rhetoric in order to score a few political points off the decision. "How many more women have to die before F.D.A. will put women's health and lives above the politics of abortion?" Wendy Wright, senior policy director of CWA, told the *New York Times*.
27. Jennifer Block, "Christian Soldiers on the March."
28. Ibid.
29. Claire McCurdy, "Concerned Women for America: A closer look at their 'concerns,'" *Planned Parenthood* 2, no. 1, April 1996.
30. "Clinton says he felt pushed into gay policy," *New York Times*, December 7, 2000.

31. Detwiler, *Standing on the Premises*, 128. Armstrong, *Battle for God*, 312.
32. *Tribulation Force*, 274.
33. *Soul Harvest*, 181.
34. Detwiler, *Standing on the Premises*, 199.
35. Durham, *Christian Right*, 52–53.
36. Hendershot, *Shaking the World*, 114–128.
37. Nicolae, 348.
38. *Indwelling*, 44.
39. *The Rising*, 252
40. *Left Behind*, 46, 93.
41. *Left Behind*, 266–267.
42. *Soul Harvest*, 220–221.
43. *Nicolae*, 295, 296, 377.
44. *Soul Harvest*, 281, 332, 363.
45. *Apollyon*, 305, 330.
46. Excerpt from *The Battle for the Family*, *Christian Inquirer* 15, no. 7.

From the Womb to the Tomb

1. "Christ Has to Be at the Center," *Der Spiegel*. March 15, 2004, www.spiegel.de/spiegel/english/0,1518,290805,00.html.
2. Armstrong, *Battle for God*, p_.
3. Harding, *Book of Jerry Falwell*, 213–218.
4. Henry Morris, ICR.
5. IRS form 990 #95–3523177, 2003; http://www.princetonreview.com/cte/profiles/facts.asp?CareerID=72
6. Cornelia Dean, "Creation and Science Clash at Grand Canyon Bookstores," *New York Times*, October 26, 2004, http://www.nytimes.com/2004/10/26/science/26cany.html?ex=1100235600&en=cba15033c261ec0a&ei=5070.
7. IRS form 990 #95–3523177.
8. IRS form 990 #95–2668328.
9. IRS form 990 2002 # 38–1856803.
10. IRS form 990 # 74–2622129.
11. David Kirkpatrick, "College for the Home Schooled is Shaping Leaders for the Right," New York Times, March 8, 2004, http://www.nytimes.com/2004/03/08/education/08HOME.html; http://texscience.org/reform/leininger.htm. In 1996, John Ashcroft, as a member of the Senate, was a key leader in getting faith-based funding into the Welfare Reform Act. Before that time churches could not

get federal funds unless they had a separate nonreligious nonprofit entity tied to it. After the act, federal money could go directly to churches as long as they didn't use it to proselytize in their community betterment activities, refuse clients, or discriminate in hiring. In September 2002, after two versions of faith-based initiative bills stalled in the Senate, President Bush announced he would implement his own program by executive order through administrative regulation, essentially ignoring Congress. While social service providers receiving the funding could not discriminate on who they gave aid to on grounds of religious faith, discrimination based on religious faith in hiring and the proselytizing limitations remain murky at best.

12. "Republican Funded Groups Attack John Kerry's War Record," Annenburg Public Policy Center, August 6, 2004, http://factcheck.org/article.aspx?docID=231.

13. Scott Gold, "Top Texas Donor's Influence Far More Visible than He Is," *Los Angeles Times*, August 8, 2004, http://www.latimes.com/news/politics/2004/la-na-perry8aug08,1,3055009.story?coll=la-politics-pointers.

14. National Committe of Responsive Philanthropy, *Axis of Ideology*, 23.

15. Detwiler, *Standing on the Premises*, 149.

16. *Tribulation Force*, 169.

17. Detwiler, *Standing on the Premises*, 173.

18. "George Bush's Secret Army," The Economist, February 26, 2004.

19. April Austin, "Homeschoolers Keep the Faith," *Christian Science Monitor,* March 23, 2004.

20. Ibid.

21. IRS form 990 for 2002 # 54–1919810.

22. LaTonya Taylor, "Christian College Denied Accreditation," *Christianty Today*, July 1, 2005, http://www.christianitytoday.com/ct/2002/008/15.16.html.

23. IRS form 990 for 2002 # 54–1919810; http://www.epm.org/randysbio.html.

The Seductive Appeal of Immiment Return

1. Hendershot, *Shaking the World*, 179–180.

2. Dr. Edward Hinson, "Why Study Bible Prophecy?" www.schoolof-prophecy.com/why_study.html.

3. "End-of-the-World Panics," OCRT, August 2004, http://www.religioustolerance.org/end_wrl3.htm.

4. The U.N. has a budget smaller than that of New York City.

5. "End-of-the-World Panics," OCRT, August 2004, http://www.religioustolerance.org/end_wrl3.htm.

6. www.mille.org.

7. "Apocalyse!" *Frontline*, PBS, www.pbs.org/wgbh/frontline/shows/apocalypse/roundtable/uno.html.

8. Gabriel A. Almond, R. Scott Appleby, and Emmanuel Sivanlmond, *Strong Religion: The Rise of Fundamentalisms Around the World* (Chicago: University of Chicago Press, 2003), 70.

9. *Soul Harvest*, 131, 135.

10. *Left Behind*, 1.

11. *Tribulation Force*, 31, 38.

12. *Left Behind*, 79, 109. 155. 125. 376.

13. *Tribulation Force*, 15. 1–2, 167, 237.

14. *Soul Harvest*, 38, 171.

15. *Armageddon*, 15.

16. *Soul Harvest*, 164.

17. *Left Behind*, 209–10.

18. *Left Behind*, 212.

19. Ibid., 214.

20. *Left Behind*, 215, 222, 394, 343-45.

21. *The Mark*, 142.

22. Ibid., 148.

23. Ibid., 343.

The Militant Jesus

1. *Glorious Appearing*, 226.

2. Paul O'Donnell, review of *Glorious Appearing*, BeliefNet, http://www.beliefnet.com/story/143/story_14331_1.html.

3. "The Greatest Story Ever Told," *60 Minutes II*.

4. Ibid.

5. *Armageddon*, 33, 258-59.

6. *Tribulation Force*, 29.

7. Ibid., 127.

8. Ibid., 362, 440.

9. Durham, *Christian Right*, 77, 72.

10. Skipp Porteous, "Field Manual of the Free Militia," January 1996, Foreword.

11. Ibid.

12. Armstrong, *Battle for God*, 312–13.

13. Dr. Gary North, "What is the Ice?", http://www.reformed-theology.org/ice/html/whatsice.htm.
14. "Dominionism," OCRT, May 18, 2005, http://www.religioustoler-ance.org/reconstr.htm.
15. CNN.com, "Left Behind' Author Jerry Jenkins on God and September 11," October 3, 2001.
16. *Tribulation Force*, 431.
17. *Nicolae*, 325, 65; The Mark, 84.
18. *Assassins*, 2, 310-11.
19. Ibid., 389, 392, 398, 410.
20. *Indwelling*, 89–90.
21. Ibid., 367.
22. *The Remnant*, 196–97; *Glorious Appearing*, 27.

Muslims, Catholics, and Jews—Oh My!

1. Tim LaHaye, "Why Babylon?" Pre-Trib Research Center, September 2000.
2. Paul S. Boyer, "When U.S. Foreign Policy Meets Biblical Prophecy," AlterNet, February 20, 2003, www.alternet.org/story.html?StoryID=15221.
3. Thomas Ice, "Myths about Israel and Palestine," Pre-Trib Research Center Newsletter. February 2001.
4. Hal Lindsay, *Blood Moon*, (Palos Verdes, Cali: Western Front, 1996).
5. David Cook, *Contemporary Muslim Apocalyptic Literature*, (New York: Syracuse University Press, 2005).
6. *Indwelling*, 166.
7. *Tribulation Force*, 216, 277.
8. *Assassins*, 174.
9. *Apollyon*, 364.
10. *Assassins*, 102.
11. Sheila R. Cherry, "Insight on the News," interview with Jenkins and LaHaye, August 26, 2002.
12. Corinne Whitlach, "Christian Committment to Peacemaking is Distrorted by Christian Zionists," PCUSA, www.pcusa.org/washing-ton/issuenet/me-030610.htm; Victoria Clark, "The Christian Zionists," Prospect Magazine UK, July 2003; Donald Wagner, "The Evangelical-Jewish Alliance," Religion Online, www.religion-online.org/cgi-bin/relsearchd.dll/showarticle?item_id=2717; Jason Keyser, "U.S. Evangelicals Back West Bank Settlements," *Washington Times*, June 29, 2003.

13. Lampman, "The End of the World."
14. "The Left Behind Books," discussion between Randall Balmer and Michael Maudlin, *Slate*, June 22, 2002, http://slate.com/id/2000179/entry/1005559/.
15. *Left Behind*, 68.
16. Gershom Gorenberg, *The End of Days*, (New York: Oxford University Press, 2002), 30–31.
17. *The Mark*, 232. 289.
18. *The Remnant*, 228.
19. Woodward, "The Way the World Ends."
20. *Left Behind*, 80.
21. Ibid., 139.
22. "Find the Antichrists: A Quiz," Frontline, http://www.pbs.org/cgi-bin/frontline/apocalypsequiz?submit=check+it+out.
23. *Left Behind*, 140.
24. *Tribulation Force*, 156, 313, 336.
25. *Nicolae*, 61.
26. Ibid, 184.
27. *Apollyon*, 6; *Glorious Appearing*, 71.
28. *Left Behind*, 301.
29. "International Religious Freedom Report: Israel," Jewish Virtual Library, 2003—www.us-israel.org/jsource/anti-semitism/relisrael03.html.
30. *Left Behind*, 312–14.
31. *Tribulation Force*, 403; *Apollyon*, 110.
32. *Glorious Appearing*, 3.
33. *The Remnant*, 81, 289, 294.
34. "The Left Behind Books," discussion between Randall Balmer and Michael Maudlin.
35. Christian Vanguard box, various copies 1972–1974.
36. *Left Behind*, 358.
37. Ibid., 152.
38. Tim LaHaye, "The Case for Imminent Rapture of the Church," Pre-Trib Research Center newsletter, March and April 2001.
39. *Tribulation Force*, 53.
40. Apollyon, 122.
41. *Tribulation Force*, 269, 275; Nicolae, 359.
42. *Soul Harvest*, 86, 284; Apollyon, 54.
43. *Tribulation Force*, 121, 221.

44. *The Mark*, 216; *Tribulation Force*, 261.
45. Andrea Smith, "Devil's In the Details," *Color Lines*, Spring 2002.

Conclusion
1. John H. McCool, "The City ABC Blew Up," October 12, 1983, http://www.kuhistory.com/proto/story-printable.asp?id=25.
2. Larry Witham, "Ghostwriting Haunts Christian Publishing," Insight on the News, August 14, 2000.
3. Malcolm, "Fearful Faith in End Times Novels."
4. Durham, "Christian Right."
5. "Born Again Christians Just as Likely to Divorce as Non-Christians," Barna Research Group, September 8, 2004, http://www.barna.org/FlexPage.aspx?Page=BarnaUpdateNarrow &BarnaUpdateID=170.
6. "Violent Crime Rates Declined Since 1994," Bureau of Justice Statistics, 2004, http://www.ojp.usdoj.gov/bjs/glance/viort.htm.
7. "Property Crime Rates Stabilized After 2002," Bureau of Justice Statistics, 2004, http://www.ojp.usdoj.gov/bjs/glance/house2.htm.
8. Marc Mauer, "Comparative International Rates of Incanceration," The Sentencing Project, June 20, 2003, http://www.sentencingproject.org/pdfs/pub9036.pdf).

BIBLIOGRAPHY

Books consulted during research for this book include:

Ahearn, Edward J. *Visionary Fictions: Apocalyptic Writing from Blake to the Modern Age*. New Haven: Yale University Press, 1996.

Almond, Gabriel Abraham, R. Scoot Appleby, and Emmanuel Sivan. *Strong Religion: The Rise of Fundamentalisms Around the World*. Chicago: University of Chicago Press, 2003.

Amanat, Abbas, and Magnus Bernhardsson, eds. *Imagining the End: Visions of Apocalypse from the Ancient Middle East to Modern America*. New York: I.B. Tauris, 2002.

Ansell, Amy Elizabeth. *New Right, New Racism: Race and Reaction in the United States and Britain*. New York: New York University Press, 1997.

Armstrong, Karen. *The Battle for God*. New York: Ballantine Books, 2001.

Balz, Daniel J. and Ronald Brownstein. *Storming the Gates: Protest Politics and the Republican Revival*. Boston: Little, Brown, 1996.

Berlet, Chip and Matthew N. Lyons. *Right-Wing Populism in America: Too Close for Comfort*. New York: Guilford Press, 2000.

Bellant, Russ. *Old Nazis, the New Right, and the Republican Party*. Boston: South End Press, 1991.

Brouwer, Steve, Paul Gifford, and Susan D. Rose. *Exporting the American Gospel: Global Christian Fundamentalism*.New York: Routledge, 1996.

Burlein, Ann. *Lift High the Cross: Where White Supremacy and the Christian Right Converge*. Durham, N.C.: Duke University Press, 2002.

Cromartie, Michael, ed. *Evangelicals and Foreign Policy: Four Perspectives*. Washington, D.C.: Ethics and Public Policy Center, 1989.

Detwiler, Fritz. *Standing on the Premises of God: The Christian Right's Fight to Redefine America's Public Schools*. New York: New York University Press, 1999.

Diamond, Sara. *Facing the Wrath: Confronting the Right in Dangerous Times*. Monroe, Me.: Common Courage Press, 1996.

Diamond, Sara. *Spiritual Warfare: the Politics of the Christian Right*. Boston: South End Press, 1989.

Durham, Martin. *The Christian Right, the Far Right and the Boundaries of American Conservatism*. Manchester: Manchester University Press, 2000.

Easton, Nina. *Gang of Five: Leaders at the Center of the Conservative Crusade*. New York: Simon and Schuster, 2000.

Emmerson, Richard Kenneth. *Antichrist in the Middle Ages: a Study of Medieval Apocalypticism, Art, and Literature*. Seattle: University of Washington Press, 1981.

Emerson, Steven. *Secret Warriors: Inside the Covert Military Operations of the Reagan era.* New York: Putnam, 1988.

Friedman, Robert I. *Zealots for Zion: Inside Israel's West Bank Settlement Movement.* New York: Random House, 1992.

Frykholm, Amy Johnson. *Rapture Culture: Left Behind in Evangelical America.* New York: Oxford University Press, 2004.

Gifford, Paul. *The Religious Right in Southern Africa.* Harare, Zimbabwe: Baobab Books, 1988.

Gorenberg, Gershom. *The End of Days.* New York: Oxford University Press, 2002.

Gzella, Holger. *Cosmic Battle and Political Conflict: Studies in Verbal Syntax and Contextual Interpretation of Daniel 8.* Rome: Pontificio Istituto Biblico, 2003.

Halsell, Grace. *Prophecy and Politics: Militant Evangelists on the Road to Nuclear War.* Westport, Conn: Lawrence Hill, 1986.

Harding, Susan Friend. *The Book of Jerry Falwell: Fundamentalist Language and Politics.* Princeton, N.J.: Princeton University Press, 2000.

Hendershot, Heather. *Shaking the World for Jesus.* Chicago: University of Chicago Press, 2004.

Jorstad, Erling. *The Politics of Doomsday: Fundamentalists of the Far Right.* Nashville: Abingdon Press, 1970.

Juergensmeyer, Mark. *Terror in the Mind of God: the Global Rise of Religious Violence.* Berkeley: University of California Press, 2003.

Kaplan, Jeffrey, and Leonard Weinberg. *The Emergence of a Euro-American Radical Right.* New Brunswick, N.J.: Rutgers University Press, 1998.

Kintz, Linda, and Julia Lesage, eds. *Media, Culture, and the Religious Right*. Minneapolis: University of Minnesota Press, 1998.

LaHaye, Tim F. *The Battle for the Mind*. Old Tappan, N.J.: Revell, 1980.

LaHaye, Tim F. *The Battle for the Family*. Old Tappan, N.J.: Revell, 1982.

LaHaye, Tim F. *The Coming Peace in the Middle East*. Grand Rapids, Mich.: Zondervan, 1984.

Lee, Harold, Marjorie Reeves, and Giulio Silano. *Western Mediterranean Prophecy: The School of Joachim of Fiore and the Fourteenth-Century Breviloquium*. Toronto: Pontifical Institute of Mediaeval Studies, 1989.

Melling, Philip H. *Fundamentalism in America: Millennialism, Identity and Militant Religio*. Edinburgh: Edinburgh University Press, 1999.

Micklethwait, John and, Adrian Wooldridge. *The Right Nation*. New York: Penguin Press, 2004.

Rossing, Barbara R. *The Choice Between Two Cities: Whore, Bride, and Empire in the Apocalypse*. Harrisburg, Penn.: Trinity Press International, 1999.

Pippin, Tina. *Apocalyptic Bodies: The Biblical End of the World in Text and Image*. New York: Routledge, 1999.

Sandeen, Ernest Robert. *The Roots of Fundamentalism: British and American Millenarianism, 1800–1930*. Chicago: University of Chicago Press, 1970.

Snowball, David. *Continuity and Change in the Rhetoric of the Moral Majority*. New York: Praeger, 1991.

VanderKam, James C., and William Adler, eds. *The Jewish Apocalyptic Heritage in early Christianity*. Minneapolis: Fortress Press, 1996.

Walvoord, John F. *Israel in Prophecy*. Grand Rapids, Mich.: Zondervan Pub. House, 1978.

Walvoord, John F, ed. *The Rapture Question*. Grand Rapids: Zondervan, 1979.

Westerlund, David, ed. *Questioning the Secular State: The Worldwide Resurgence of Religion in Politics*. London: Hurst, 1996.

Wilcox, William Clyde. *God's Warriors: The Christian Right in Twentieth-Century America*. Baltimore: Johns Hopkins University Press, 1992.

Zamora, Lois Parkinsons, ed. *The Apocalyptic Vision in America : Interdisciplinary Essays, on Myth and Culture*. Ohio: Bowling Green University Popular Press, 1982.

Zeidan, David. *The Resurgence of Religion: A Comparative Study of Selected Themes in Christian and Islamic Fundamentalist Discourses*. Boston: Brill, 2003.

Michael Standaert lives in Monterey, California, where he works as a writer. His first novel, *The Adventures of the Pisco Kid*, is forthcoming from Arriviste Press.